T0272622

SEASONS OF LOVE

SEASONS
OF LOVE

Why **Rent** *Matters*

Emily Garside

APPLAUSE
THEATRE & CINEMA BOOKS

ESSEX, CONNECTICUT

APPLAUSE
THEATRE & CINEMA BOOKS

An imprint of Globe Pequot, the trade division of
The Rowman & Littlefield Publishing Group, Inc.
4501 Forbes Blvd., Ste. 200
Lanham, MD 20706
www.rowman.com

Distributed by NATIONAL BOOK NETWORK

Library of Congress Cataloging-in-Publication Data

Names: Garside, Emily, author.
Title: Seasons of love : why Rent matters / Emily Garside.
Description: Essex, Connecticut : Applause Theatre & Cinema, 2023. | Includes
    bibliographical references and index. | Summary: "Rent's importance transcends the
    musical and its fans-it was and is one of the most important musicals of the twentieth
    century, and its impact resonates far beyond its own productions. Seasons of Love
    offers analysis on why Rent has had such a profound impact on the landscape of
    musical theatre" —Provided by publisher.
Identifiers: LCCN 2022033443 (print) | LCCN 2022033444 (ebook) | ISBN
    9781493064618 (cloth) | ISBN 9781493064625 (epub)
Subjects: LCSH: Larson, Jonathan. Rent. | Musicals—History and criticism.
Classification: LCC ML410.L2857 G37 2023 (print) | LCC ML410.L2857 (ebook) |
    DDC 792.6/42—dc23/eng/20220713
LC record available at https://lccn.loc.gov/2022033443
LC ebook record available at https://lccn.loc.gov/2022033444

∞™ The paper used in this publication meets the minimum requirements of American
National Standard for Information Sciences—Permanence of Paper for Printed Library
Materials, ANSI/NISO Z39.48-1992

To every person who found this show when they needed it.

Contents

CONTENTS

Acknowledgments

This book is for my Rentheads past and present. If this show ever found you, you probably needed it. Thank you for keeping it alive with all of us, from the lines outside the Nederlander to the fan art to countless versions of "Seasons of Love."

To every cast member who has been part of this show over the last twenty-five years, you were someone's Maureen/Mark/Roger/Squeegee man, and you all mattered to us.

To everyone who helped put this book together, offering their time, thoughts, and feelings on this show, and helped me create this story.

To my musical theater family, who let me talk about this show and create more trivia questions on it than is healthy and who let me cry on them when we see it live too.

Always, to Jonathan for what he made.

Measure in love.

Introduction

The Musical That Defined a Generation

The marketing tagline for *Rent* came true—at least for a musical theater generation. For those who were in their teens and twenties across the twelve years *Rent* ran on Broadway, it was a rite of passage. It was the musical that taught them not all musicals sounded like Sondheim or Lloyd Webber (eliciting varying degrees of relief and elation).

Its significance is marked by its impact on musical theater and the dedicated following it created. These "Rentheads" grew up with the show—starting as teenagers and becoming the young adults the show depicted. Many were young New Yorkers and Londoners, but many more found the show through the cast album and connected through the internet in the earliest days of online theater fandom. As much as the musical itself, they were trailblazers, and they are as much a part of *Rent*'s story as the performers and the show's creator, Jonathan Larson. The story of *Rent*, the musical that rewrote musical theater and responded to collective grief and crisis like no other work had done, deserves to have its story told, as do the fans who helped it become what it was.

The story is theatrical legend by now. It is the story of Jonathan Larson, the young composer working in a diner when *Rent* became his big off-Broadway break, the composer who was mentored by Sondheim but still struggled to break through, the young man who finally got the show that would make it all happen but tragically died the night of its final dress rehearsal. It is the small off-Broadway musical that swiftly moved uptown without its composer, broke box office records, and won every award in the book.

The importance of *Rent* musically and culturally is often overlooked. It is reduced to parody and has been pulled apart for its narrative in ways other classics have not. There are serious questions as to why *Rent* is taken less seriously than other musicals of its caliber and importance. It may have had a "romantic," "media-friendly" subplot, but musicals do not win the Pulitzer Prize for column inches. *Rent* is a robust, significant work of musical theater, and one whose history and significance should be recorded.

Rent broke many molds. Musically, it was an evolution—the rock musical that reflected musical tastes rather than the Andrew Lloyd Webber approximations of previous years. It was also the first musical of significance since *Hair* to portray real people. And not just real people—the outcasts of society. The characters in *Rent* were the people many areas of American society were choosing to ignore: drug addicts, gay people, trans people, and people of color. *Rent* throws them all center stage. More importantly, it shows them as young people taking center stage. It gave young people a voice on the musical theater stage and on Broadway, which had been deafening in its absence. *Rent* gave Broadway its first same-sex love song and its first same-sex kiss. *Rent* said "AIDS" on a Broadway stage when America's president could barely bring himself to say it. *Rent* had more to say than it has been given credit for. It changed history, and it is time to record that change and what it meant to audiences.

Jonathan Larson wanted to be "the future of musical theater," and while we never got to see that actualized, he lives on in his influence. He can be found in the "Lin-Manuel Mirandas" of the world, in the actors who passed through *Rent*, in the work that was influenced in even the smallest way. He was the future in every person who loved *Rent*, for one night or twenty-five years. The musical asks, "How do you measure a life?" You measure Jonathan's and the life of *Rent* in the people who loved it, how it changed their lives, how it influenced them as young people, and how it is a constant years later. You measure in the love of generations of Rentheads.

The year 2021 marks the twenty-fifth anniversary of *Rent*, now a whole generation away from its opening. All the teens and twenty-somethings who grew up with the show are not grown-ups. It's a suitable distance from all the events of note: the film debut in 2007, Broadway's closure in 2008, the revival in 2012, London's revival three years ago, and the Fox TV special in 2019. Enough time has passed for us to reflect, but the fans are still young enough that those formative years loom large in their memory. The cast is still working on Broadway, for Disney, and beyond. We can see how their lives panned out in parallel to the lives of fans.

It would also be remiss not to mention a pandemic. Larson was writing in response to a plague, and soon new writers will be writing about a new one. He witnessed an emergency in New York that nobody was responding to, as are we. We look to what united us in the past in response to devastating losses in our community, and we prepare to do that again. As we look to older works for inspiration and hope to fill our theaters again, the way we view Larson's work about another pandemic will have shifted. The true perspective on these parallels may take another twenty-five years to see, but the living, breathing nature of theater is that it takes on the influence of the world around it. Larson's bohemian celebration of love in the face of loss certainly feels relevant once again as it hits its quarter century.

Rent might not have had the twenty-fifth anniversary celebrations it would have had in an alternate time line, but it's a milestone worth celebrating nonetheless. In this book, we look at the story of *Rent*, the stories the musical told, and why they matter.

1

"DECEMBER 24TH, 9 PM"

Rise of *Rent*

Rent was a huge hit on Broadway, winning three Tony Awards, including Best Musical, and earning composer Jonathan Larson the Pulitzer Prize for Drama. *Rent* engaged audiences through its medium—the musical—and its approach to AIDS. It is also inseparable from the untimely death of Larson, who died the night of the final dress rehearsal, never getting to see his show fully realized.

Larson's story is part of *Rent*'s story, no doubt. The Broadway program notes that "Larson's life is a finite chapter in the show's on-going story." As a composer, his background impacted the production and depiction of AIDS; his tragic death following the final dress rehearsal of *Rent* overshadowed the production. Larson studied drama at Adelphi University and originally envisioned being an actor. During his time there, he began writing musicals. Before graduation, he wrote a letter to Stephen Sondheim, who, upon meeting Larson, advised him to focus on his writing, telling him: "there are a lot more starving actors than starving composers."

But *Rent* is also notable and separate from this tragedy; it is a musical that rewrote rules of what musicals looked and sounded like. It was also the musical that changed conversations about AIDS and is an enduring legacy to those lost to the worst years of the AIDS pandemic.

The original conversation around *Rent* began with a conversation about the opera. *Rent* is well documented and is based on Puccini's *La bohème.* The original idea came not from Larson himself but from playwright Billy Aronson. Aronson said of the idea as Larson pitched it:

> The similarities between those artists and their poverty and New York in the 1980s really struck me. The numbers of homeless people were shooting up and people were dying all around us. There was AIDS and a lack of government support for the arts. I wanted to rework the plot of the opera, which is very choppy like a Samuel Beckett play. One thing that excited him [Larson] is that it was both highbrow and lowbrow. (McDonnell & Silberger, 1997)

This approach appealed to Larson's concern with contemporary social issues. In discussion with Aronson, Larson convinced Aronson to alter his setting of the new *La bohème* from the prestigious Upper West Side to the more artistic, grungy East Village. Larson felt that the population of the East Village was more on par with the characters from Puccini's opera and Henri Murger's novel than those in the more bourgeois Upper West Side. The idea of adapting a classic also coalesced with Jonathan's artistic outlook, as close friend Eddie Rosenstein comments:

Jonathan's idea was that you have to look at the classics. He was a student of the Aristotelian dramaturgy and felt that you structured everything after the classics. Once that was complete, you departed. (McDonnell and Silberger)

Ian Nisbet explores the musical relationship between Larson's writing and Puccini's opera (2011). In his analysis, Nisbet details both the plot and musical similarities to illustrate how Larson, as in Rosenstein's remarks above, took direct influence from the classic he appropriated for *Rent*. It does not serve the analysis of Larson's depiction of AIDS to consider in detail his direct musical transposition of Puccini; however, his transposition of the narrative and the connotations of disease and social status that Puccini explored certainly resonate in Larson's updated depiction of illness through AIDS. The title *Rent* is used for its double meaning, first to do with the payment for accommodation that is a running theme in the "bohemians'" problems, and secondly for its meaning of to "tear apart," as a metaphor for the community torn by AIDS.

On October 4, 1991, Aronson signed a letter agreeing that Larson would continue to work on *Rent* alone. Even so, Aronson is still credited for his initial contribution and the songs he worked on with Larson (McDonnell and Silberger). When Larson asked Aronson for permission to continue with *Rent,* four of Larson's close friends had been diagnosed with HIV. Indeed Larson himself had confronted the fear of an HIV diagnosis as one of those friends was an ex-girlfriend, which meant that Larson had been exposed to the virus as friend Victoria Leacock Hoffman recalled in McDonnell and Silberger (Leacock Hoffman,

"Rent Is Real," in Larson 2008, p. xiii). This personal closeness to the AIDS epidemic pushed Larson to continue what he and Aronson had begun, as Hoffman describes in her introduction to the text: "[*Rent* is a] canvas large enough to honor his [Larson's] friends and to raise awareness about AIDS and the social injustices he saw every day"(Leacock Hoffman, "Rent Is Real," in Larson 2008, p. xiii).

NYTW AND *RENT*'S BEGINNINGS

Larson began looking for a place to produce *Rent* in early 1992. He approached Jim Nicola of New York Theatre Workshop, a small off-Broadway theater based in the East Village. The company had recently moved to the East Village, and Nicola thought *Rent* would be a good fit as a piece that would reflect the community in which they were now based. It wasn't an immediate hit as the folklore might suggest. Instead, it took a couple of years of workshopping and an exclamation of theatrical magic (or nepotism, depending on your point of view) from one Stephen Sondheim.

It became part of Larson's legacy then, too, that indirectly through the theater his work has helped shape the landscape of New York theater going forward. Notable productions from NYTW include American premieres of work by leading British and European theater makers like Caryl Churchill (an associate artist), Mark Ravenhill, and Ivo Van Hove (an associate artist) while also being a hugely significant theater for developing American work from established writers like Tony Kushner, another associate artist, to being the development ground for newer playwrights. In the 2018/2019 season alone, both *What the Constitution Means to Me* by Heidi Schreck and *Slave Play* by Jeremy O. Harris were breakout plays in American theater; both originated in NYTW within months of one another. Maintaining the legacy of being a space to develop new musicals, the theater in recent years developed *Peter and The Starcatcher* and *Hadestown* (Anaïs Mitchell) as well as *Lazarus* (David Bowie and Edna Walsh). These and other musical projects went on to great success, including *Once* (Enda Walsh, Glen Hansard, and Markéta Irglová). NYTW became the home *Rent* needed because of its artistic ethos but also was able to carry on the ethos of *Rent* in its future work.

Larson submitted the script to NYTW in 1992, and through the theater's new work support group, known as "The Usual Suspects," a reading of *Rent* was offered to Larson. Thus, the first public reading of *Rent* took place the following summer, on June 17, 1993. It was directed by Christopher Grabowski, an associate director of the theater and the literary manager. The cast included Beth Blankenship, James Bohanek, Angel Cuban, Jon Cavaluzzo, Bob Golden, Tony Hoyle, Bami Jones, Clinton Leupp, David Levine, Rusty Magee, Joel Newsome, Nancy O'Connor, Karen Oberlin, Chiara Peacock, Anna Seckinger, and Robert Tate.

The next steps beyond the workshop weren't clear—musicals are big and expensive to produce, and there wasn't at that time full confidence in the musical as is. Larson was undeterred, perhaps sensing he finally had momentum for the piece. But with the kind of dogged determination—and at times perhaps the overconfidence that shaped his entire career—he set about raising funds for the workshop.

Larson then returned to the Richard Rodgers Award for Musical Theater. He had already won for *Superbia*, but when he'd applied with *Rent* in 1993, he had been rejected. The rules technically prohibited reapplication for the same piece. Still, Larson, again displaying a mixture of confidence and perhaps sheer brazenness, asked Sondheim, who was on the selection panel, to make an exception: proof that talent only gets you so far in theater and who you know gets you over the finish line all too often. Sondheim, of course, supported Larson, and he was awarded the 1994 Richard Rodgers Development Grant of $45,000, which made it possible for NYTW to fund the full workshop production.

Aside from the money, the key component in the workshop production was securing a director. When Michael Greif came on board, Jim Nicola felt confident in the future of *Rent*. One of the key elements in producing the piece was a sense of "authenticity" in a conversation that has become more heated in the last twenty-five years; there was the question of who gets to tell what stories. Larson was a white, straight, cisgender man telling a story that involved highly emotive queer issues and would come to include a variety of BIPOC characters. For Nicola, in particular, the AIDS storylines and associated queer characters were a concern when told only from Jonathan's perspective. That is not to suggest that Jonathan was appropriating the stories or, in some ways, was unqualified—after all, he had based *Rent* on a good deal of his own experience and drew on the lives of friends. But Nicola was keen for someone from the gay community to have a voice in the room. Greif seemed like a natural choice.

What Greif (with help from Nicola) also gave Larson was the kind of dramaturgical support he needed to shape the script fully. Overall, the songs were solid, but Larson struggled with the story and book, which was understandable given the numerous narrative strands and

Larson's attempt to give all the characters adequate space for their stories. The union of Larson and Greif also did what all good director/ writer partnerships do: they balanced out each other's traits. Larson's naturally heart-on-sleeve sincerity combined with Greif's wry, dry look at the world prevented *Rent* from being saccharine and gave it a bit more sharpness than Larson was perhaps naturally inclined to. (Although some critics would still find it too sentimental.) Overall, Greif brought what Larson could not: insight into the LGBTQ community and a certain balance to the production. With Nicola's help (his experience as a director also helped the process), *Rent* was ready for its workshop production.

CASTING *RENT*

The show was cast with some of the actors from the workshop reprising their roles. Casting is significant in an original production. The acting of the original cast not only influences how the roles will be created but also acts as a physical and stylistic blueprint for future productions. Bernard Tesley was brought on board to cast the show after starting his own casting agency in 1988. (Tesley would go on to be one of the most successful casting agents for Broadway but at the time his own company was in its infancy.) Tesley and Greif were keen on what they called "authentic" casting, so they began to look around at other types of performers for some of the roles not cast from the workshop. And that truly is the important thing. We don't need to pretend that the casting of *Rent* was some utopian inclusive, diverse process to appreciate its impact. In a way, it's more influential the way that it did happen—the team wasn't seeking token "minority" actors to flesh out a show and tick boxes. The casting of *Rent* genuinely came from the people who fit the roles. But the impact of that was highly significant in two ways. First, as the show was still a work in process, the casting of Mimi, Angel, Collins, and Benny as people of color did affect how those characters were shaped. Collins as a Black professor at MIT has a different resonance with an audience and for his character than a white man in the same role.

The original cast influenced how the roles were created and acted as a physical and stylistic blueprint for future productions. Anthony Rapp comments that Larson told his family that "we [the cast] were the sexiest, most talented, most exciting group of people he had ever seen assembled." Because the cast was young and urban like Larson himself, they had personally experienced many of the themes of *Rent*. Like Larson, they were members of a generation who had seen the effect of AIDS from their teenage years into their twenties. They were people who had lost and would go on to lose friends to the disease, and they were also the first generation whose lives were affected by AIDS.

NYTW RUN

Rent began rehearsals in January 1996. At this point, the story of *Rent* turns into something of a Broadway legend. After watching the final dress rehearsal of *Rent* the night before the first full production was staged, Larson was interviewed by the *New York Times*. Then he went home, suffered an aortic aneurism, and died. Larson was discovered by his roommate at 3:30 that morning. The following day NYTW decided to continue with the production, reflecting what Larson had sought to represent: the community pulling together in crisis and the influence of art on people's lives. During the day, people—the cast as well as Larson's friends—gathered to talk about Larson. In the evening, they were joined by the Larson family, as they performed his work.

That night the cast performed the entire show; initially, they sat and sang, but eventually, they got up and performed. Many of the cast and people associated with the production felt that Larson's death truly galvanized his message of "no day but today" (McDonnell and Silberger). Anthony Rapp (the original Mark in *Rent* and friend of Larson's) too, remembers Al Larson (Jonathan's father), who said after the performance, "You have to make this a hit," and Rapp echoes this, saying he felt, "We have this to do for as long as we can now, and we have to do it as best we can" (Rapp in McDonnell and Silberger). The effect of Larson's death was profound on the cast and influenced the course of *Rent*'s production.

Jonathan Larson's death certainly was an issue for *Rent*'s development: losing the composer at a critical stage in development meant that the remaining creative team had to judge what Larson would or wouldn't have wanted when making changes. It is also likely that they were more hesitant in reworking the text following opening night and in the move to Broadway. If Larson had lived, it is likely the version of *Rent* that was staged on that opening night would have been altered directly afterward, and certainly, by the time it moved to Broadway, changes would have been made. This is not meant to disparage the version of *Rent* Larson produced to this point; it is merely to state that it is standard practice to continue reworking a new musical, particularly when moving from off-Broadway to Broadway.

Alongside the problem that losing a composer gave the production team in terms of reworking Larson's text, Larson's death also gained early press attention for *Rent*. Cynical responses have always protested that the "romanticizing" of Larson's death is the sole reason for the success of *Rent*. It cannot be denied that the story was newsworthy and brought in press coverage and that the themes of *Rent* and affirming life in the face of death brought attention. However, Larson's death alone would not be enough to sustain the kinds of ticket sales that expedited its move to Broadway and sustained it once the transfer was made. The musical connected with the audience downtown. Jim Nicola recounts how the most successful previous shows at NYTW had ticket sales of around $8,000 while *Rent* took close to $40,000 (Nicola in McDonnell, *Rent,* 1998, p. 56). Because of its success, the producers began looking for a bigger venue. Still, at this point, the show's future was uncertain, with strong feelings on both sides as to whether it should remain a downtown show, move to a bigger theater, or move uptown and possibly Broadway. Eventually, it was agreed that *Rent* would move to Broadway's Nederlander Theatre.

MOVING UPTOWN

Rent was a sensation downtown. Whether drawn in by Larson's story or the promise of a new musical, people were intrigued and responded to it. Normally, the idea of a Broadway transfer would be a no-brainer. It's the dream, after all, to go from downtown show to uptown smash. And indeed, for Larson, who sought to be "the future of musical theater" that would have been what he wanted. But concerned with the legacy again, the team owed it to Jonathan to do it properly. But also there was the question, did this "downtown" and "East Village" show belong on Broadway? Would the transfer work? Would audiences follow it uptown? Would uptown audiences like it? Was it selling out?

The Nederlander was considered among the most "downtown" of the "uptown" theaters. The theater venue was also carefully considered, so its downtown origins should be reflected, even when playing uptown. Today, West 41st Street, where the Nederlander Theatre stands, has been enveloped by the radical redevelopment of Times Square. Chain stores and restaurants dominate the area. On the other hand, when *Rent* first moved uptown, the Nederlander was still part of Times Square's more dilapidated lower end; the nearby 9th Avenue and Port Authority bus terminal reflected the run-down, slightly scruffy aura of the East Village. The producers didn't pay for renovations within the theater, which had been empty for several years, retaining the run-down image, choosing to decorate instead with artworks from New York artists.

The money involved in staging a musical is substantial. This was also a major concern of Seller's when *Rent* was transferred uptown. In his work on the commercial element of Broadway theater, Steven Adler broke down the cost of staging a new musical on Broadway in 2003–2004 and estimated the amount as $14 million (2004). Allowing for inflation since *Rent* was staged, this is still an extraordinarily large sum of money to gamble away, which is why, as Adler notes, revivals of musicals and staging straight plays are far more common than new musicals (2004). Although *Rent* had performed well off-Broadway, the economics and audiences of Broadway and off-Broadway are very different.

Jeffery Seller commented on how difficult it was for the producers: "One million people said don't go to Broadway. They said the downtown people wouldn't go up and the uptown people, because the subject matter won't come . . . I was scared to death" (Seller, quoted in Trachtenberg1996). Seller here indicates the risk new musicals undertake in being staged on Broadway. In part, he is pointing out the authentic roots of *Rent* and the connection with the neighborhood audience it had at NYT; that it was inextricably linked to the place it was originally conceived and performed was a worry in moving uptown. Specifically, the producers were concerned that *Rent* would lose the connection to the people it depicted and therefore lose its connection with an audience. This fear was also a concern when transferring it to Britain, with the potential that the connection to both audience and the place it came from would be lost.

However, choosing the Nederlander in part strengthened *Rent*'s transfer. Don Summa, press agent for *Rent,* commented: "The show seemed stronger in a Broadway house, and I never thought it would have." The Nederlander, he noted, is on a block that is "not unlike an East Village block—it was kind of rundown, it was—still is—inhabited by homeless people." Summa concludes that they found the right theater and the right surrounding area (Summa, quoted in Wollman 2006, p. 30).

This setting proved key in cultivating the image of *Rent* for marketing purposes too. Carlson notes in his work that the physical surroundings of a play can influence the reception of a performance. The physical location was a significant factor in deciding on the New York theater locations for *Rent* for the NYTW production and the Broadway transfer. Although the theater selected was partly chosen for convenience, availability, and price, the setting also became an integral part of the *Rent* experience for audiences. Helen Lewis and David

Savran have found this "lifestyle experience" related to the environment of *Rent* problematic; *Rent* is no guiltier of this than any other theater performance, particularly musical theater. In selling theater as a commercial commodity, producers sell an artistic experience, often of a world considered different or exotic to the audience. Savran compares *Rent* and its depictions of race to *South Pacific;* however, it is arguable that the minority cultures in *Rent* are less commoditized than Savran suggests. The point is that all artistic works—particularly those in the commercial theater—can be accused of co-opting the people or issues they represent.

The Nederlander, post-*Rent*, will forever have connotations of the musical. But as soon as it opened, *Rent* began to create new connotations for this particular performance space. The theatrical space can influence audiences and be used to create associations, but it cannot erase personal connotations with a particular space. However, because the Nederlander was empty for some years before *Rent* moved in, there were no recent performance associations in that space, and *Rent* was freer to make its architectural mark. The Nederlander became part of the "*Rent* experience": fans left messages on a wall in the theater for the cast to see and offered comments about the show. *Rent* was not designed as a site-specific or immersive theater; the same time, the surroundings of the Nederlander may have added to the experience for some, but it was not necessary for *Rent* to be effective.

While it was not an "immersive" experience there were some site-specific elements that added to the experience at the Nederlander. One famous example being the *Rent* Wall, or walls as it eventually became. Starting as a unofficial guest book, the wall spread out (literally) to the front walls of the theater, and fans started to add their messages. This also began listing names, of themselves and of their friends or messages to the cast or Jonathan. But it also evolved into messages about what the show meant to them, about their own stories. The tributes to Jonathan made the *Rent* wall an ever-evolving and living memorial to Jonathan and to those he had lost and written about the show and what it meant to the fans.

It's unclear whether this was directly related to something that the Public Theater incorporated into *The Normal Heart* a decade earlier or another coincidence. At *The Normal Heart*, Larry Kramer's important play on AIDS, theatergoers were invited to write the names of people they lost to the AIDS epidemic on the wall. This was political statement and memorial, a memorial because none existed at the time for people who had died of AIDS and a political statement because it was a way to visually illustrate a government committed to inaction and the real-life consequences of its actions. This type of action has been replicated at other productions of *The Normal Heart* and it had clear parallels to the *Rent* wall.

The wall also became part of the bigger conversation *Rent* was having and the unique way it engaged with fans beyond the show. As explored later, the engagement of fans was integral to *Rent* and the feeling that fans were woven into the building; the environment that *Rent* deliberately built around itself was also critical to this.

The downtown-uptown feel of *Rent* was part of the marketing of the show, and it's not without comparison to what Disney does—albeit on a much smaller budget. The experience of seeing *Rent* was just that—an experience. But it also formed something particularly special for fans—an attachment to the physical space no matter how many times they went to the Nederlander, no matter how renovated the theater might be. And indeed, no matter if it's an actual Disney show (*Newsies*, which had a suspiciously *Rent*-like scaffolding set) or Harry Connick Jr. crooning (he had a residency at the Nederlander in 2019).

Hindsight is wonderful; we know the answer was yes, the audience would follow it; newer uptown audiences (and beyond) would love it too. As for selling out? Larson wanted to be the "future of musical theater." It was hard to do that from a two-hundred-seat downtown venue. There was, of course, the option of moving to another off-Broadway venue with a bigger capacity. But the nature of Off-Broadway is to both be smaller and to mount largely short-term house runs. To guarantee *Rent* a longer future, that wasn't an option. Another option that now in the days of many more site-specific and immersive style theater events looks like a brilliant, almost obvious solution was to use a bespoke space. There was talk of a warehouse or club-like space for *Rent* specifically jumping in part off the Donmar/Sam Mendes version of *Cabaret* that turned the theater into the Kit Kat Club. Off-Broadway would take this approach down the line in shows like *Natasha, Pierre & the Great Comet of 1812*, which created its own space on a disused parking lot (a very *Rent* idea in itself). But despite the success downtown the budget wasn't sufficient for a bespoke space at the time. For long-term financial viability, Broadway looked like the strongest option. For both Larson's legacy and the dreams of the young producers, it seemed like the only goal too. Everyone knew it was Larson's dream, but Jeffery Seller, in an interview with Robert Simonson of Playbill.com, also recalled how important it was to him:

Kevin [McCollum] and I felt it was our mission to go to Broadway. We felt that, if *Rent* can't be on Broadway then the Broadway we grew up loving so much cannot accommodate us that we cannot work on Broadway. And we wanted to work on Broadway.

Would audiences come? It was fair to say *Rent* was unlike other Broadway offerings at the time. As Patrick Pacheco reported on the show in the *Los Angeles Times*, the show was considered a risk "with its very different demographics," which was possibly code for "not white and middle class." He went on to say, "Broadway ticket users hardly seem to be hungering for a musical in which four of the seven leads are HIV positive, the central romantic couple meets over a bag of heroin and vagrants snarl out Christmas carols." No *Rent* does not exactly have tourist and marketing copy-friendly written all over it. But what exactly were audiences watching at that time? There was a definite trend for a certain kind of musical output, led by Andrew Lloyd Webber and Cameron Macintosh. Then again, musical theater was not without a bit of subversion at the time. This period also saw successful revivals of the previously mentioned *Cabaret* (in London first and later Broadway) and a critical, if not commercial, success for Terrence McNally's *Kiss of the Spider Woman*. Both productions are significant for their portrayal of homosexuality; their authors' other work also centered on AIDS. Elsewhere in musical theater, the notable but small-scale AIDS musical *Elegies for Angels, Punks, and Raging Queens* made its debut.

Despite the phenomenal commercial success *Rent* went on to achieve, there was honesty in its roots that shows like *South Pacific* or even *Hair* (with its fringe theater and political roots) both lack. *Rent* was created with a similar motivation to the earlier AIDS plays: Larson was seeking to commemorate those he had lost and use his artistic voice to discuss the issue of AIDS. That *Rent* became so successful should not detract from that fact, nor should it make it a somehow lesser depiction of AIDS.

Also in the mix was the emotion of having lost Jonathan so suddenly and the instinct from his family to preserve his work. The team was conscious of that, too, as Tim Weil said in an interview with Michael Portantiere for *Playbill*, "With deference to his family and friends and the graceful dynamics of the situation, we were faced with the fact we had to present the showing the best possible light." And that was all anyone could do. *Rent* was always destined to be an unfinished work because we cannot know what Larson might have changed or added. This also goes for the critiques or how it stands the test of time, explored later in this book. Larson may have adapted things, as other composers have (Lin-Manuel Miranda adapting and changing elements of *In the Heights* for the film, but also to reflect changing attitudes and changing times), but that is if a composer is living. The work is also living and being produced. It is the composer's prerogative to keep the piece alive and changing. Instead, *Rent* remains frozen in a moment with its composer.

Moving uptown could have been a chance to feed off audience responses and create a better version of the musical. In front of an audience, does anyone figure out what works? Only by seeing it performed can the smaller details be worked out, as well as the bigger ones. Would Larson have changed Roger's final song "Your Eyes," which is widely considered not to be reflective of Roger spending a year on it after all? It pales in comparison to Roger's opener, "One Song Glory." What else structurally might have changed? Would songs have shifted? Would "Seasons of Love" have stayed, moved, or been part of the narrative? Would scenes change between characters, and would songs change? Nobody will ever know the answer.

We are left with a musical that feels "rough around the edges" for Broadway. Even after all these years, it feels a little bit like a "downtown tryout." And if Larson had lived, the temptation from other creatives and producers (especially in the move to Broadway) would likely have been to polish it up a bit more, make it a bit more Broadway. So as tragic as it was, perhaps Larson's death preserved some of the authenticity of the piece.

2

"MUSETTA'S WALTZ"

Form and Reception

RENT AND *LA BOHÈME*

Anthony Tommasini said in his *New York Times* profile:

> After that final dress rehearsal, Mr. Larson gave an interview
> to the *New York Times* at the workshop, in which he spoke of
> "La Bohème," which he first saw when his parents took him to
> a puppet version for children.
>
> As he grew older, he said, he realized that Puccini's bohemi-
> ans were not just four wisecracking guys who wear one anoth-
> er's clothes, eat one another's food and spend one another's
> money when they have any. He recognized himself and his
> East Village artist friends in the story: struggling young people
> who hold down numbing jobs to support their artistic dreams,
> while coping with drugs, poverty, sexual confusion and AIDS.
> (Tommasini 1996)

In adapting *La bohème* and developing the first of the original songs, Larson and Aronson worked to adapt these ideas to the musical theater form. In the beginning of this adaptation, Larson and Aronson composed drafts of three songs that still remain in *Rent*: the title song "Rent," "Santa Fe," and "I Should Tell You." These numbers cemented the style of pop-rock-musical that *Rent* was to become. The collaboration with Aronson allowed the initial concepts and musical identity to take shape, but Larson quickly developed strong ideas about the project, influencing Aronson to change the location. He also developed the title and began to shape the story of *La bohème* on his own terms, specifically that Mimi should live at the end, unlike the opera and novel.

In the end, the AIDS narrative brought Larson back to *Rent*. By 1991, he'd learned that many of his friends were sick, and he saw clear parallels in Mimi's story. Larson felt strongly he wanted to write a piece about hope rather than despair, an element that would set *Rent* apart. Larson was also queering the existing text by including the gay and lesbian characters and a drag queen.

There are several similarities with *La bohème* peppered across *Rent* both thematically and in little nods to the narrative. There is also an interesting concept: usually in an adaptation, we expect the characters to live in a "parallel" universe where the original version of their story doesn't exist. In *Rent*, the characters know *La bohème* exists and reference it. A salient example is when Mark mocks Roger's composition skills and inability to write anything that isn't reminiscent of "Musetta's Waltz." *La bohème* exists, but the characters aren't conscious of their similarities to the story. For a whole generation of musical theater fans, maybe they will one day see an opera set in France about a seamstress and her suitor where she dies tragically at the end and wonder, "Why did they rip off *Rent* and give it such a sad ending?" Larson's skill as a storyteller and composer enabled him to authentically integrate elements of an art form he had little experience with, particularly in terms of musical elements. It shows his passion for taking musical theater to the next level. Working on the opera adaptation allowed Larson to consider what elements could be updated and repurposed and use them to push the form of musical theater.

Some narrative elements mirror the opera almost exactly. "Light My Candle" parallels the meeting between Rodolfo and Mimi in the opera and Roger and Mimi in the musical. The character dynamics are slightly different: in the opera, Rodolfo pursues Mimi, while the play has it the other way around. In the opera, a key is lost, not drugs, but the principle remains the same. Rodolfo's aria in "Che Gelida mania" has subtle echoes in "Light My Candle." Lyrically, "cold hands" is also in the opera, and "they call me Mimi" is a direct translation of the original operatic end to the scene. In both narrative and music, Larson gave Mimi and Roger a love duet, "I Should Tell You," corresponding to Puccini's "O soave fanciulla." He also gives Mimi her farewell "arias." Although in Puccini it is "D'onde lieta usci" and her final farewell, Mimi also gets a similar set of laments in "Without You." "Goodbye Love" has several different characters singing musical lines all while furthering the story—a technique used in opera called "ensemble," but not one used extensively in musical theater. Boublil and Schönberg use this technique extensively in *Les Misérables*, which has operatic sensibilities. *Hair* and *Jesus Christ Superstar* also use an ensemble, both of which are "rock operas" in style, which proves this term has roots other than the slightly dismissive use of musical theater purists. While Larson—unlike

Aronson—didn't start as an opera aficionado, he was grounded in an appreciation of the musical storytelling form.

The "one great song" that Roger seeks to write includes elements of "Musetta's Waltz" despite his best efforts. The great eleven o'clock number that Larson gives Roger and Mark, "What You Own," is a lyrical parallel to "O Mimi, tu pie non torni." In Puccini, the friends lament their lost loves invading their mind, making it impossible to work. For Larson, the outside world, the demands of capitalism, and the commercialization and relentlessness of modern life prevent the two from creating. A parallel to Puccini, outside of the duet, is their love for friends and lovers in Angel, Collins, and Mimi that brings the two back to their work and their sense of self.

Some of Larson's changes are a bit more tongue in cheek: the scenes in Puccini with a band of merry shopkeepers and toymakers played by the chorus are replaced by the drug dealers and homeless street vendors in St. Mark's Place. The choice to shift Mimi from a "humble seamstress" to an S&M club dancer no doubt raised a few eyebrows with traditionalists. He makes throwaway references across the musical; Musetta (Maureen) has a song about attracting admiring glances ("Take Me or Leave Me"). "Tango Maureen" is a nod to the dance.

In terms of characters, Larson drew upon parallels, but his updating of the characters was integral to create a new musical that reflected the era he lived in and the social and cultural points he was making. Roger (Rodolfo) who is Puccini's poet becomes a rock musician. Larson makes Roger sick, which is a natural change reflecting the AIDS epidemic rather than tuberculosis. Mimi and Roger share their diagnosis, and their shared issues with addiction is a solid reworking of the original. Their romance is powerful, and the "I Should Tell" you conversation works because they share a the same "fate" and prejudices. Mimi surviving the condition she shares with her love is an important part of that message—unlike Rodolfo, doomed to heartbreak, the hope in Larson's piece is also in Mimi having Roger to share the journey with her illness, for however long it lasts.

One misconception is that Puccini's Mimi is more "innocent" than Larson's. In the opera, Mimi has a relationship with a rich viscount. She (and other ladies in similar positions) would strike up relationships with wealthy men in exchange for protection and the perks of being in their company. Mimi's on-off relationship with Benny (which Roger is so jealous of) reflects this arrangement. Benny provides protection and financial help, especially when Benny says, "I'll pay" when she wants to go to rehab. In terms of character, Mimi is bolder and brasher than her operatic counterpart, and her job (dancer at an S&M club) worlds away from Puccini's seamstress.

For Larson, in the face of AIDS and the loss he himself had seen, the message of hope in having Mimi live became integral to his story. Of course, Angel, another key character, doesn't live. Larson shifts the tragic scene and aria of Puccini's ending to the midpoint of act 2 when Collins sings "I'll Cover You" at Angel's funeral. Angel, for the most part, is based on Schaunard in *La bohème*. Angel Schunnard is a violinist who also acquires additional cash as the result of an animal death. While not exactly "drag," Schunnard does sing in falsetto at the ball scene. There's no indication of Schunnard's sexuality, but there's also no refuting of it either. Colline is great friends with Schunnard, and Larson "queers" the existing source material by drawing on the unspoken. Colline, who becomes Collins, has the least in common with his operatic counterpart. He is a philosopher, but less anarchist in nature and far more mild mannered. Neither Schunnard nor Colline are ill in Puccini, but in *Rent* their new alter egos, Angel and Collins, both have AIDS—again an important element of his commentary on the impact of the disease. Similarly, Benny doesn't share much with his operatic counterpart Beniot. He's a landlord, but the similarities end there. In Puccini, he is an old codger who is mocked and taken advantage of. Larson's Benny is a trendy, intelligent "yuppie" who married his way to wealth. Larson used the idea of a landlord as a jumping-off point to consider capitalism versus the bohemian lifestyle, as well as the impact of gentrification on New York. Benny may also be a subtle dig at those he felt "sold out" post-college for "sensible" jobs that bring in money. Much like Benny/Beniot, the character Musetta (Maureen) leaves Marcello (Mark) for, Alcindoro, is so similar to Benny/Benoit that they're often played by the same actor.

Marcello in Puccini becomes our narrator Mark. A painter in the opera, he is a filmmaker in Larson's story—reflecting both his friends in real life and a neat update of someone capturing a "version" of the world around them through their art. Both versions of Mark are unlucky in love, opening the story recently dumped. Mark was left for another women, which allowed Larson to explore the diversity of the community he sought to capture. In both versions, Mark's lovelorn artistic block is a strong opener for the story, leading to the debate between commercialism versus art. In Puccini, Marcello sells his painting to a pub. In *Rent*, he sells his footage to cable news. In both, Mark is the center of the friendship group. He pulls the group together, and although this parallels the opera, this could also be how Larson saw himself within his own friendship group. As much as Larson was "updating" Puccini, he was also trying to catalog the world he lived in and the friends he knew and lost.

CRITICAL RESPONSE BROADWAY

During the transfer period from NYTW, it was announced that Larson won the Pulitzer Prize for drama, which garnered even more attention for the show. *Rent* opened on April 29, 1996, attended by numerous celebrities including George Clooney, Sigourney Weaver, and Isabella Rossellini (McDonnell, Rent, 1998, p. 63). As described by Anthony Rapp in his autobiography, cast and producers anxiously awaited the *New York Times* review. Upon reading Ben Brantley's review, which called the show "exhilarating" and "vigorous" and said it "rushes forward on an electric current of emotion," Anthony Rapp said, "That's what we needed" (Rapp 2006). Although the reviews made much of Larson's death, John Lahr said, "Larson's death does not diminish the phenomenal achievement of *Rent*." Others followed, praising *Rent* and citing its revolutionary approach to the musical, including Michael Feingold in the *Village Voice*:

> With few exceptions *Rent* is the only important event in the rock musical since *Hair*. And thanks to its Sondheimian formal sense, it's a work of consistently higher quality than Hair, which shot off in all kinds of exciting new impulses but barely followed them up. (Feingold 1993)

That the *Village Voice* already placed *Rent* alongside both Sondheim and *Hair* indicated a high-quality new musical. As a "rock musical," *Rent* would inevitably be compared to *Hair*, but this review considers it superior in quality to the current benchmark of its genre. It also highlights that *Rent* was significant as much for its innovation and quality in musical theater as it was for its depictions of AIDS. In making comparisons to *Hair*, which took on the politics of Vietnam and the era of the hippie, the review cast *Rent* as a significant work of musical theater.

Amid the praise for *Rent* and Larson's style heralding it as the dawn of a new age of musicals, there was a sense of sentimental lament among the reviews for the loss of a young talent. The sentiment is apparent in this review, and the account moved beyond the production onstage to the real-life events that colored it. It is difficult to imagine Michael Billington or Nicholas de Jongh responding the same way in the *Guardian* or the *Evening Standard*. In Britain, scandal and sentiment are the fuel of the tabloid press, although London reviewers and theatrical criticism tend to shy away from such personalization. British critics were perhaps harsher given the associations of Larson's death and its publicity when producers Seller and McCollum took *Rent* to London.

One critic less than enamored with the show was John Simon of *New York* magazine. He commented that Larson's death was "doubly sad when you consider that the cited young man was groping his way to a unified personal style that this uneven, scattershot show does not yet achieve." He was wont to say, "*Rent* profits from the Bohème infrastructure, it is also hampered by it, as the author is obliged to think up clever parallels or disheveled variation that invite unfavorable comparison with the original."

John Lahr also wasn't sold on the format of the piece. "Inevitably the theatrical shorthand of *Rent* makes it wobble. What you get is a song cycle tricked out into a notional story whose events are not so much dramatized as indicated." It's unclear whether it's the story or the form that didn't work for Lahr, but he was clearly unconvinced by Larson's style. For him, the "narrative overload" of the eight stories proved too much, but he was also resistant to the "challenges" of using rock music to bring the stories to life. However, he was ultimately moved by Larson's story: "The aroma of *Rent* may not be sweet, but it is also not sour. Larson's gift was the elegiac which celebrates both grief and gladness. He uncovers the poignance in his characters' panic—a manic quality that suits rock's electrified sound."

Jeremy Gerard of *Variety* further praised Larson for improving the state of American musical theater. He declared, "*Rent* makes the musical theatre joyously important again." John Istel, for the *American Theatre* magazine, wrote of Larson's sentimentality as his strength: "Larson was a severe romantic and a shameless sentimentalist. . . . His East Village Romantics are Rodgers and Hammerstein versions." Istel refutes the idea that sentimentality was either a bad thing, or unusual in musical theater—or theater in general. Istel also praises Larson's technical ability regarding the ending and Mimi's recovery: "Ah, the American musical ending! This is pure arts, as in artifice, and Larson, so well-versed in the musical and structural material of the genre in which he worked, knew it."

Istel enjoyed the social and political vision that Larson's piece demonstrated for the true social conscience and commented that the piece proved Larson was "deeply disturbed by a society that could become obsessed with an exclusionary notion of "family values" while alienating itself from the fundamental human values of community, caring, and love." Istel's response is in tune with what audiences would come to love and connect with. Reviews were vital to the show's success— particularly in the pre-internet (or early internet) age that *Rent* opened in, where word of mouth was slower and the age of social media promotion was not yet upon us. What worked in *Rent*'s favor was an array of critics like Istel who seemed in tune with what *Rent* stood for and what audiences saw in the show.

The story that *Rent* accidentally gave Anthony Tommasini helped the relationship with the *Times* enormously. What had begun as a small arts piece on an opera and a rock musical—cute, niche interest with a bit of human interest—had broken to be the biggest arts story of the year on Larson's death. That piece brought Ben Brantley to the show at NYTW and the interest of the *Times* at the off-Broadway level, which was not unheard of but it was unusual. So, Brantley's reviewer hailing it as a landmark was one of the first critical signs the show might be truly "going places." Brantley said that it "restores spontaneity and depth of feeling to a discipline that sorely needs them. People who complain about the demise of the American musical have simply been looking in the wrong places." He also was among the first to praise Larson's writing and how it elevated the source material, saying, "Puccini's ravishingly melancholy work seemed, like many operas of its time, to romance death; Mr. Larson's spirited score and lyrics defy it." This high praise catapulted *Rent* to be recognized as something new and important.

When Brantley revisited, he didn't blindly praise the piece, and this adds weight to his review. He is still enthusiastic about the work, but it is modulated as any of his famously honest and in-depth reviews are. This showed that the praise he gave to the Broadway production was earned. Is his re-review of the production, he said, "What makes *Rent* so wonderful is not its hipness quotient, but its extraordinary spirit of hopeful defiance and humanity."

The *New York Times* was clearly on board in its support of *Rent*, and they dedicated various articles to it over the coming months, including most of a Sunday arts and leisure section. Accompanying the review from Brantley, there would later be a longer op-ed from Frank Rich, the former chief theater critic, who praised the social and political ethos of *Rent* along with its artistic merit in a piece called "East Village Story": "*Rent* is all the critics say it is. It takes the very people whom politicians now turn into scapegoats for our woes: the multicultural, the multi-sexual, the homeless, the sick—and without sentimentalizing them or turning them into ideological symbols of victims, lets them revel in their joy, their capacity for love . . . all in a ceaseless outpouring of melody."

PULITZER PRIZE

Rent is one of a handful of musicals to win a Pulitzer Prize. One quirk of the Pulitzer is that if the jury finds no work worthy of award, then they don't award in that category. For the drama category, the award is "for a distinguished play by an American playwright, preferably original in its source and dealing with American life." Since the award began there has been roughly a musical per decade to win the prize: *Of Thee I Sing* (1932), *South Pacific* (1950), *Fiorello!* (1960), *How to Succeed in Business Without Really Trying* (1962), *A Chorus Line* (1976), and *Sunday in the Park with George* (1985). Since *Rent*, it has been awarded three times: *Next to Normal* (2010), *Hamilton* (2016), and *A Strange Loop* (2020). Among those, a few overlap with *Rent*, including *A Chorus Line*, the first Broadway musical to have an overtly gay storyline. *Sunday in the Park with George* was by Larson's mentor Sondheim, and Larson paid tribute to him in *Tick, Tick . . . Boom!* with "Sunday," a parody of the Sondheim song of the same name. *Next to Normal* was directed by Michael Greif and starred *Rent* alumnus Aaron Tveit. Hamilton creator Lin-Manuel Miranda cites Larson's work as his key musical theater inspiration. Miranda also directed the film version of *Tick, Tick . . . Boom!* The Pulitzer musical theater family is a small one and illustrates Larson's prominence in the landscape of American musical theater.

The point of the Pulitzer was not necessarily monetary reward (the award came with a $3,000 prize) or ticket sales but rather critical endorsement. It was a way of "proving" that *Rent* was a legitimate and worthy piece of work. In all the hype as it transferred to Broadway and in the rumblings of accusation around the impact of Larson's death being responsible for its success, the Pulitzer was a stamp of quality. Because the prize and committee are independent from the theater community—unlike the Tony Awards—it helped brush away doubts or any lingering elements of Broadway Imposter Syndrome.

The award was bittersweet according to Jeffrey Seller in an article by Robert Viagas of *Playbill*:

> First and foremost this prize belongs to Jonathan Larson. We are continually gratified that so many people, both in and out of the theater community, have expressed so much support and love for this incredible show. In a year that has brought some of the greatest highs and lows of our professional lives, his prize will go down as one of the highest highs yet. (Viagas 1996)

Awards season for the show was a predictably busy affair. In addition to the Pulitzer, it went on to be awarded in almost every major category of the New York theater world. Interestingly, the small gap between off-Broadway and Broadway meant it was eligible across both kinds of awards. *Rent* was given three Obie awards (awards for off-Broadway shows) for Book and Music, Direction, and Best Ensemble performance. Adam Pascal and Daphne Rubin-Vega won Theatre World Awards, which recognize significant debuts. The Drama Desk Awards are one of the biggest awards and usually an indication of Tony Award success. *Rent* predictably did well, winning for Outstanding Musical, Outstanding Book of a Musical, Outstanding Orchestrations, Outstanding Lyrics, and Outstanding Music—a clear recognition for Larson's work above all else. There were also nominations for Greif, Adam Pascal, and Daphne Rubin-Vega, while Wilson Jermaine Heredia won for his performance.

Moving on to the Tony Awards, which were announced just ten days after the Broadway opening, the show was nominated for ten and won four. Larson posthumously won Best Musical, Best Book of a Musical, and Best Original Score. The other award went to Wilson Jermaine Heredia for best featured actor. On the performance side, *Rent* wasn't as recognized as others, but a full "sweep" of the Tonys for a musical is very rare. *A Chorus Line* won nine in 1976, and then *Hamilton* recorded sixteen nominations in 2016, winning eleven. The only true "sweep" in Tony Award history is the record-holding show *The Producers*, which was nominated for twelve and won eleven. Tonys voters rarely seem to go in one direction, but Larson's writing received the stamp of approval. Julie Larson accepted the award for best score on his behalf and said he had "worked very hard for fifteen years to become an overnight sensation." She acknowledged other artists still struggling and said on Jonathan's behalf, "Stay true to yourselves and to your dreams and know they can come true; this is for you."

MUSICAL THEATER FORM

The form that *Rent* takes is of the "sung through" musical, which means that instead of dialogue interspersed with song, *Rent* is predominantly sung, with minimal spoken dialogue. This approach is fitting given its operatic roots. Music becomes the primary means of communication, characterization, and narrative. Without dialogue, the music conveys information and develops the character of the musical. The pop-rock music married the early 1990s pop-rock style with musical theater influences.

The musical theater form became a new way of engaging with AIDS and as a means of reaching diverse audiences. In the move to Broadway and later London, the audiences that Larson's musical connected with were potentially different and more diverse than the traditional audience of the "AIDS play." The musical theater form demands a different approach to performance in general and, by association, the depiction of AIDS. In musical theater the narrative is driven forward by musical numbers, sometimes allowing characters to convey emotions impossible through traditional speech.

The "sung through" approach also lends itself to the musical theater Larson was aiming to create. He was trying to engage with and create a different form of musical theater as an antidote to the overblown spectacle-heavy productions of the era. In creating an antithesis to current trends in the pared-down style of *Rent*, Larson and Greif's design team showed an awareness of the musical theater form and the ability to adapt this theatrical approach. The pared-down approach served the narrative function of showing the gritty East Village location. It also suited the production budget while providing an alternative approach to the form. For this and its rock music approach, *Rent* was set apart from other examples of the musical theater genre of this period. *Rent* also became part of a new chapter in LGBTQ musicals onstage, as explored in the next chapter.

STAGING

The staging of *Rent* is important in understanding the tone and approach of Larson's depiction of AIDS. *Rent* is staged with a minimalist set. The stage is bare and industrial in appearance; the dominant color is gray, and the set has a scaffolding platform above the stage with a staircase leading to it. A metallic sculpture/structure to one side becomes a Christmas tree at one point. The action transforms the areas of the stage through the use of minimal props. The four-piece band sits onstage, visible to the audience, and seems to blend into the action as part of the East Village landscape. Two large metal tables form various pieces of the set, from a bed to a door. Any set that not made by use of tables and simple props is suggested by the actors' movements. The staging is similar to the National Theatre's production of *Angels in America* as it is actor-driven and minimalist. In this, *Rent* contrasts with the traditional staging of musicals, which is often opulent and spectacular. By stripping back the production, *Rent* emphasizes the music and narrative, focusing an audience's attention on issues, including AIDS.

David Savran describes the staging as "toward the emblematic and presentational." What Savran is referring to is *Rent*'s stark and minimalist staging. This was, in many ways, a diversion from the traditional musical theater approach to staging, particularly the more specular staging of the "mega musicals" of the 1980s. Thus, the staging of *Rent* contrasted with the dominant stylistic approach to musical theater, which is, as mentioned, traditionally more opulent and grandiose. The musical theater format also allows productions to take the opposite approach and become "emblematic and presentational" rather than realistic, an acceptable artistic approach within the musical theater style and particularly the case within sung-through musicals such as *Rent*. In these examples, an element of realism in performance is lost, allowing for this more "presentational" and "minimalist" approach to emerge. This serves *Rent* well in several aspects of the production, working with the overall "suspension of disbelief" that accompanies the musical theater genre in terms of song replacing dialogue. This "presentational" style of musical theater also gives *Rent* a more distinctive musical theater identity and sets it apart from its contemporaries as something different in both style and substance.

Savran aligns *Rent*'s staging and style with a self-aware and postmodernist approach to the musical. While a valid interpretation, the staging can also be seen as a reflection of the community it aims to depict and its origins at NYTW. Although we can read *Rent*'s staging in the fashion suggested by Savran, the reality is that, rather than being a self-reflexive artistic decision as he suggests, it is more likely a matter of convenience and economy. The off-Broadway production budgets would not allow for elaborate sets or costumes, which was retained in the move to Broadway and eventually London.

"How do you measure" a year in love, the show asks . . . but also how do you market a show about AIDS?

CRITICAL RESPONSE

Rent did prove to be incredibly successful on Broadway. Integral to any theatrical success in New York is for a review to appear in the *New York Times*. As described by Anthony Rapp in his autobiography, the cast and producers anxiously awaited the review. After reading Ben Brantley's review, which called the show "exhilarating" and "vigorous" and said it "rushes forward on an electric current of emotion" (Brantley, *New York Times*, February 19, 1996) Rapp said, "That's what we needed" (Rapp *Without You*, p. 140). Although the reviews made much of Larson's death, it certainly gained the show additional press interest it would not otherwise have had but reviewers also praised the show itself. As John Lahr said: "Larson's death does not diminish the phenomenal achievement of *Rent*" (Gerard 1996.) Others followed, praising *Rent* and citing its revolutionary approach to the musical, including the *Village Voice*, which stated: "With few exceptions, *Rent* is the only important event in the rock musical since *Hair*. And thanks to its Sondheimian formal sense, it's a work of consistently higher quality than *Hair*, which shot off in all kinds of exciting new impulses but barely followed them up" (Michael Feingold, *Village Voice*, May 18, 1993).

That the *Village Voice* placed *Rent* alongside both Sondheim and *Hair* indicates the high quality of the musical. As a new "rock musical," *Rent* would inevitably be compared to *Hair*. Still, the review here considers it superior in quality to the current benchmark of rock musicals, which indicates the kind of impact *Rent* was having.

The *Village Voice*, perhaps feeling close to the composer and his material as a defender of the same downtown sensibilities as itself, ends its review with the following:

Any rejoicing over *Rent* comes attached to a tragic sense of loss: we lived to see it, and its author did not. I said this review wasn't about death, but it is. I loved *Rent* and Jonathan Larson's dead, and yes, I'm crying. (Feingold, *Village Voice*, May 18, 1993)

The sentiment is apparent in this review; the account has moved beyond a review of the production onstage to the real-life events that colored it. However, it is difficult to imagine Billington or de Jongh responding the same way in the *Guardian* or the *Evening Standard*. In Britain, scandal and sentiment fuel the tabloid press. London reviewers, and theatrical criticism on the whole, tend to shy away from such personalization. As will be seen in the analysis of the British reception of *Rent* later in this chapter, critics were perhaps harsher given the associations of Larson's death and the publicity that was seen to have fueled *Rent*'s progress. Because *Rent* did indeed progress, and its success in New York soon led producers Seller and McCollum to look to a London production.

Critical opinion is important for box office sales and, therefore, for the success of a work, but it is not the only factor. Critics cited here reflect an element of audience response but do not represent the entire audience. The comments about *Rent* indicate that its approach to depicting AIDS on the theatrical stage was successful. Larson's text made a broader political and social statement about AIDS while connecting with an audience on an emotional level. So even when the show moved uptown, even down the line where celebrity casting, *Rent*-like clothing lines at Bloomingdales, or celebrities in the audience might have created cries of "selling out," there still was a level of authenticity in the piece being firmly rooted in a moment downtown—and forever preserving that piece of downtown uptown. All musicals are a product of a particular moment. *Rent* is not different in that respect, but being aware that might have been part of the reason for its longevity.

Broadway is a big business, and an expensive one at that, and an ability to claw back the money the show had cost, also to put money in the bank to guard against dips in ticket sales, and also to ensure the future of the show was going to be seized upon by the producers. At the same time, nobody knew how long the show would last. For the young cast and creative team, there was a sense of "seize the moment" to capitalize on what they had. And so while some decisions might not, in hindsight, have particularly been in keeping with the overall "brand" (saying that in itself seemed like a contradiction), they were also part of the machine of keeping *Rent* going.

Part of the ongoing success was that *Rent* entered into something of a PR machine in its first year on Broadway. Not unusual, certainly by today's standards. But what was unusual was the level of interest from the "mainstream" press. While theater blogs existed, they were small-scale at the time and online content was minimal. In the early 1990s, most of these were in their infancy regarding online content, which has since proliferated. However, there was still a steady output from publications like *Playbill* and *American Theatre*, focused specifically on New York theater within their remit for obvious reasons. Usually, aside from reviews, a new show might get one or two articles in the "mainstream" press; this would include local publications in New York like the *Village Voice* and other regional magazines and newspapers. Of course, press interest is always more for bigger shows, particularly those with "celebrity" casting, but the level of interest for a cast of young unknowns was unheard of.

The production and cast had photo shoots in *Harper's Bazaar*, the *New York Times*, *Out*, *Rolling Stone*, *Time Out*, *Vanity Fair*, and *Vogue*. You can't help but think that Larson would have been impressed but also confused by that array—his rock musical about addiction and AIDS in *Vogue*? Larson had ambitions, but the world's premier fashion magazine probably didn't feature in them.

Integrated into the sometimes ridiculous nature of the press machine was the idea of sharing a legacy that Larson never envisioned. So while Larson probably didn't dream of *Vogue*, he did dream of being the future of the American musical, and you only get to do that if your show makes a splash. So while there was a sense of fun, a sense of the slightly ridiculous about the PR machine the young cast got swept up in, it's also true that there was still a sense they were doing this for Jonathan. A sense that if they gave that part of the job their all as well, then Larson's message could be spread far and wide, and his legacy was also secured with it.

The media attention can be seen as a blueprint for newer musical theater hype. This crossover text transcends the regular interest in the genre, the niche fan interest, or passing tourist trade into something else. And yes, to a degree, the mega-musicals of the 1980s had an element of this—a wider popular appeal with a sense of a show as the celebrity. But the next show to replicate this kind of "beyond the bubble" interest was, of course, *Hamilton*. With the breakout success of the album and the crossover appeal of the show more broadly, there was a sense of the same kind of ubiquitous element with that show, augmented by the age of social media.

In the summer of 1996, John Istel wrote a piece in *American Theatre* asking, "Did Jonathan Larson's Vision Get Lost in the Media Uproar?"

Istel (who also reviewed *Rent* elsewhere) rightly asked if the surrounding conversation (and yes, hype) around the show and Larson's death obscured was he was trying to do. He adds, "In the last few months, I have often wondered what the audience and critical reception of *Rent* would have been if that aneurysm hadn't developed in Larson's aorta. Were that the case, you obviously wouldn't be reading a year-old interview with him—Larson would have been more than willing to give an update on his mission."

Istel goes on to rightly note that before Larson's death, hardly anyone had heard of the composer or the musical he was working on with NYTW. Istel wrestles with the sentimentality around Larson's death—and indeed, the column inches generated, along with the somewhat irrefutable proof of awards and continued ticket sales, seem to show there is something in Larson's work beyond a good story to pull people in. At the time of Istel's piece (in the summer of 1996, not long after *Rent* transfers), he had no answers and in fact, was forced to rest on the same story of Larson's death and the tragedy as everyone else: "I implied that Mimi died in *Rent*. 'She doesn't die in my version,' he reminded me. And that]s the ultimate tragedy: that we can't rewrite his story to make a happy ending. The sad fact that Larson's demise is irreversible highlights just how far his art diverged from his life" (Istel, *American Theatre*).

Istel's analysis tells us that we can't separate Larson's story from *Rent*; they are entwined forever. More so perhaps with Lin-Manuel Miranda's adaptation of *Tick, Tick . . . Boom!* And the integration of Larson's story even more so into the legend and legacy of *Rent*. And maybe we shouldn't. Perhaps we should accept that tragedy got *Rent* attention; it got Larson's voice heard in a way it hadn't before. While that story can't be rewritten, as Istel says, we can, like *Rent*, find hope in the tragedy.

Rent exploded into the mainstream when it moved uptown. A inevitable part of the success was a shift away from the downtown roots of the show. But between the design of the space, the keeping of the original cast, and the way Greif structured his direction, *Rent* managed to maintain its downtown feel. And we must remember that "the future of Broadway" is what Larson dreamed about.

3

"I'LL COVER YOU"

Rent and LGBTQ Musicals

HISTORY OF LGBTQ MUSICALS AND RENT

Until this point, portraying LGBTQ characters was a rarity. They were either a "joke" character or a villain. Understanding the significance of *Rent* and its portrayal of queer characters and the importance of it as a queer musical text requires the context and history of these characters onstage. There is a long history of queer stories. Larson didn't burst onto the scene with nobody before him. And given that he was a straight, cisgender writer, we should remember he stood on the shoulders of many queer writers before him who couldn't bring their whole selves to their work, but whose queerness still became entwined with their musicals.

One of the earliest examples of a "homosexual" character in a musical was in *Patience* (1881). Gilbert and Sullivan gave audiences the first effeminate lead character in an English-language musical: Reginald

Bunthorne. Of course, there were LGBTQ audiences at this time, and long before that they were intrinsic to the theater, both as creatives and as audiences. There was a scattering of similar caricatures across this period, but it wasn't until much later in the twentieth century that we see fully rounded gay characters onstage in any form.

There were many LGBTQ writers (as well as directors, actors, designers, etc.) in theater. These writers were often either not including their real identities in their work or doing so in coded forms. One such writer was Cole Porter, who separated his life as a gay man from his "wholesome" musicals. However, Porter included coded references for those in the know. In the "coded" years, Cole amused himself by pitching his words on two levels, so that the "coach party" audience was content with the obvious, while the "in" group relished the real meaning. Noël Coward also wrote "coded" elements in his musicals about gay men. *Bittersweet* (1929) featured a quartet of overdressed 1890s London fops, who referenced (in coded terms) gay life. Porter and Coward existed in a similar theatrical space to Tennessee Williams, hiding in plain sight. Many people knew their "secret," but they couldn't incorporate openly queer themes into their work.

As a straight man, Larson was in a position of privilege to both openly integrate gay characters with less fear for his personal safety and his career. For writers like Williams or Porter, despite their sexuality being an "open secret," integrating it into their work was dangerous and possibly career suicide. Larson didn't have to think about that equation. Being a straight man protected his career. We know that queer artists still struggle with having their voices heard authentically. Objectively it isn't right that one of the first gay stories in musical theater came from a straight man because gay writers weren't afforded the opportunity to write their stories. However, it is important that Larson was able to use his privilege to do that. Larson didn't have to contend with active censorship and the fear of persecution for what he wrote.

Opportunities for queer writers and stories with queer characters had slowly begun to change in the run-up to Larson writing *Rent*. Following a wave of conservatism in the 1950s, the mid-1960s saw the first public manifestations of a gay rights movement with the Stonewall Riots in 1969 that became viewed as a "watershed" moment in gay liberation. In fringe theater, this new age of permissiveness and openness began a shift. The mainstream musical was a slower ship to steer. The same year as the riots, René Auberjonois played Sebastian Baye in *Coco* (1969), the first openly gay character in a Broadway musical, even if it was written as a hateful caricature. A year later in the Tony Award–winning *Applause* (1970), Lee Roy Reams played the hairdresser Duane, the first likeable openly gay character in a Broadway musical. *Applause* also included a scene in a gay bar. A few years later, Tommy Tune won his first Tony portraying an explicitly gay choreographer in *Seesaw* (1973). *A Chorus Line* (1974) was the first major Broadway book musical where gay characters discussed (in both dialogue and song) the sexual aspects of their lives.

Across the early 1970s and 1980s, there were an array of off-Broadway "gay plays" that represented this era of "liberation." However, little of this translated "uptown" to Broadway or to musicals. The first musical written by and for a gay audience to receive mainstream attention was off-Broadway's *Boy Meets Boy* (1975). This charming hit by Bill Solly and Donald Ward imagined what the 1930s might have been like if gay and straight lifestyles were equally accepted, allowing two men to have an Astaire and Rogers–style romance. Off-Broadway's *Gulp!*

(1977), which took a musical comedy look at the trials and tribulations of a gay lifeguard, was coauthored and produced by John Glines—the same gay impresario who later brought Harvey Fierstein's *Torch Song Trilogy* (1982) and William Hoffman's *As Is* (1985) to Broadway.

As the wider world slowly became more accepting, so did theater, and artists were able to tell stories that reflected a range of identities and their own. Of course, many LGBTQ writers were still not putting their own stories into their work. Larson's own mentor, Stephen Sondheim, never wrote a "gay" musical despite being a gay man and being out for many decades. We don't consider Sondheim's works of art lesser for this. His works reflect human experience, as most artists aspire to do, regardless of his sexuality. Had Sondheim (and indeed Larson) been writing in another era, perhaps their respective approaches would have been different. There is often a lot of pressure on LGBTQ artists to write their own experiences, and often their own trauma, into their work. Not all, Sondheim included, wish to do that.

Other shows had their problems. The adaptation of Christopher Isherwood's semi-autobiographical short stories into the musical that would become *Cabaret* had issues of queer erasure. This show crosses over gender and sexuality representation and is an undeniable part of the through line of queer stories onstage (and beyond). The book was adapted into the Tony Award–winning musical *Cabaret* (1966) and the film *Cabaret* (1972) for which Liza Minnelli won an Academy Award for playing Sally. Bob Fosse directed the movie and won the award for Best Director.

Cabaret was a forerunner to the bohemian life that the characters in *Rent* look for. The Emcee specifically can be viewed like Angel as the performer who takes elements of their stage self and their true self to defy clear labels and classification.

Despite Isherwood being one of the first openly gay high-profile writers in America, some of the "queerness" was damped down in adaptations such as *I Am Camera* (1951). Crucially this involved Cliff, a character who, in various edits, has been in and out of the closet.

As Hal Prince, producer and director of the original stage production of *Cabaret*, remembers, "We persuaded ourselves that the musical comedy audience required a sentimental heterosexual love story with a beginning, middle and end to make the concept palatable. In my opinion, we were wrong" (Prince 2017).

Prince continues: "Were I to do *Cabaret* now, I would take the opportunity . . . to restore the original gay subplot. But putting Nazis on the stage in a musical seemed like a big enough step at the time."

They weren't alone in a hiding, or at least diluting queer identities. Larson existed in an in-between time, where writers were "out" but little "gay work" was being made. Now, twenty-five years on, queer writers have more freedom to move between telling "queer stories" and just "stories." So, while Lisa Kron wrote *Fun Home* with an emphasis on telling lesbian stories, Benji Pesak wrote *Dear Evan Hansen* with no queer themes (but one or two awkward homophobic remarks). We can also encourage straight/cisgender writers to include queer stories, like David West Read with *& Juliet* and Irene Sankoff and David Hein including gay characters in *Come from Away*.

Rent was clearly part of a through line in telling queer stories in musicals. But where does the show fall in terms of the characters and stories it depicts?

LESBIANS

Queer happy endings are a rarity in any media, and lesbian characters disproportionately die first or go back to their man. *Rent* was significant for showing lesbians . . . having a relative happy time. Previous examples of lesbians in musical theater had also been a rarity and, by the 1990s, they were even subject to more clichés than their male counterparts. Lesbian-coded characters existed, such as the gym teacher in *Hairspray* (2002), a clichéd stock character; or Mama Morton in *Chicago* (1975), not named as a lesbian but queer coded; or Lorraine in *Nick and Nora* (1991), who dies and whose death is played over and over. There was a love story in Andrew Lloyd Webber's *Aspects of Love*, but it was fleeting. The most positive portrayal of lesbians at this point were the "lesbians from next door" in William Finn and James Lapine's *Falsettos*.

Following this list, Maureen and Joanne are a continued evolution. Cordelia and Charlotte are important characters, but they form part of a gay, male-led story. Meanwhile, Maureen and Joanne have their own story, a revelation in musical theater and broader culture. Their story does not end up in a breakup (at least not permanently) or someone dying. In fact, Maureen and Joanne probably have the "easiest" and happiest storyline out of everyone in *Rent*. This was no small thing for most queer women watching the show, used to seeing their representation as secondary, ending in disaster or death.

Maureen and Joanne aren't perfect characters. Maureen can be viewed as "problematic" because she falls into the "slutty bisexual" trope: she sleeps around and cheats on her partners. However, we could reframe this with a twenty-first-century "sex positive" outlook and say Maureen embraces her sexuality. Larson was writing from Mark's point of view, which colors how we see Maureen. She still gets a happy ending with Joanne, so this point is a minor gripe in the bigger picture of queer female representation onstage (and beyond). Joanne feels ahead of her time—she is a Black lesbian lawyer from a "sensible" middle-class background. Her parents, despite comments about "Doc Martens and a bra" haven't rejected her for her sexuality, and she's clearly "out" to them. That's no small thing for 1994, and the representation Joanne offered for queer women, particularly queer women of color, was monumental.

Both characters are a benchmark for future queer female representation in musicals. Following *Rent* there were forward steps for lesbians in musicals, though admittedly not as much as their gay male counterparts. Michael John LaChiusa broke ground in *The Wild Party* by depicting a female same-sex couple and characterizing their sexual relationship. In 2013, Alison Bechdel's graphic memoir *Fun Home* was turned into a musical, putting a lesbian story at the heart of a musical. An adaptation of Alice Walker's novel *The Color Purple* (2004) meant that a Black lesbian protagonist was finally seen in a musical, though it took the revival in 2016 to bring the musical the critical attention it deserved. These musicals are a huge leap from when *Falsettos* was leading the depiction of lesbian characters.

The Prom (2018) foregrounds a lesbian high school romance, with the narrative centering on a young girl wanting to take her girlfriend to prom. It parallels the UK's *Everyone's Talking about Jamie* (2017), with its queer teenage representation. Similarly, *Be More Chill* (2017) features a bisexual character and many other queer-coded characters in the young cast. These shows that represent queer teenagers and their experience feel like an extension of what *Rent* began: showing young people in the moments of discovering themselves and their identities and giving them the art to reflect that. Teenagers flocked to it largely because there was nothing—not in musical theater, not in more mainstream settings—to represent their queer experience. Now, there is a plethora of representation in TV and film—still not nearly enough, but much more than in the 1990s.

DRAG AND TRANS CHARACTERS

There has been much debate over how to categorize Angel as a character. Angel originally was read as a drag queen by many reviews and fans alike, which is factually correct: Angel performs drag, and their performance persona (and outfits) are an integral part of their identity. Many productions now interpret Angel as a trans/nonbinary character. The latter identity seems to make most sense for a person who embraces the fluidity of gender in their expressions. It seems safe to also assume that Larson simply lacked the language we have twenty-five years later to articulate who Angel was. He clearly integrated sexual fluidity into their character but lacked the "labels" we have for nuanced identities today. Today it comes more naturally to play them—and more importantly to cast them—with this in mind, much like the Hope Mill Theatre production in 2021 did by casting a nonbinary actor in the role. This is a solid step forward to acknowledge what we now understand about Angel's character.

Drag and gender nonconformism have long been a part of musical theater. In the UK pantomime dames—a man dressed as a woman—are a staple of the theater calendar. We must emphasize the difference between drag and Angel's gender identity because being a drag performer is a part of their identity. In the scope of musical theater representation, the lines of gender expression, drag, and trans and non-binary representation, Angel has helped evolve the conversation.

The Rocky Horror Picture Show (1973) is an example of the changing conversation and language. It is a musical that is "controversial" in many ways, and its language about gender identity no longer fits contemporary discussions, but it is no less important for it. The label—at the writer's own insistence—is not "drag" (as it might appear in context) but transvestism: "Nobody is in drag, that's how they dress in Transylvania" (Sokol 2019). This sparked conversations around gender, identity, and how we portray it. The show, which premiered at London's Royal Court in 1973, went on to be a huge cult hit. The idea of personal expression in dress and gender performance became an integral element of fan engagement. It was designed to be subversive and provoke conversation, and it is a queer show from a queer creator. Like Angel, the show was a queer awakening for many.

Another historical precursor to what Angel represents onstage was *La Cage aux Folles* (1985). It is about a drag queen (Albin) in the more traditional sense—Albin performs in a drag club and identifies as a gay man. He also appears in female clothing, adopts feminine mannerisms, and takes up the mantle of "mother" figure in the family outside of performance. Like Angel, Albin's use of drag goes beyond a stage performance and is an aspect of their gender identity. Written in the 1970s, it lacks nuance and occasionally plays elements of Albin's identity for laughs, but under the moments that aged poorly is a story about embracing who you are.

In another parallel to *Rent*, *La Cage* features a gay couple as the central romantic pairing. It is an unapologetic celebration of a gay love story, and with it a celebration of love and queer joy that was—and continues to be—rare. It is an important through line in cultural and musical theater history that allowed *Rent* to come to be.

Without *La Cage aux Folles*, later musicals such as *Falsettos* and *Fun Home* would not have succeeded with LGBTQ characters as the leads. In the words of Harvey Fierstein, the librettist for *La Cage* and an out gay man, gay sensibility was always in the theater. *La Cage aux Folles* made money, which catapulted the musical from the subculture into the mainstream. Had it not been such a hit, the Broadway shows today that represent LGBTQ culture would not have survived in the mainstream world of theater.

The representation of nonbinary genderfluid and drag characters has continued post-*Rent* and evolved. *Priscilla, Queen of the Desert*, in the 2006 adaptation of the 1994 film, features a trans character who performs drag, as well as cisgender drag queens. The film and the musical are a joyous commentary on drag and trans identities and continues to be a popular show. It continues to hold importance as the narrative moves away from genderfluid and queer characters only existing and finding acceptance in big cities and shows tolerance can be found in many places. Much like *La Cage*, it might read as idealistic, but it seeks to lead by example and embrace diversity. Both contrast *Rent* by showing queer communities outside of big cities like New York, but their themes of chosen family and community transcend setting.

Rent has inspired many other musicals both in style and content. Probably one of the biggest followers to *Rent* in style and following was *Hedwig and the Angry Inch*. The show debuted off-Broadway in 1998, became a film in 2001, and had a Broadway production in 2014. The time lines and the parallels with *Rent*—a slightly scrappy, subversive off-Broadway piece with queer themes—is apparent. With music and lyrics by Stephen Trask and a book by John Cameron Mitchell, the musical follows Hedwig Robinson, a genderqueer East German singer of a fictional rock-and-roll band. The musical explores queer identity and challenges the notion of rock culture being separate from live theater. It adds to the increasing number of mainstream films and media that questions dichotomous views on sex and gender. *Hedwig and the Angry Inch* provides a space for openly queer performers in this alternative theater movement and punk subculture that is often labeled as queercore.

Fans of the play and film refer to themselves as "Hedheads." In Korea and Japan, a number of teen idols and respected actors have played the role and inspired a large number of young, female Hedheads. This devoted musical theater following, especially from younger fans and LGBTQ fans, is part of *Rent*'s legacy. While *Rent* didn't invent theater fandom, the young people devoted to the musical in person and online are an important part of its legacy.

Two examples of musicals with drag and queer characters at their core are *Kinky Boots* (2012) and *Everyone's Talking about Jamie* (2017). In *Kinky Boots*, the performance emphasizes drag, and the theme focuses on acceptance. In *Jamie*, which is set in a high school and aimed at younger audiences, the central theme is "being who you are." The musical *& Juliet*, which premiered in London in 2020, features a nonbinary character called Mae. Mae was originally cast with a cisgender actor and was ill-defined in the musical; the producers and writers were open to feedback and made changes. When the show returned in 2021, they cast a nonbinary actor Alex Thomas Smith . . . who coincidentally had just played Angel in The Hope Mill Theatre's production of *Rent*.

Though *Rent* did not start this conversation, its characters were an important depiction of trans/nonbinary characters and the celebration of queerness.

AIDS MUSICALS

Rent was innovative in its portrayal of AIDS. It was far from the only theatrical/performance-based text to take on AIDS, but alongside *Falsettos*, it was the only "mainstream" musical to do so. There had been many fringe-style plays and musicals (including the memorably titled *AIDS: The Musical*), but Broadway producers did not see AIDS as a marketable topic. Despite shifts in what musical theater could look like, there was still a trend toward the mega musical and the spectacular.

Falsettos unapologetically depicted the gay experience of AIDS. In the story, Marvin falls in love with Whizzer and leaves his wife Trina in act 1. By act 2, the impact of AIDS on the gay community has grown, and Whizzer becomes sick and their potential future is derailed. It is an unflinching, emotional, and honest response to what William Finn and James Lapine had seen unfold in the years they worked on the show. Like *Rent*, *Falsettos* shows a real love story between two men. *Rent* often gets credited with being the first gay love song and kiss in a Broadway musical, but *Falsettos* has that honor. Several songs explore the love and loss between Whizzer and Marvin. In "Unlikely Lovers," they reflect on how their love affair should never have happened, but how it's exactly what they needed. In "What Would I Do," Marvin reflects on his loss—having finally found love only to lose it so quickly.

Falsettos centered AIDS in the narrative of its unapologetically gay love story—a story that includes both gay men and gay women. Without

Falsettos, we can speculate that *Rent* would not have found its place on Broadway. This landmark musical on AIDS was written by William Finn, a gay man who has been open about his sexuality for most of his career.

Rent was not the last Broadway "AIDS musical." *The Boy from Oz* (1998/2003) is a jukebox musical based on the life of singer and songwriter Peter Allen, featuring songs written by him. The original book is by Nick Enright, with a revised book by Martin Sherman. Premiering in Australia in 1998 and starring Todd McKenney, the musical opened in a revised version on Broadway in 2003 with Hugh Jackman in the title role. It also manages the feat of being a musical about AIDS that never actually mentions AIDS.

ROCK MUSICAL LEGACY

The significance of *Rent* on the musical theatrical landscape can be seen through the continuation of the "rock" genre. The most successful "rock musical" in Britain is *We Will Rock You* (2002), based on the music of Queen and cowritten by Ben Elton. It ran for twelve years in London and had a successful international touring life.

Original composition in musicals has continued to lean toward the pop-rock style of contemporary music, with leading pop stars branching out into musical theater. Elton John collaborated with Disney on both *The Lion King* (1997) and *Aida* (2001) as well as his work on the adaptation of *Billy Elliot* (2005). This cross-genre writing by leading musicians such as Elton John and Bono indicates the influence of contemporary music and a progression in the prestige of the genre.

Subsequent "rock opera" or "rock musicals" such as *American Idiot* (2004) and *Spring Awakening* (2006) fuse controversial subject matter with a rock score, while also focusing on young people's experiences. The most natural successor to *Rent* is *Next to Normal*. It deals with difficult subject matter against a backdrop of a rock-pop score. This show deals with the subject of mental illness, depicting a family's struggle with their mother and wife's bipolar disorder. Directed by *Rent*'s Michael Greif, it is the only musical since *Rent* to win the Pulitzer Prize for drama.

Rock musicals have become fairly mainstream. The idea that a musical is just tap dancing and romance is thankfully a thing of the past now.

RENT AND LGBTQ CHARACTERS IN MUSICALS

After *Rent* there has been a steady—but still not representative—flow of musicals that feature LGBTQ characters.

One of *Rent*'s natural successors was *Spring Awakening*, an adaptation of the music by Duncan Sheik and a book and lyrics by Steven Sater. It is based on the 1891 German play *Spring Awakening* by Frank Wedekind. The queer plot is a subplot but still significant. The show had the same youthful appeal as *Rent*. Like *Rent*, its stars went on to success beyond the show. Lea Michele landed a part on the 2000s hit musical TV show *Glee*. Jonathan Groff originated the role of the king in *Hamilton*, as well as having an array of TV roles. Groff has been open about his sexuality as a gay man early on in his career and has taken many LGBTQ projects, including HBO's *Looking*, which centered on contemporary gay life in San Francisco. Groff is part of a younger generation of actors who are "out" from a younger age and take LGBTQ roles alongside "straight" ones.

Bare is one of the most important musicals of our generation, and it's an underappreciated gem. It is also one of the most "queer" musicals since *Rent*. This pop/rock musical tackles issues like bullying, stigmatization, rape culture, religion, sexism, and coming out. At its center, *Bare* is a love story of two teenage boys named Peter and Jason who are attending a private religious high school. It's structured as a modern-day *Romeo and Juliet*, and its original 2004 release gained a cult following before it was revived in late 2012. It has a similar feel to *Spring Awakening* but with a more focused LGBTQ angle. While *Bare* and *The Prom* might skew to the teen market, *Rent* also opened doors for other queer musicals.

Kiss of the Spider Woman, A Man of No Importance, A New Brain, and the incredibly significant historical piece *The View Upstairs* forefront LGBTQ experience across all ages and eras in the post-*Rent* era. These importance pieces curate and continue a line in musical theater that tell existing LGBTQ stories (*Spider Woman/Man of No Importance*), new stories with LGBTQ threads (*A New Brain*), and historical stories (*The View Upstairs*). However, only one (*Spider Woman*) had a Broadway run. A surprising addition to the LGBTQ canon was *The Full Monty*.

In the film adaptation, gay playwright Terrence McNally adds a budding gay romance. While attending a coworker's funeral, two unemployed steelworkers realize their love for each other in the song "You Walk with Me." They join hands—a daring gesture at a steelworker's funeral. Instead of condemning them, their butch friend (the lead character in the show) remarks, "Good for them," providing a watershed moment of quiet affirmation and understanding. This marked a stream of more "incidental" inclusion in musicals, where the gay character is a part of the plot.

Some shows included queer characters for other reasons. *Avenue Q* and *Book of Mormon* both have jokes at the expense of gay characters.

Avenue Q does this with a sense of love and includes a happy ending for its gay character Rod. Later *Come from Away* cemented proper use of "incidental" gay characters, with its tapestry of characters including a gay couple. The plot also achieves this in the scene where they discover an array of allies and gay people in rural Canada, showing that there are ways to integrate allyship subtly without making it the sole point of the musical. The film *In the Heights* (2021) is another good example of "incidentally gay" characters. Carla and Daniela, who run the salon (Daniela played by Daphne Rubin-Vega), are in a relationship. No overt comment is ever made about it—they simply exist as a couple. This collection of examples proves that progress comes in many kinds. Not all representation is about having a "gay musical," but rather about including LGBTQ people as they would be in "real life."

The most recent LGBTQ themed musical is *The Prom*, with music by Matthew Sklar and a book by Bob Martin and Chad Beguelin, who also wrote the lyrics. The musical made its debut in Atlanta in 2016 before moving to Broadway in October 2018 and officially opening on November 15. It is based on an original concept by Jack Viertel and follows Emma as she tries to take her girlfriend Alyssa to their high school prom. The school, however, will not allow this and tries to cancel the prom. With the help of Broadway stars, the students eventually convince the school to put on an inclusive prom that allows LGBTQ students to bring their same-sex dates to the prom. The musical was performed as part of the 2018 Macy's Thanksgiving Day Parade, where they made history as the first LGBTQ kiss to ever be featured at the parade. Though the kiss "sparked homophobic remarks on social media" (Romano 2018), it also brought joy to the LGBTQ community and received praise. In 2020, it was made into a Netflix film starring Meryl Streep, James Corden, and Nicole Kidman. While the film had mixed reviews, it was the first musical with a lesbian protagonist on the streaming service.

We have come a long way in the representation of LGBTQ characters on Broadway. As we gain a more accepting audience, more faithful representations of these characters will continue to be brought to the stage. The AIDS epidemic is used less as source material these days, and characters in the LGBTQ community find realistic representation that is not offensive or stereotypical. *Falsettos*, *Rent*, and *Fun Home* have inspired a new generation of LGBTQ artists to show the world the ups and downs of the LGBTQ community, and they will continue to do so as we grow and develop as a society.

We will not make inclusive LGBTQ theater until all identities are represented, as the controversies in two musicals recently illustrated. In the UK's production of *& Juliet*, a nonbinary character was played by a cisgender actor. The book of the musical did not make it clear that the character was nonbinary and the resulting song moment of "I'm Not a Girl Not Yet a Woman" looked like a joke about the character. Following the 2020 shut down, the producers, writers, and director responded to feedback from the trans community and reassessed the situation, cast a nonbinary actor and redirected the scene to make the intention and inclusivity clear. In that show, all actors can choose to display their pronouns in their bio. Compare this to *Jagged Little Pill*, the adaptation of Alanis Morrissette's eponymous album, which was fraught with controversy on many levels. In a similar note to *& Juliet*, they wrote an explicitly nonbinary character into the role and cast a cisgender actor.

Unlike the team behind *& Juliet*, the creative team has not altered the casting or script, illustrating that the post-*Rent* musical landscape still struggles with representing the broader LGBTQ community.

There is however a lot of hope—the amount of representation onstage and the high-profile adaptation of stories means progress has been made. *Rent*, while not the start of the conversation, was an important turning point.

4

"LIFE SUPPORT"

AIDS in *Rent*

AIDS HISTORY

Context

In America, the first reports of AIDS came from a *New York Times* article in 1981 that ran the headline "Rare Cancer Seen in 41 Homosexuals" (July 3). By 1982 in America, 452 cases in twenty-three states had been reported to the Centers for Disease Control (CDC). There was little understanding of what caused the increasing incidences of immune deficiency and resulting illnesses. Answers did not emerge until 1984 when Dr. Robert Gallo announced the discovery of the virus. It was another two years until the virus was known by its current name: HIV. Once scientists became aware that the condition was not exclusive to gay men, the narrative around it began to shift. As one representative for the CDC noted, "When it began turning up in children and transfusion recipients that was a turning point in terms of public perception. Up until then it was entirely a gay epidemic, and it was easy for the average person to say, 'So what?' Now everyone could relate." The late 1970s and early 1980s were marked by fear and uncertainty.

When it began to be seen across the wider population, AIDS moved into public consciousness in America. However, knowledge of the condition was still limited. A lack of research created frustrations, as did problems associated with access to treatment and a lack of awareness. That President Ronald Reagan did not mention AIDS in an official capacity until 1985, and then only did so in response to reporters' questions, fueled anger. This lack of engagement from government agencies to combat AIDS led to the early years of activism, which sought to compensate for government inaction while also providing care for those affected by AIDS.

Performance aspects were an integral part of the response to AIDS, as described by Román (1998). He states that "the social ritual of gathering people into a space of performance to raise money, were, along with memorial services, the first acts of intervention in the fight against AIDS."

These events form the backdrop against which early AIDS plays were created. There was then slow but steadier progress in AIDS research and treatment in America. ACT UP and other campaign groups like Gay Men's Health Crisis maintained a high profile; attempting to combat discrimination in healthcare against those with AIDS and the accompanying homophobia. In 1992, the election of Democrat President Bill Clinton seemed to signal hope for a new age, as detailed in David Román's account of seeing *Angels* on the eve of Clinton's election.

Despite this progress, however, by 1994, when *Rent* began workshop productions, AIDS was the leading cause of death for twenty-five- to forty-four-year olds.

The following texts also formed part of the theatrical exchange on AIDS: Paul Rudnick's *Jeffrey* (1996), Steven Dietz's *Lonely Planet* (1994), and Terrence McNally's *Love! Valour! Compassion!* (1995). The early works on AIDS were by necessity small-scale productions, therefore prohibitive to musical theater, which generally requires greater resources. Two of the most important AIDS plays, and probably the best known aside from *Rent*, are Larry Kramer's *The Normal Heart* (1985) and Tony Kushner's *Angels in America* (1994). *The Normal Heart* is a seminal text in AIDS theater. Originally staged at the Public Theater in New York—a not-for-profit off-Broadway theater—it is a piece of white-hot anger and activism cataloguing the early years of AIDS and includes an autobiographical element of Kramer's own experiences. In Kushner's *Angels in America*, he mixes the realism of gay men's experience with fantastical elements (angels crashing through ceilings) and politics (diatribes against the state of America). Alongside *Rent*, Kushner's seven-and-a-half-hour epic spectacle is one of the best-known theatrical productions about AIDS.

PERFORMANCE AND AIDS

Performance aspects were an integral part of the response to AIDS. As described by David Román in his book *Acts of Intervention* (1998), "the social ritual of gathering people into a space of performance to raise money, was, along with memorial services, the first acts of intervention in the fight against AIDS" (Román, 1998, p. 10). The vigils and fund-raising events of early AIDS activism had performance elements at the center of their activities. Many used performance as the event through, for example, cabaret fundraisers, or incorporated a performance element into protests. Román credits ACT UP with opening up the fund-raising and associated performance beyond the small core group of original activists and fundraisers.

Performance was integrated into fundraising from the start and remained an integral part of the AIDS protest movement in America. Drawing on the protest movements of the 1960s, "die-ins" were organized. These were reminiscent of the "sit-ins" of the 1960s, but participants would obstruct businesses or streets rather than simply "sit in." In addition, "political funerals" were held, which turned the memorial services of people with AIDS into a political protest. Activist David Wojonarowicz described them thus:

> To turn our private grief for the loss of friends, family, lovers and strangers into something public would serve as another powerful dismantling tool. It would dispel the notion that this virus has a sexual orientation or a moral code. It would nullify the belief that the government and medical community has done very much to ease the spread or advancement of this disease. (Wojonarowicz, via ACT UP website)

Wojonarowicz speaks here of the powerful awareness-raising power that events like political funerals, and the other more performative elements of protest, could have. Wojonarowicz's funeral took place in New

York on July 29, 1992. The funeral procession was led with a banner proclaiming: "David Wojonarowicz 1954–1992 Died of AIDS due to government negligence." Political funerals combined traditional memorial processions with political protest. Processions of mourners with banners and other effigies of the deceased, these memorials to friends or relatives became, in part, a form of political protest. Wojonarowicz was an artist and activist, so it seems logical his death would take on political and artistic meaning. ACT UP's work continues today, still with a performance element to it, details of which are documented on their current website. The online information includes images showing some performance-based elements of recent demonstrations.

By 1986, there was some progress in American approaches to AIDS. President Reagan finally acknowledged AIDS in an official public address. The first antidiscrimination case about AIDS was won, and the first significant treatment progression since the virus was identified was made with AZT trials. AZT also marked progress in the social and ethical treatment of people with AIDS, as the clinical trial was stopped early when it was determined unethical to give placebos to people with AIDS.

Theatrical responses to AIDS began to evolve into full-scale productions. Rebecca Ranson's full-length play *Warren* in 1986 and Rebecca Headehorn's *One* in 1989 were both early examples. Unusually these early plays were written by women whereas men would later dominate the area. Either way, playwrights sought to illustrate the problems of AIDS as it affected communities while also educating people about the stigma associated with AIDS. Other, earlier productions between 1983 and 1985 included the poorly received surrealist piece *Night Sweat* by Ron Chesley (1984) and *Fever of an Unknown Origin* by Stephen Holt

(1984). These plays, initially on a small scale, were usually performed at specialist theater companies like Theatre Rhinoceros in San Francisco and, later, at the Gay Sweatshop in London.

The first significant work on AIDS was the American play *As Is* by William Hoffman, the start of the "AIDS Play" genre—plays that deal directly with AIDS and its impact on characters in it. This was followed by other plays in the early 1990s, including Paul Rudnick's *Jeffery* (1996), Steven Dietz's *Lonely Planet* (1994), and Terrence McNally's *Love! Valour! Compassion!* (1995). McNally's text, in which a group of gay men meet over a summer and eventually come to terms with the AIDS diagnosis of one of their group, was well received. McNally's play was later turned into a film featuring most of the original cast. McNally, a prolific playwright, previously wrote *Andre's Mother*—another early AIDS play.

The early AIDS plays were, by necessity, small-scale productions prohibitive to musical Theatre Rhinoceros, which generally required more significant resources. However, *Rent* is not the only musical to deal with AIDS, nor is it the first. Previously, there had been the smaller scale *AIDS: The Musical* followed by *Falsettoland* by William Finn. The latter musical won two Tony Awards in 1992 and was first produced in London in 1998. Similar to other plays dealing with AIDS—such as *As Is* or *Love! Valour! Compassion!*—it concentrated on the personal and social impact of AIDS. In terms of musical style, Finn followed a more traditional American musical format than Larson in *Rent*. However, his use of the musical format to address AIDS was innovative.

The Normal Heart, by Larry Kramer, is a seminal text in AIDS theater. Originally staged at the Public Theater in New York, a not-for-profit off-Broadway theater, in 1985, *The Normal Heart* was first staged in Britain at the Royal Court theater in 1986 and starred Martin Sheen as Ned Weeks. In New York, its first major revival was also its Broadway premiere. In America, *The Normal Heart* made funding and the eventual staging of *Angels in America* and *Rent* possible by showing that theater provided an essential medium for responses to AIDS and would also attract audiences.

Original British theatrical output on AIDS is limited to Kevin Elyot's *My Night with Reg* (1994) and Andy Kirby's *Compromised Immunity* (1986), both created with the previously mentioned Gay Sweatshop Company. Elyot's work was moderately successful; it spawned a film version and transferred to New York, albeit in a small off-Broadway theater. In other British writing, the closest any other text comes to being an "AIDS Play" is Mark Ravenhill's much later text, *Some Explicit Polaroids* (1999). While AIDS is not the central focus, the death of a character from an AIDS-related illness is a significant focal point within the play. The play also marks an evolution in AIDS theater and the British take on presenting AIDS onstage. In *Some Explicit Polaroids*, AIDS has become a part of life. It is still presented as a deeply tragic element of his characters' lives, but not the play's primary focus. Rather, AIDS is part of the tapestry of the characters' world. Like Elyot, the focus was how AIDS affected the characters' lives rather than on politics or health.

LARSON AND AIDS

Larson left university in 1982, the same year the Centers for Disease Control and Prevention identified and named the AIDS virus. By the early 1990s, Larson began incorporating the effect of the AIDS epidemic into his work. Larson himself had confronted the fear of an

HIV diagnosis, as one ex-girlfriend had also been diagnosed with HIV, which meant that Larson had been exposed to the virus. This personal closeness to the AIDS epidemic pushed Larson to continue what he and Aronson had begun.

In adapting *La bohème* and developing the first of the original songs Larson and Aronson worked to bring these ideas to the musical theater form. They composed drafts of three songs: the title song "Rent," "Santa Fe," and "I Should Tell You." These musical numbers cemented the style of pop-rock-musical that *Rent* was to become. The collaboration with Aronson allowed the initial concepts and musical identity to take shape. Still, Larson quickly developed strong ideas about the project, influencing Aronson, as noted, to change the location. He also developed the title and began to shape the story of *La bohème* on his terms, specifically, that Mimi should live at the end, unlike in the opera and novel. Larson felt strongly he wanted to write a piece about hope rather than despair, an element that would set *Rent* apart in terms of other AIDS performances. By featuring gay and lesbian characters, including a drag queen, Larson was also queering the existing text; an element explored in more detail later in this chapter.

Some writers, such as Ian Nisbet, have explored the musical and thematic connection between Larson's work and Puccini's opera in more detail. Nisbet discusses both the plot and musical similarities to illustrate how Larson, as in Rosenstein's remarks above, took direct influence from the classic he appropriated for *Rent*. It does not serve the analysis of Larson's depiction of AIDS to consider in detail his direct musical transposition of Puccini's work; however, his transposition of the narrative and the connotations of disease and social status that Puccini explored certainly resonate in Larson's updated depiction of illness. The title *Rent* is used for its double meaning: first to do with the payment for "commodation that is a running theme in the "bohemians" problems, and second for its meaning "to tear apart," a metaphor for the community torn by AIDS and other social problems in the narrative.

As previously noted, by 1991 four of Larson's close friends had been diagnosed with HIV (Hoffman Leacock, "Rent Is Real," in Larson 2008, p. xiii). What Larson was also attempting with *Rent* was a new engagement with AIDS through musical theater. *Rent's* theatrical form is equally as important as Susan Sontag's influence on Larson's work. He sought to produce new work in musical theater as much as he sought to depict and alter perceptions of AIDS. In addition, Stephen Sondheim also heavily influenced Larson's creative life. Larson met Sondheim while studying at Adelphi University; the composer became a mentor. Sondheim encouraged Larson to pursue writing (rather than acting), and it was through this influence Larson began to consider ways to put his own stamp on the musical theater genre. Larson had a "vision for musical theatre that was both political and aesthetic" (McDonnell and Silberger 1997, p. 14). He felt frustrated by the current form and state of musical theater, dominated as it was by big-budget sensational productions that lacked content or "highbrow" music. The drive to change the musical theater aesthetic became wedded with the desire to effect change in perceptions and depictions of AIDS.

AIDS AND *RENT*

The impact of AIDS was the chief reason Larson went back to *Rent* after Aronson stepped aside. Larson had, by this point, lost many friends. Writing *Rent* became a way of facing, channeling, and responding to the fear and grief of the AIDS crisis. Three of his friends had already died by the time the musical opened, showing how quickly the illness took its toll. Matt O'Grady, thankfully, has lived a long life with HIV. The production invites companies to substitute names in the "Life Support" scene with people they knew and lost. As memories of that time fade, there are fewer that choose to do that, but it still retains an element as a living memorial.

Victoria Leacock Hoffman describes in her introduction to the published version of *Rent*: "[*Rent* is a] canvas large enough to honor his [Larson's] friends and to raise awareness about AIDS and the social injustices he saw every day" (introduction in Larson, *Rent Is Real*, 2008, p. xiii). Larson's 1992 statement on the concept for *Rent* echoes the focus on HIV/AIDS he would bring to it:

> Inspired in part by Susan Sontag's 'AIDS and its metaphors' the aim is to quash the already clichéd "AIDS Victim" stereotypes and point out that A. People with AIDS can live full lives' B. AIDS affects everyone-not just homosexuals and drug abusers; C. in our desensitized culture, the ones grappling with life and death issues often live more fully than members of the so-called "Mainstream." (Larson in McDonnell and Silberger)

This description illustrates the motivation behind Larson's work; he was working from personal experience of the AIDS epidemic and its effect on his peer group. He also draws, as he notes, on Susan Sontag's work, using the consideration of cultural meaning attributed to illness that Sontag explores in both *AIDS and Its Metaphors* and the earlier

Illness as Metaphor. What Sontag considers in both works is the type of language used to talk about AIDS and how, as a result, society views these illnesses.

One of the key elements of Sontag's argument is the idea that feared diseases such as AIDS result in the dehumanizing of its victims. Larson's work intersects with Sontag's thinking. In the above quotation, Larson expresses the need to remove the concept of an "AIDS victim," a dehumanizing idea. Sontag also makes the analogy of AIDS as taking over a person's entire identity, exploring the stigma as in Larson's description of the "clichéd AIDS victim" that surrounded those with AIDS. Larson, as mentioned above, was dealing personally with the effects of losing friends to AIDS. That Sontag discusses AIDS and challenges society to consider a different way of thinking about those with AIDS could have inspired Larson's thinking on the nature of the person with AIDS that he depicts in *Rent*.

Larson notes in his manifesto above that he wishes to depict people with AIDS as individuals, not as victims, and to show their diversity. Again he draws on Sontag's idea of relative perceptions of diseases. Sontag writes about those diseases that society finds most terrifying, which may not be the most widespread or the most lethal, but are still seen as dehumanizing. Larson's work reflects this through the idea of people with AIDS being more than just "victims" and being beyond the perceived groups of homosexuals and drug users. In actuality Larson's characters do not transcend the categories of homosexuals and drug users. However, they do transcend the identity of "AIDS victim." Larson's characters respond emotionally to the impact of AIDS, as explored further in this chapter, and in so doing *Rent* is a response to the type of "dehumanization" Sontag discusses. In presenting, through art, characters that counteract this dehumanization, Larson is attempting to reverse the negative way society has talked about AIDS and that Sontag writes about. How society views AIDS can be closely linked to cultural and artistic depictions. If the only depictions of AIDS continue to be the dehumanized image of the "AIDS victim" that both Sontag and Larson wish to dispute, then there will be little progress in cultural understanding of the condition or empathy for the people that it affects.

Though Larson does not explore these elements explicitly in *Rent* in relation to AIDS, he does explore the idea of society perceiving people with AIDS as outsiders from mainstream culture and excluding them from society. Both elements could be viewed as inspired by Sontag's work. What Larson takes from Sontag is a crystallizing of ideas based on his own experience. His characters share this experience, and though not written primarily as an educational conduit, the work, in part, does function in the broader reeducation of society about the dehumanization of the AIDS victim.

Rent, through its depictions of characters with AIDS, shows the personal emotional impact their illness has and takes AIDS away from the dehumanizing aspects that Sontag's work discusses. In drawing on Sontag's criticisms of how cultural language and illness (specifically AIDS) impact those affected, Larson can offer a counterargument. *Rent* offers the potential for audiences to connect with the emotional impact of AIDS without needing to know or understand the finer medical facts that had been the dominant cultural discourse to this point. Larson's work, therefore, contributes to a shift in the depiction of people with AIDS.

SCHULMAN CASE

The early AIDS stories largely came from within the gay community. Gay men typically wrote them (though, not exclusively, as women like Paula Vogel also wrote prominent pieces). Some felt *Rent* was a "straightwashing" of AIDS, much like the film *Philadelphia*. Larson, a straight cisgender white man, writing about the characters did not sit well with everyone.

Novelist and activist Sarah Schulman has decried this commercial "commodification of homosexuality," stating that *Rent* depicts "basically straight-made homosexuality for predominantly straight audiences." While Larson stated that his inspiration for *Rent* came from Puccini's opera, Schulman also accused Larson of stealing narrative material, particularly in Act I, from her novel *People in Trouble*, as some characters in *Rent* and their relationships to one another bear a striking resemblance to those in the novel.

Schulman, in her book *Stagestruck: Theater, AIDS, and the Marketing of Gay America*, writes extensively about how stories of AIDS have been told, holding people she believed to be profiting from them accountable.

Schulman's criticisms of Larson's work merit consideration, and they are shared by others. Her irritation at a similar story being hugely successful is understandable: she was trying to get an operatic version of her novel made around the same time Larson was making *Rent*. It's no great stretch to appreciate that theater was perhaps not receptive to an opera about AIDS and that a lesbian writer outside the circles of power wasn't invited into the right rooms. Larson's connection to Sondheim was instrumental in getting *Rent* to a workshop, and there is no denying his personal connections helped get the show off the ground. He was in the right place at the right time and had access as a straight white man in the 1990s that a lesbian theater maker did not.

Schulman arguably has a right to feel defensive, insofar as she had "authentic" insight into the world that she wrote about. As a founding member of ACT UP, she demonstrated, wrote, and was involved in gay American life and AIDS activism in a way that Larson was not. We should absolutely question why her story was never staged while Larson's succeeded. Nonetheless, in my view, the extent to which *Rent* incorporates the plot of *La bohème* strongly suggests that the opera is the key source for his work, not her book. Schulman's case rested on the anecdotal evidence that Larson owned the book, which while suggestive, was far from outright proof.

Schulman's other critique of *Rent*—that it wasn't subversive enough— is a valid one coming from someone on the "front lines." Because later works came from and spoke to that audience, we can argue that the strength of *Rent* is its ability to speak to broader audiences. Although less confrontational than works made for and by the community, the impact of *Rent* is still significant in its contribution.

Rent engaged audiences through its approach to the effect AIDS had on its characters, which became a universalizing force. With more characters living with AIDS than in previous plays, the work reflects the demographics hardest hit by the disease: gay men, women of color, IV drug users, Latinos, and African Americans. Alongside his main characters, Larson paints a wide-ranging picture of people with AIDS. The balance of HIV-negative characters in *Rent* is also significant. Of the central characters, four are HIV-negative: Mark, a straight white man; Benny, a straight Black man; Maureen, a bisexual white woman; and Joanne, a lesbian Black woman.

Roger is a musician and a former drug addict. In the opening song, he is "just coming back from half a year of withdrawal" and his girlfriend April has died, committing suicide after finding out she had AIDS. Roger's story is a harsh, almost brutal, introduction to the character's situation and the depiction of AIDS. Roger demonstrates a departure from previous characters with AIDS depicted onstage. Overwhelmingly, these roles had been white, middle class, gay men. Roger is heterosexual, thereby presenting a challenge to one stereotype but perpetuating the stereotype of another, in this case a drug addict. Here, there is no perfect concept of "representation," only a striving to do more.

Larson's work does seek to incorporate a range of demographics affected by AIDS. Roger's love interest Mimi is potentially an unsympathetic character as a dancer at an S&M club and a drug addict. The audience is not given information on how Mimi contracted AIDS, but as a female character, she offers an alternative to the predominantly gay males depicted in AIDS dramas. Mimi is also Latin American, another demographic that was neglected in previous works.

RENT'S QUEER CHARACTERS AND AIDS

Rent engaged audiences through its approach to the condition's impact on its characters, which became a universalizing force in its depiction of AIDS. *Rent* has more characters with AIDS and characters from more diverse ethnic groups and backgrounds than previous works, which mainly had situated themselves in the world of white middle-class gay men. The key characters with AIDS in *Rent* are Roger, Mimi, Collins, and Angel and various ensemble characters with AIDS.

Rent contains more characters with AIDS than previous plays that labeled themselves as "AIDS plays." As highlighted by Román, the characters in *Rent* reflect the demographics hardest hit by AIDS: gay men, women of color, IV drug users, Latinos, and African Americans. Alongside his main characters, Larson paints a wide-ranging picture of people with AIDS across the musical. This works against what Douglas Crimp called the "preponderance of AIDS as a gay disease," which Crimp believes underscored cultural depictions and cultural understanding of AIDS. Larson's work begins a move away from this.

Larson queers the source text of *La bohème*; presenting a character in drag is a powerful tool in his AIDS narrative. Following Butler's notions of drag as subversive, Larson may have deliberately left Angel's gender identification slightly ambiguous to enforce this. As Butler highlights, drag challenges notions of fixed and binary gender by illustrating the constructed nature of gendering. In discussing AIDS, these gender debates draw on Foucault's ideas in *Discipline and Punishment*, with external powers acting on regulating bodies. In presenting drag about AIDS, ideas of deconstructing gender identity alongside AIDS challenge the cultural expectations surrounding both.

Depicting AIDS across various genders and ethnicities offers an alternative to previous theatrical representations of AIDS, including Kushner's. In diversifying those characters with AIDS in his play, Larson is widening the spectrum of those representations, a progression in depictions of AIDS onstage. The ethnic diversity of Larson's writing also sits neatly alongside the queering of the text. Larson was reflecting the world as he saw and experienced it in his writing, and for audiences, in the NYTW production, this would likely have been the same. As the musical moved uptown and to London, however, the audiences changed, and this diversity became part of what *Rent* presented to theater audiences and the theatrical landscape. The world the audience is confronted with—where this depiction of AIDS sits—is diverse in every way. It may not be, as noted, the world with which the audience is familiar, but it has diversity in race, gender, and sexuality, which makes for a believable world created onstage.

The relationships between characters with AIDS and the impact of AIDS on their relationships in *Rent* are a driving force in the narrative. It is, in fact, the center of Larson's account of AIDS. As *POZ* magazine described: "By facing AIDS as yet another of life's uncertainties, *Rent's* HIV-positive pairings love each other with a sexual passion that not only turns on Broadway audiences but brings them to their feet."

The center of Larson's plot is formed from how its two central couples, one gay and one straight, deal with their AIDS diagnoses and how it affects their lives and relationships. The relationship between Collins and Angel is significant in its depiction of characters with AIDS. Collins and Angel's treatment in the story, and the development of their romantic relationship in the face of AIDS, is given equal time as the heterosexual love affair between Roger and Mimi. Larson presents a far more balanced text regarding those affected by AIDS than previous works centered on the gay male experience. In depicting Roger and Mimi's experience, Larson is widening the demographic beyond those groups already addressed. Though Larson cannot hope to encompass the spectrum of those affected by AIDS, his work extends that depiction in theatrical works (Stefani Eads, *POZ*, August/September 1996, quoted in Román, 272).

Mimi's words in "Out Tonight" and "Another Day" show recognition of the limited time and a determination to embrace life. In a more reflective declaration of seizing the day, she says, "I can't control, my destiny." This comment further illustrates the darker side of Mimi: the loss of control that AIDS creates in her life replaces her previously seemingly carefree, possibly reckless attitude. Mimi believes in living in the present in the face of a fatal illness but she also has a broader message. Mimi uses this carefree attitude to convince Roger to take her out. Despite her best efforts, Roger rejects her, feeling that his condition means he cannot start a relationship with her. Roger has closed himself off to the possibility of love and life due to his AIDS diagnosis. He laments that "It'd be another song; we'd sing another way." In a meta-narrative on the use of song to discuss AIDS, Larson draws attention to the different types of musicals he would be writing without AIDS.

The next chapter takes a "deep dive" into how Larson used that approach.

5

"WITHOUT YOU"

AIDS and Emotional Impact in *Rent*

In his analysis of *Rent*, David Roman states: "Although AIDS does not drive the plot of *Rent* AIDS informs and helps to shape it" (Román, 1998). Román argues that this constant presence of AIDS woven into the plot of *Rent* is intrinsic to its impact. AIDS in *Rent* is not treated as a separate "issue" or "message"; instead, it is a continual part of the narrative. Narrative and structural content and even its genesis, the topic of AIDS seems hard to avoid. In fact, AIDS saturates *Rent*. *Rent* engaged audiences through its approach to the condition's impact on its characters, which became a universalizing force in its depiction of AIDS.

In *Rent*, AIDS is a clear and constant presence without becoming overbearing in either a "political" or "educational" manner. It becomes a central issue in the text because it is essential to the characters. For Larson, AIDS is engrained in the world he is depicting, and his language reflects this. Instead of detailed descriptions or medical analyses, there are fleeting references to AIDS throughout the text. These references range from the veiled: "One song, before the virus takes hold to the blatant, "My body provides a comfortable home for the Acquired Immune Deficiency Syndrome." These two phrases indicate that AIDS is implicitly and explicitly referenced in *Rent* but that, as noted, the medical or graphic depiction is not as detailed as in other texts. This reflects the piece's style and does not lessen its impact.

DEPICTIONS OF THE AIDS IN MEDICAL TERMS

Rent's depiction of AIDS in physical or medical terms differs from its predecessors in performance. In a stylistic choice that fits with the musical theater style, Michael Greif's direction does not rely on details, instead using a minimalist set and props to give an impression or overview. This complements Larson's writing style, which leaves much of the detail unsaid in its sung-through approach. The minimal style extends to the depictions of AIDS, which do not dwell on the overt medical symptoms of AIDS like other dramas did. Again, Larson can be viewed as drawing on the influence of Sontag; he is looking at the social impact and perceptions of the disease rather than the exact medical details. As Sontag highlights in her work on AIDS and previous work on cancer, it is, at times, the social and cultural perceptions and impact of a disease that is more difficult for a sufferer to deal with than the physical impacts.

It appears, therefore, that his skirting of the physical detail of AIDS in favor of exploring the social impact of the condition is a deliberate effort to force audiences to confront the kinds of "metaphors" and connotations that Sontag discusses.

The audience sees two characters being physically affected by AIDS during the performance. Angel during "Without You," Mimi during

"Your Eyes/Finale B." Neither of these is a graphic portrayal, as both actors give the impression of being weakened by their illness but little more. Again the symbolic gestures associated with the illness are more significant to Larson than the realistic depiction. In both cases, the person affected is cared for and literally carried by their lover, Angel by Collins and Mimi by Roger, as symbolic gesture again takes precedence over realism. The mirroring in the staging of Collins and Roger carrying their dying lover draws attention to their shared experience as people with AIDS and Larson's equal treatment regardless of sexuality.

Angel's death is acted out across two musical numbers and departs from the expected illness narrative of a dramatic, emotional deathbed scene. In "Without You," there is a more traditional, emotive lament. The emotion of Angel's death is still felt in "Without You": from the beginning of this number, as Mimi and Roger fight, Angel is seen now dressed in white pyjamas and lying on a table covered with a white sheet. It becomes apparent Angel's health has deteriorated; he is seen, and stage directions dictate, coughing with Collins attending to him, picking him up, and carrying him the length of the stage before lying next to him on another table. As he does so, Mimi laments, "Without you, The moon glows, The river flows, But I die without you." This brings home to the audience the emotional resonance of Angel's death. The movements and performance at this point are slightly stylized yet still give a strong indication of the physical toll AIDS has taken on him.

In "Contact," which directly follows "Without You," Angel, dressed in white, is surrounded by company members. They wrap him in a sheet and participate in a "sensual life and death dance" (as Larson described it in his stage directions). The other actors speak passionately before Angel emerges upstage from the sheeted group. In a metaphoric approach to

Angel's death, Larson uses the accompanying musical number's words to communicate and depict ideas about AIDS. In sensual language such as "Touch! Deep! Dark! Kiss! Beg! Slap! Fear! Thick!" Larson equates the sexual element of AIDS with the bodily impact of AIDS.

The crescendo of the music and the words of the sexual dialogue of "Contact" meld into Angel's dying lament. Angel ends euphorically on these notes as the music swells; his words are then echoed by the company whose repetition of the words "It's over" signal his death and the song's true meaning. Collins's final words segue the music into a refrain from their love song, "I'll Cover You." The emotional impact and broader social commentary, the link between sexual expression and death caused by AIDS, is achieved here by Larson without graphic medical depictions. The following funeral scene and the impact on Collins and the other characters are, as already explored, emotionally powerful. Therefore, the graphic depiction of the exact physical impact of Angel's illness is redundant in making Larson's point here.

The only other character the audience sees physically affected by AIDS is Mimi. Larson keeps the deterioration of her condition off-stage in the time lapse between Halloween and Angel's funeral when Mimi is said to be going to rehab and Christmas Eve when Maureen and Joanne find her unconscious in the park. The shift from Mimi's previously healthy appearance to being close to death provides the emotional climax of *Rent* without Larson having to deal with the medical details. Much has been made of Mimi's "miraculous" recovery; Larson maintained that *Rent* was about life rather than death, which explains his dramatic reasoning. Mimi's death and resurrection are dramatic and sentimental; she wakes after being serenaded by Roger, claiming a vision of Angel brought her back. Mimi is brought back both by the love Roger convey in his song and by a vision of her best friend, Angel. Clearly, this is a romanticized and unrealistic depiction of AIDS, particularly given we are told moments earlier that Mimi has been living rough and presumably, therefore, not receiving any treatment. However, the details of the medical impact of AIDS are not Larson's key concern in his depiction of AIDS. Larson seeks to represent the community response to AIDS and how friendships and romantic relationships endure in the face of AIDS—and even flourish. It is for this reason that he insists Mimi lives in *Rent*.

Wollman refers to this "miraculous recovery" in her analysis of *Rent*, noting it is one of Larson's departures both from musical theater and source material traditions (2006). It is also in keeping with the overall positive attitude of *Rent*. In Mimi's recovery, Larson uses the depiction of community seen in his and other musicals. Drawing on Kirle's work on Broadway musicals, *Rent* works according to the model laid down by *Oklahoma!* in which the authors' mythologize community and the unification, acceptance, and tolerance of all who agreed by the social contract (*Unfinished Business: Broadway Musicals as Works in Progress*, 2005). Within the social contract, Larson's imagined community onstage and that of the audience "in residence," which he depicts, becomes an agreed mythologized version of the reality it draws on. It is not in the stylistic nature of *Rent* to present an audience with the kind of medical details about AIDS they were perhaps used to from television dramas. Or even the kind of slower-paced exploration of the impact on characters physically and mentally that other AIDS dramas were inclined toward.

Larson does create a world where these references to AIDS are that of those accustomed to the condition. Again, we come back to the point that AIDS just "is" for these characters. They do not question its existence or dwell overtly on medical facts, instead commenting on the effects, creating an emotional connection with the audience. This helps its transference to the British stage. Recalling Jones's introduction to her work on "Second Generation" AIDS plays (1994). The language of *Rent* has moved away from the medical issue in favor of talking around its impact, allowing for humor, satire, or, in Larson's case, song. The audience's connection to *Rent,* therefore, comes from an emotional rather than medical understanding and offers a far stronger chance of transatlantic translation.

LANGUAGE AND AIDS

Depictions of the medical aspects of AIDS in *Rent* were already outdated when it was staged. Criticism of the content is based mainly on the treatment depicted for AIDS. In *Rent,* the characters are shown taking AZT, but the drug was slightly outdated for AIDS treatment by 1996. The fast-paced changes to understanding AIDS across the early 1990s, and the subsequent changing treatments, mean that any text dealing with AIDS struggled to keep up. Nevertheless, this inaccuracy or anachronism in its medical depiction doesn't detract from *Rent's* impact as a text on AIDS. As previously explored, the world of *Rent* is so permeated with the impact of AIDS that it is almost intrinsically interwoven to the point that the audience may overlook it. However, how the characters talk about their condition can be used to assess

Rent's impact and how it may communicate effectively with a specifically British audience on this issue.

These references peppered across the text act as subtle reminders of the characters' condition, rather than Larson spending time detailing the condition. There is also an expectation that at this stage, the audience will have enough basic awareness of AIDS as a condition to understand the medical references, at least in the broadest sense. In keeping with this, *Rent* is rarely overt in its medical references to AIDS. This is partly due to its musical format, which doesn't allow for much exposition, nor do medical terms generally lend themselves to rhymed dialogue.

The first song to address a character's emotional response to AIDS is Roger's rock ballad lament, "One Song Glory." As the second major musical number, performed early on in the musical, it sets the tone for Roger's character and his response to AIDS. At this point, the audience knows that Roger is a musician and former drug addict with AIDS. His song—sung after he refuses to accompany Mark out—is his lament, seated on the table in their apartment, accompanying himself on guitar. It is about unfulfilled promises as a musician but also illustrates his thoughts about his condition. He sings, "Find one song before the virus takes hold" and "One song to leave behind." He sings about needing to leave an artistic legacy as well as a longing for personal fulfilment in what he knows will be limited time. In "One Song Glory," Larson illustrates the frustration of young people with AIDS: the idea of "another empty life" that Roger sings about, and the idea that "time flies—time dies," emphasizing the people whose lives were being cut short.

In contrast to Roger's approach in "One Song Glory," Mimi's attitude to her own life and having AIDS is quite different, as illustrated in "Out Tonight." Echoing Roger's "time flies," Mimi sings, "Get up life's too quick," summarising her attitude. Mimi implores Roger to take her "out tonight"; she intends to win Roger over and enjoy her night. Her plans or intentions do not extend beyond the present as she declares, "in the evening I've got to roam" while dancing. This contrasts with Roger's subdued lament for his lost life and legacy. Mimi is intent on existing in and enjoying the here and now, wanting to "find a bar so dark we forget who we are." Her behavior clearly is a means to forget her situation, and it may be argued that it is equally unhealthy as Roger's subdued response. What Larson does in Mimi, however, is present an example of someone for whom life does not simply stop at an AIDS diagnosis.

This is a theme Larson maintains across other musical numbers. While Mimi and Roger are still coming to terms with their feelings for one another, Collins and Angel declare their love, illustrating that love and AIDS are not mutually exclusive. It becomes a coming together for Collins and Angel—a bonding moment over their shared condition. They sing the song while walking down the street together, arm in arm or hand in hand, and end it with a kiss. This unashamed declaration of their love is part of Larson's unapologetic depiction of a gay relationship in what became a mainstream musical. It is as important for depictions of homosexuality in theater as it is about AIDS.

By depicting AIDS but also showing a romance that doesn't end with an AIDS diagnosis, Larson makes a statement of defiance. Other plays had often depicted the struggles and often the untimely demise of relationships, but none had shown one beginning and strengthening. This somewhat idyllic, romantic scene is bookended by Collins singing, "When you're worn out and tired, when your heart has expired"—indicative of the loss they know awaits them. The poignancy of Collins repeating these lyrics at Angel's funeral during the song's reprise is heightened by their use at the otherwise promising start of the character's relationship. The three songs highlighted here illustrate the three facets of relationships between the romantic leads and their different attitudes to having AIDS.

Mark and Roger's relationship is equally significant in *Rent*'s depiction of AIDS; likewise, the musical number that addresses this, "What You Own," is important to Larson's connection with the audience. In "What You Own," Mark and Roger, who separated after Roger left to move to Santa Fe, vent their frustrations with the world around them and each other. Both lament the other's artistic problems and frustrations with each other—a play on the traditional love duet. The phrase, "I don't own emotion, I *rent*," even links back to the musical's title and the several meanings of "rent," referring both to temporality and tearing apart. The emotions surrounding their friendship are always temporary, given Roger's condition. Larson echoes Mark's earlier comment, "[m]aybe it's because I'm the one of us to survive." Through the two friends, Larson again highlights the impact of AIDS and its emotional impact on all relationships, not just the romances at the center of his narrative.

SEXUALITY AND AIDS

Rent is open about its characters' sexual identities without being overtly sexual. Larson's characters are sexual beings: they are contemporary characters in all respects, and Larson deliberately doesn't shy away from their sexual identities. Mimi and Roger's relationship is perhaps the most sexual of relationships between lovers. Partly because of her occupation as an S&M club dancer, Mimi is immediately associated with sex and the taboos of sexuality as she performs. In aligning Mimi with these taboo sexual expressions, Larson again draws on Sontag. The taboo nature of Mimi's sexuality is highlighted in both her occupation and her HIV status. Her HIV status has links through cultural association with Mimi as both a drug addict and in her occupation within the sex industry (though there is no indication from Larson her work as a dancer extends to prostitution). In her drug use and employment, Mimi is a prime candidate for cultural judgment of AIDS as punishment. In Mimi's personal rejection of this attitude and in her embracing of her sexuality, Larson rebukes the kinds of cultural judgments and metaphors Sontag discusses. And in Mimi's character, he does so with force. This again alludes to Sontag's notion that when AIDS is seen as affecting a "risk group," it brings back the historical idea that the "illness has judged" (1991). In Sontag's reading, the sexually transmitted nature of AIDS makes the metaphor of illness and punishment clear.

Mimi engages with and embraces her sexuality as an expression and defies society's expectations of her. Mimi's first musical number, "Out Tonight," is fueled with sexuality in both its lyrical content and her performance. Mimi dances provocatively above Roger on the upper levels of the set's scaffolding in various sexualized moves. Mimi is obviously not shying away from her sexuality, and it is Roger's reluctance to engage in this, as a way of removing himself from living life, that Larson uses to extend his "no day but today" metaphor.

In "Out Tonight," Mimi's dance and lyrics are one of only two overt depictions of sexuality in *Rent*. The second, a clear and none-too-subtle metaphor of the link between sex, AIDS, and death, is in the musical number "Contact." The overtly sexual lyrics and movement in "Contact," the only clearly choreographed dance number in *Rent,* depict sexual acts and sexuality. Meanwhile, it soon becomes apparent that Angel is dying. Dressed in white and physically lifted up by the company, Angel sings their portion of the number.

Angel's swan song is both a vivid sexual expression and a dying cry. In creating a parallel between sex and Angel's death from an AIDS-related illness, Larson acknowledges the connection and shows defiance in the face of it. This number, the lyrics, and the performance of Angel's death seem to say that death and sex may be inextricably linked. Still, this will not prevent people from living and having sexual experiences. In a theatrical sense, linking the two also acts as defiance to critics and broader popular culture that might wish all references or depictions of sexuality to be erased in the face of AIDS.

EMOTIONAL IMPACT AND AIDS

These three relationships—Mimi with Roger, Collins with Angel, and the platonic relationship between Roger and Mark—both universalize and normalize AIDS. Once the audience moves past the nature of the illness, thinking only about the humanistic element of the text, of love and loss. In *Rent,* the couples are driven together and apart by their AIDS diagnosis. For Collins and Angel, it's a sign to grab what they have with full force. This acts as a bonding tool for Collins and Angel, their shared AIDS diagnosis meaning it is easier for them to begin a relationship. This is a logical step for many people with AIDS as it seems easier to maintain a relationship with someone who doesn't have to fear infection and understands its impact. Naturally, another impact of the disease is also the potential, or during the time when *Rent* was written, of the inevitable loss of that person. Roger and Mimi use their illness as a shield from their true feelings. In both cases, Larson seems to be using AIDS to talk about the nature of love rather than the disease. They are brought together after discovering their mutual condition. Their diagnosis does not define or drive their relationship.

Angel and Collins depict an idealized version of a couple living with AIDS, which could be interpreted by some as over-romanticized or simplified. However, their romance and Mimi and Roger's echo *La bohème*'s source material and characters. Larson deviates from the narrative enough to accommodate the modern era. Unlike Mimi and Roger, for who AIDS is a barrier for love, Collins and Angel love each other despite the circumstances. They also appear to live healthily despite their illness and are monogamous, which means they are not putting others at risk of infection. This can be read as problematic from a political point of view and even unrealistic that AIDS seemingly doesn't affect these characters. However, from a narrative point of view, they counter Mimi and Roger's fraught relationship. Angel and Collins are a nonthreatening, strong image of people living with AIDS that can confront an audience—whether familiar with the condition or not—and challenge expectations and stereotypes. They also emotionally handle both living and dying with AIDS well. Angel and Collins are pragmatic but also live their life fully. They embrace support for their condition and thrive when they attend the "Life Support" group. Their philosophy of "no day but today" influences how they live and conduct their relationship. In this case, AIDS informs but does not shape the narrative; it permeates it but does not override it.

The romantic pairings of *Rent* form the center of Larson's narrative; however, he is equally concerned with the impact of AIDS on the community and friendships. This is shown most clearly in the relationship between Mark and Roger. Following the opening number, their conversation sets the tone for their friendship and the impact of AIDS on it. Amid the friendly bantering, Mark reveals Roger's AIDS diagnosis to the audience and then reminds him to take his medication. His concern for his friend's well-being is clear from this short exchange; he has taken on the role of carer for his friend, especially after Roger's loss of April, his previous girlfriend. Larson also indicates the role of friends in caring for people with AIDS. As in Kushner's depiction of Belize assisting Prior—the strength of a friendship in caring for those with AIDS—Mark and Roger's relationship is as significant, if not more so, than the romantic parings at the center of the narrative.

The relationship between Angel and Collins shows an audience, despite its ultimately tragic consequences when Angel dies midway through Act 2, that AIDS does not necessarily mean the end of love and relationships for all people. Angel's death and funeral constitute one of Larson's most powerful statements on AIDS. The response of friends and Collins to Angel's death is a powerful emotional moment. The connection between the characters and their obvious grief at the loss of Angel is punctuated with Collins's heartfelt eulogy. Collins stands at the funeral, holding the coat that Angel bought him before singing a reprise of "I'll Cover You," which blends into "Seasons of Love." Larson transforms the heartfelt lyrics of love between the two men earlier into expressions of Collins's grief; the song ends in a repeat of the phrase: "Oh Lover I'll cover you," which becomes a lament, transforming their love into grief.

Through Collins's and Angel's relationship, Larson makes a connection between the audience and AIDS—first with love and then with grief. By connecting with these characters, the audience also becomes connected to the loss felt at Angel's death. Through this elicited sympathy, they also formed an understanding and empathy for the impact of AIDS.

Through Mimi and Roger, Larson shows the opposite effect: rather than the seize-the-day mentality that brings Collins and Angel together, the idea of AIDS as a life sentence drives Mimi and Roger apart. Mimi shares a similar attitude with Angel, desiring to seize the day and lose herself in the moment.

Mimi embodies the musical's slogan, "no day but today" in that living with AIDS does not mean ceasing to live the life she currently has. The mortality that AIDS forces her to face is met with an embrace of her current life. There is certainly a darker side to Mimi's seize-the-day attitude; in both "Out Tonight" and "Another Day" Mimi recognizes the limited time she faces but she is also determined to embrace life.

Mimi and Roger's romance is not without its problems, and while the issues they face as a couple are not necessarily derived from their AIDS diagnosis, they are augmented by it. Mimi's drug addiction, and Roger's fears she is cheating, are both brought into harsher focus by their shared condition. Essentially, Roger and Mimi's reaction to their AIDS diagnosis and its impact on their attitude to life and love makes them incompatible.

The role of Mark as caregiver is not overemphasized by Larson in the narrative but serves as a subtle message that not only romantic relationships are affected by AIDS. In response to Roger's accusation of being "detached," Mark says, "Perhaps it's because I'm the one of us to survive (Larson, "Halloween").

AIDS here, in Larson's depiction, moves out of the gay or drug user connotations of the lovers' quarrels and into the profound sadness a young man feels losing a friend. This differs from other AIDS dramas focusing on romantic, sexual, or familial relationships. Mark and Roger's resolution at the end of the piece is as powerful as the reunion of the lovers. The audience becomes as emotionally invested in their friendship as they do in love affairs. In showing this breadth of impact and experience of AIDS, *Rent* reaches beyond the demographics previously reached by AIDS drama; this wide-reaching scope also assisted its transference to the British stage. All three relationships focus on the emotional impact of AIDS. This allows an audience to empathize with the characters regardless of their experience with AIDS.

Moving away from the source material in *La bohème*, Larson has Mimi come back to life following Roger's declaration of his love with his song "Your Eyes." This depiction of AIDS is a departure from previous models where a character's death from AIDS is a central trope. Larson does this with Angel's death, but in dramatizing Mimi, Roger, and Collins's lives, he shows that people can manage to live with AIDS. Offering hope is essential. If an audience is left thinking all is lost, the text is not as effective in engaging and, in particular, motivating an audience. And here, we see Larson's more political attitude to AIDS.

POLITICS AND AIDS

Larson's broader attitudes to AIDS and his ideas about how a community should respond to them assume a very different approach than previous AIDS plays. While other plays with AIDS as a theme, notably

Angels in America and *The Normal Heart*, take on the political systems and attitudes of the day, Larson focuses on the community's response. As Larson himself said: "In these dangerous times, where it seems the world is ripping apart at the seams, we can all learn how to survive from those who stare death squarely in the face every day and (we) should reach out to each other and bond as a community, rather than hide from the terrors of life at the end of the millennium" (Larson in McDonnell and Silberger 1997).

Larson's concern is the "personal as political" stance. The use of the support group to represent groups for people with AIDS is significant. Larson places it centrally in his narrative, indicating his thoughts on the importance of such groups to the community he depicts. In so doing, rather than showing the characters involved heavily in activism—as such individuals may have been—Larson emphasizes care and the community responsibility of care. There is an innate sense of politics here, which Larson depicts, and it is not divorced entirely from AIDS activism as a broader spectrum. This approach also translates internationally. In the UK, ACT UP wasn't as significant an organization as in America; British audiences were unlikely to be universally familiar with organizations such as the Terrance Higgins Trust or Stonewall.

Larson does reference the political activism group ACT UP when Collins reprograms the MIT computers to broadcast "ACT UP fight AIDS." By doing so, Larson illustrates his support for the activist and political side of AIDS awareness without having to integrate it into his play. His characters would have been aware of its existence, perhaps even participated in it. Still, Larson stays away from the potentially contentious or complicated associations that a more detailed reference to the organization would hold. Instead, by referencing his characters' political and activism awareness about AIDS, Larson creates a realistic portrait of the characters' political sensibilities regarding AIDS and gives a subtle but meaningful facet to his work's political dimensions.

The depictions of AIDS activism, as seen in plays like *The Normal Heart* or the approach in *Angels in America*, show the politics of AIDS in a particular political moment in America. While having a political stance, Larson's work is more generalized; a heavy-handed or specific political approach is also not in keeping with Larson's overarching and inclusive attitude. Although Larson depicts a particular community, his ethos was that of inclusion or certainly reaching as wide a demographic as possible. Larson's message of the community as a force for action and caring can be staged anywhere. *Rent*'s enduring and worldwide success after these initial productions showed a universal appeal that transcends any specific community. In using community action, Larson allows his text to be both specific to the East Village and a message that can be understood regardless of location. Larson's theatrical approach to depicting AIDS in *Rent* is emotionally accessible to any audience.

6

"ANOTHER DAY"

Rent in London

The London transfer of *Rent* took place in 1998, two years after the Broadway production opened; the show ran between May 12, 1998, and October 30, 1999. While this cannot compete with the twelve-year Broadway run, *Rent*'s tenure in the West End, both in its original run and in its subsequent tour and revival in its original format, is still healthy. Looking at it here, in the context of *Rent*'s broader impact, illustrates the global but often highly personal impact *Rent* had. Discussions of three London revivals in this book—the infamous *Rent: Remixed* experiment and the post-COVID-19 Manchester production in 2021, also shows its global reach.

The musical was transferred as a carbon copy of the Broadway production, aside from minor adjustments to the set to fit the London theater, and included several members of the original Broadway cast. Although riding on a wave of publicity from its New York run, it needed more to guarantee success in Britain. Benedict Nightingale pointed out in his review that producers did not take any chances, bringing members of the original Broadway cast as "insurance."

Rent ran for fifteen months in London, closing in October 1999. Limited revivals occurred at the Prince of Wales Theatre from December 4, 2001, to January 6, 2002, and from December 6, 2002, to March 1, 2003, following a UK tour. There was also a successful production in Manchester in 2006, with an additional "goodbye" performance in 2008 from the Manchester cast. Though not as impressive as the fifteen-year run of the Broadway production, this was still a successful run by West End standards, where often a year is considered a lengthy run.

The success of *Rent* in New York was well known when the show arrived in London; many London reviewers commented on the New York production in their reviews, often questioning *Rent*'s ability to succeed in London. David Gritten commented, "*Rent* will clearly not storm London just because of the raves from across the pond"—though, in fact, *Rent* sold well based on its American success and did establish a solid business for its year and a half run. The press response indicates a level of skepticism around *Rent,* but this was to be expected with a musical that pushed boundaries in form and content.

STAGING IN LONDON

David Savran described *Rent*'s staging as "toward the emblematic and presentational" (2002). with a self-aware and postmodernist approach. The staging was also a reflection of the community it aimed to depict and its origins at NYTW. Although we can read *Rent*'s staging in the fashion suggested by Savran, the reality is that, rather than being self-reflexive artistic decision as he suggests, it is more likely a matter of convenience and economy. The off-Broadway production budgets would not allow for elaborate sets or costumes, which was retained in the move to Broadway and eventually London. In bringing the show to Broadway, while there was more budget to change sets and costumes, *Rent* was still funded on a comparatively low scale; the budget was not in the realm of its Andrew Lloyd Webber or Cameron Macintosh counterparts. The existing set was cheap and practical and could be maintained for years with minimal cost and effort. Keeping to the same set also created a sense of continuity between the productions. In so doing, some of the authenticity of the original was retained.

There was also skepticism of the ability of *Rent* to translate to the British theatrical landscape. Joanna Coles in the *Guardian* wondered whether it would work in London, suggesting three reasons why it might not. London, she noted, was less collectively traumatized by AIDS. Further, there was a cultural difference, or distance, to the East Village lifestyle portrayed (1998). These two reasons are valid observations; however, despite not being as directly affected by AIDS, Britain was affected and aware of the impact of AIDS worldwide. The idea also that to connect to a musical, British audiences needed to be directly affected was a narrow view. As a comparison, Britain was far less affected by Vietnam, yet Boublil and Schönberg's *Miss Saigon* was a massive success in London. Likewise, the success of *Angels in America* a few years earlier indicated that despite the differences in experience, British audiences were receptive to American depictions of AIDS. Coles's pointed out that *Rent* was an unfinished work. This is a fair point: as explored previously, *Rent* could have taken on a different shape had its creator lived to make alterations. Coles, in her review, highlights some of the concerns and criticisms of the British press that, in essence, *Rent* would not translate effectively for a London audience.

Aspects of *Rent*, particularly about depictions of AIDS, were communicated effectively to British audiences. Still, reviewers reacted adversely to the content itself, albeit more about the style of Larson's text than the broader themes. Charles Spencer said: "I have a horrible suspicion, however that the grotesque sentimentality won't prevent *Rent* from becoming a huge hit in touchy-feely post-Diana Britain" (1998). While being slightly patronizing to the British theatergoing public, Spencer's statement that the emotional resonance in *Rent* was central to its appeal is reasonably accurate and not a reflection on the transfer of the text to Britain but rather an issue of personal taste. The idea of a post-Diana Britain is an interesting approach regarding audience reaction. Spencer is alluding to the public outpouring of grief about the death of Diana, Princess of Wales, in 1997. In breaking with traditional British reserve, the public mourning of Diana's death marked a transitional moment in the public consciousness.

What Spencer alludes to here, albeit sarcastically, is a shift in public trends and perhaps a desire for a more emotional approach to life. In this public mentality, Spencer reasons that what he views as a highly sentimental musical might appeal to the theatergoing public. John Peter also has issues with what he views as an overly sentimental approach in *Rent*. He says that at times it is "from your heart sincerity" but that "well-meaning but oppressing political correctness made him 'recoil in despair'" (1998). Here, Peter points out that *Rent's* emotional approach may appeal to only some audience members. For some, it will be too heavy-handed or too saccharine. However, such matters of taste apply to any theatrical performance and audience group.

The reviews highlight the links between American and British productions. Alastair Macaulay comments that the West End version, though "virtually identical [to Broadway], looks rather feeble and obscure" (1998). Macaulay's comments have a slight contradiction at heart. If Rent is "virtually identical" in London, his judgment that it looks "feeble" and "obscure" is possibly more influenced by its perceived effect than actual appearance. What Macaulay alludes to is that Rent was less impactful when it transferred to Britain, rather than any differences in the quality of the musical production. Prejudice relating to Rent on Broadway seems to relate little to the content and depiction of AIDS.

It is reasonable to ask whether Macaulay does have a point: is the West End version always destined to be if not "feeble," certainly somehow a lesser copy? This question is addressed when considering the revived text in the next chapter. It is a fair assessment that a restaged version of a theatrical text, particularly when exported to a new country or on tour, will never quite capture the original. In the case of Rent, particular status comes with the original cast and production. They are the only actors to have worked directly with the original composer on the piece. They also had the experience no subsequent cast could have of working on the production in its original East Village location, a facet which, combined with the fact that they were working directly with Larson, lends a certain authenticity to the performance. Those following the original cast will inevitably be a somehow "lesser" copy. In staging the performance elsewhere with another cast, though, the production gains other elements through the performers involved and the environment in which it is staged.

The comparison of the productions by the press and the, at times, the negative reaction it garnered is relevant in considering the text's transfer to Britain. Some critics, such as John Peter of *The Sunday Times*, took precise issue with the show's inherent "New York" feel, saying: "You can take the show out of New York, but you can't take New York out of the show" (1998). Peter felt that the musical was so attached in its location that the transfer to London didn't work. Again, this is problematic given many examples of New York or American, based musicals that have been successful in Britain. From Sondheim's *Company* to *Hair* (with which *Rent* was frequently compared) to *Guys and Dolls*, which was revived at the National in 1996, resolutely "New York" musicals had found success in Britain. David Benedict of *The Independent* also noted the "hundred and one local factors" ("The American musical comes of age," 1998) in *Rent* that he believed both explained its success but also caused him to question whether it would travel well. These comments highlight the potential issues of staging the production in London. There was an element of artistic judgment on the production and perhaps a reference to the content about AIDS not functioning as well in Britain. However, there was little mention of the part AIDS played in Larson's text within the press analysis. For some, like the American reviewers, AIDS became a label to categorize the musical. One such critic was Nicholas de Jongh, who wrote, "This famous, mid-Nineties American musical that makes a song and dance affair of AIDS and drug addiction with young lovers, straight gay and lesbian, not to mention a frisson of transvestitism" (1998).

Thus, for a number of reviewers, AIDS was one of a list of factors that contributed to their reaction. Still, for many, AIDS no longer seemed a central focus of their analysis in contrast to responses to *Angels in America* a few years earlier. This partly may be due to the point at which it was performed in Britain, at a point when the urgency of the early days of the epidemic was over and where treatments were improving. In Britain particularly, there did not seem to be as strong an urgency by 1998 around AIDS. Therefore, *Rent* as a theatrical text had a different function in Britain when it was staged. David Thomas, in his review for *The Times*, asks: "New York went crazy for the tale of doomed love, Aids and drug addiction that is *Rent*. But will the hit Broadway musical have cynical British theatregoers queuing round the block for a ticket?" (1998).

Thomas indicates here that the content, specifically including AIDS, may be an alienating factor to British audiences. He also observes that Larson's approach may be equally problematic for "cynical" British audiences, as he refers to them. According to Thomas, the sentimentality associated with musicals and American theater contrasts with what he views as British audience sensibilities. Thomas's view is open to debate, and universalizing statements about audience behavior are dangerous; however, this may be accurate about other texts on AIDS and theatrical trends outlined elsewhere. Thomas's assessment of British audience trends is also based on personal experience as a theater critic and, thus, may hold weight.

Thomas goes on to examine what he and other reviewers in Britain saw as a critical error in *Rent's* depiction of AIDS: its approach to the condition and whether it was both realistic and political enough. In his review, Thomas comments, "Ironically, though, the problem with *Rent* is not that it is radical, but that it is not radical enough." He compares *Rent* with the film *Trainspotting*, which he sees as Britain's response to the same era. In this comparison, Thomas highlights how British culture, when faced with troublesome issues, such as "a generation racked by drugs and disease," came up with the grittier realism of *Trainspotting*. In comparison, Thomas says, "Given the same situation, Broadway proved that there is no circumstance so vile that America cannot sanitize it, glamorize it and successfully commercialize." Thomas sees *Rent* as reductive, as he seems to want more realism and less sentimentality. This may be a fair comment, but Larson's central aim was to depict a story of hope about AIDS. Thomas is also drawing national lines in his criticism, attributing what he sees as shortcomings to the American origins of the piece. Thomas's points are, however, backed up by British theatrical traditions. The work of Edward Bond in addressing the darker elements of society and human behavior, and comparable work by Mark Ravenhill, which addresses issues of sexuality, including that of AIDS in modern cities, offers a far darker outlook.

There is further derision at the approach taken to representing AIDS from other reviewers who mention it. John Peter was puzzled at the approach *Rent* takes to AIDS:

'This is exactly the kind of soppy exhibitionism that has done the cause of Aids sufferers so much harm; and it is strange that a show that first opened as late as 1996 could still indulge in it" (1998). Peter's point is that given the time it was written, *Rent* should have been more progressive and probably more political than it is to be considered a meaningful statement on AIDS.

Nevertheless, while *Rent* can be considered a sentimental piece, I disagree that the musical does people with AIDS harm. The representation and effect that *Rent* has in depicting AIDS are good for those with the condition, particularly those in Britain. The representation, the emotional attachment, and the development of those groups depicted helped bring greater awareness of AIDS to the general public. Billington goes on to call it "*Hair*, with added Aids" (Billington 1998). In this context, it is not a reference or compliment to Larson's piece continuing the legacy of the 1960s rock musical, but rather a disparaging comment on the (lack of?) political content. Peter sees *Rent* as existing in a commune-like setting separate from the reality of the world it claims to represent, concluding that it is problematic as a text on AIDS. He suggests that watching *Rent* for British audiences in 1998 may be like watching the revival of *Hair* more than a decade later in 2010, a nostalgic fiction idealized but with little reflection of reality or real political message. Though British audiences viewed *Rent* as a slightly historical piece, this was not detrimental to its impact. *Rent* did not, as illustrated, need to be realistic or have a direct political message to be a compelling depiction of AIDS. It is fair to say that the sentimental element was not to everyone's taste, as reflected in critics like Peter.

Therefore, the British press response was mixed at best. On the other hand, some critics embraced *Rent*. Michael Billington wrote, "Once you strip away the hype and hysteria you find a genuinely enjoyable anthem to modern youth: a touch sentimental and self-admiring but full of melodic invention." Billington here highlights one of the problems for critics and audiences seeing *Rent* in Britain, the initial hype surrounding it and the subsequent negative press, which somewhat blurred views of it. Billington reflects on the show becoming a phenomenon in New York. Billington's response reflects a more measured and fairer approach. Although he is not heralding *Rent* as the savior of musical theater as some American colleagues did, Billington recognizes *Rent* as a quality musical that appealed to a general audience.

One powerful critique of *Rent* in the British press was in an editorial from Joanna Coles of *The Guardian*. As mentioned in the introduction to this chapter, Coles draws on Sarah Schulman's book about Larson's alleged plagiarization of her work. Coles's article draws on the problems and criticism of Larson's work. Coles uses Schulman's complaints to discuss what she deems "the most compelling criticism of Larson's work." She goes on to say "that if, as he insisted, he was genuinely trying to portray life in the East Village, what actually appears on the Broadway stage is arguably something of a travesty . . . It could be a fiction storyline: Struggling young writer-composter dies on the eve of phenomenal success" (1998). These comments see *Rent* as appropriating a culture, and Larson's work detracting from the actual lived experience of those he depicts.

Coles quotes East Village residents and some people with AIDS to support her argument. Some described their unhappiness with Larson's portrayal. One commented that it had been "Disneyfied," then goes as far as to say, "I feel like I've been raped." The issue with Larson's portrayal of AIDS, for some, is that it is sanitized and favors the straight characters, such as Mark, as integral to fighting AIDS and Schulman says it is "like a Benetton ad." This latter comment by Schulman may be viewed as a double-edged comment highlighting the trendy sanitized element of *Rent*, which is reminiscent of Benetton's campaigns in the 1990s—and which also references the controversy over the 1991

Benetton advertisement that used an image of an AIDS sufferer in a hospital. Both aspects indicate a "commodification" of AIDS. The idea that *Rent* took the real lives and experiences of people with AIDS and used them for commercial gain was problematic for Schulman and Coles. However, Larson's work is not, in my reading, exploitative. How *Rent* drew on the experiences and lives of those affected by AIDS was no different from *Angels in America*, *The Normal Heart*, or any other performance piece. Tony Kushner does not have AIDS but was affected by losing those who did, and so was Larson.

The reactions in Coles's article are extreme, and there is no indication that other critics saw Larson's work as exploitative. The people cited in Coles's piece have particular grievances against Larson's work; one comment is perhaps pertinent to a British audience: "I think the history of Aids should be taught in schools. More people know and think they understand Aids through *Rent* than will ever know about it truthfully." In the British setting, with *Rent* coming later in the epidemic and appealing to a younger demographic, the danger of the minimal information about AIDS is worrying. However, as with many second-generation plays, this was designed as something other than an information service to the audience. Once again, realism, or educational content, is one of many markers of a successful piece. *Rent* did not strive for gritty realism or detailed medical or political information. What *Rent* did deliver was an emotive, character-driven work on AIDS.

These criticisms of *Rent* as an educational work on AIDS and its perceived shortcomings were accompanied by other articles whose criticism was based more on artistic merit than content. David Gritten failed to be won over:

It has been hailed as the saviour of the musical but despite the nobility of its conscience too much of the show is laudable for its attempt rather than its realization. (Gritten, *Rent* review, 1998)

Such criticism is justified and perhaps expected for a musical that, if not it did not break the mold, certainly strayed from the expected norms of the genre. There were bound to be critics who disliked, as with any artistic or theatrical endeavor, the approaches of the composer and director. Updating *La bohème*, as Macaulay highlights, also garnered negative attention from opera purists. However, the criticism on an artistic level did not completely negate *Rent*'s artistic merit.

Despite the negative reviews, critics recognized that there was an appeal to the show. Some reviewers praised Larson's musical ability as well as the work as a whole. Nicholas de Jongh commented that Mimi's "Light My Candle" "captures a mood of sexy, wistful yearning more powerfully than any West End Musical song this decade" (1998). This is a powerful compliment, indicating that Larson's piece displayed a high musical talent. In highlighting the musical ability of the composer, de Jongh draws attention to the importance of *Rent* as a work of musical theater. This is also seen in Billington's assessment, who praises Larson with the remark: "He also writes powerful and romantic songs including a deeply Sonheimite one *Without You* in which love is designed by a series of negatives" (1998). Other critics paid much more attention to the hype surrounding *Rent*.

In comparing Larson's song to Sondheim, the leading American composer of previous decades, Billington praises Larson's work. There were certain elements to praise in *Rent*, and as producer Jeffery Seller noted, they weren't selling out on Broadway three years in on hype alone; people were coming on the strength of the show (Seller, in Benedict, May 5, 1998). Tempering the criticism of Larson's style elsewhere, Benedict comments that hit rock musicals are rare (Benedict, April 19, 1998). By saying this, he indicates that the critical issues that Larson's musical encountered may, in part, be related to the form as much as his own content and style.

RENT, AIDS, AND THEATER IN BRITAIN

The press evaluation of *Rent* in Britain, as shown above, did not echo the rave reviews in New York. There was trepidation due to the hype surrounding the New York production and the success of *Rent* in America. British reviewers also were cautious about whether the musical would translate well to British audiences. And yet, despite some negative reception by critics, the production still connected with fans in Britain. The love for the show and the strength of support from those who loved it played a strong part in *Rent*'s success in New York and London, as Anthony Rapp comments. "People have said to me afterwards that it has changed their life. If people are going through difficult times the show can be a source of great comfort and cathartic for them" (quoted in Fanshawe 1998). Rapp indicates a far more important element of *Rent*'s success—the connection with fans.

Critical opinion is important for box office sales and, therefore, for the success of a piece, but it is not the only factor. Critics cited here reflect an element of audience response but do not represent the entire audience. The reflection on the text of *Rent* indicates that its approach to depicting AIDS onstage was successful. The emphasis on the personal, emotional connection to AIDS meant that transposing to the British stage was in some respects easier than for *Angels in America* with its more detailed medical and political focus. Larson's text still made a broad political and social statement about AIDS while connecting with an audience on an emotional level. Fans of *Rent*, just as in America, were affected strongly by the show and were very loyal to it. As will be explored later in relation to discussing the revivals, this dedication to *Rent* by fans is intrinsic to its long-ranging effects, both as a depiction of AIDS and on the wider theatrical landscape.

7

"I HEAR SPIKE LEE'S SHOOTING DOWN THE STREET"

Rent on Film

Rent once again was a trailblazer. Long before Tom Hooper got his hands on *Les Misérables* and *Cats*, there was Chris Columbus and *Rent.* The story of the film is a protracted one as these things tend to be. From the moment it was clear *Rent* was a hit rumors of a film circulated. Still, these things take time, and ultimately it was ten years later that fans finally got a film version directed by Chris Columbus, known then for *Home Alone,* and later for *Harry Potter.* There was much criticism of the film—both from film and theater critics, and fans themselves. But equally the adventure in getting there, and the importance of the film is still significant—both for the history of *Rent* itself and to the people who love it.

As the hottest ticket on Broadway, *Rent* was an obvious candidate for movie adaptation. As soon as the success seemed apparent, studios were approaching the Larson family about rights. But there was one issue: nobody was making musicals any more. This was before a few of the big hitters made their way to film, before *Phantom*, before *Les Mis*, and before *Cats* was committed to film. The year *Rent* moved to Broadway *Evita* was released in cinemas and became the most successful and most prominent musical film in some time. But really the "peak" years of musicals occurred in the 1960s and 1970s. At that point a slew of classic musicals were being made into films—the back catalog of the 1940s and 1950s Rodgers and Hammerstein classics were all made in this period, along with other now-iconic musicals like *West Side Story* (1961) and Lionel Bart's *Oliver!* (1968). Moving into the 1970s a few more "experimental" musicals were made, including *Cabaret* (1972) and *Jesus Christ Superstar* (1973) along with *The Wiz* (1978), which despite being groundbreaking on numerous levels, was a commercial flop in its initial run (though has seen considerable success since) was also among a number of musical flops that would continue into the 1980s and 1990s. Around this time, too, *Grease* (1978) was released. More than a decade earlier, *The Sound of Music* was one of a handful of musicals that became iconic on film almost separate from its stage roots similar in fact to *Rent*'s original cast and their future careers.

In truth, the late 1980s and the 1990s were something of a wasteland for musical theater. Musicals that in theory should have been a critical and commercial success like *Annie* or *A Chorus Line* flopped—*Annie* has had a solid life on VHS/DVD and TV reruns and remains a childhood classic for many while *A Chorus Line* could generously be termed a cult hit. Other niche films did make more of a splash in this period. *Newsies* (which would go on to live at the Nederlander Theatre after *Rent*) became something of a cult hit in the 1990s; meanwhile, the film version of the record-breaking Off-Broadway musical *The Fantasticks* also became a cult hit when released on DVD in the early 2000s.

Box-office wise the biggest musical "hit" in recent memory when *Rent* was onstage was *Evita*—peak 1990s in every respect (it came out in 1996) with the combination of the heavy-hitter Andrew Lloyd Webber and his mega-musical juggernauts, alongside pop star Madonna, who used the film as a vehicle to cement her acting career (it wasn't the success she'd hoped for). The biggest musical theater film success in recent memory before *Rent* was the adaptation of *Chicago* (2002). Directed by Rob Marshall, it featured a cast that included a mixture of Hollywood stars with a theatrical background (Catherine Zeta-Jones, Christine Baranski) alongside bankable, but appropriately cast "names" (Richard Gere perfectly cast as Billy Flynn, Renée Zellweger proving her acting ability once again as Roxie) with an array of Broadway veterans in the chorus as dancers, and cameos from the likes of Chita Rivera (the original Velma) and even Taye Diggs as the bandleader. *Chicago* is now considered a watershed moment in musical theater on film. Unfortunately, as the much-mocked Tom Hooper ventures with *Les Mis* and the later outright disastrous *Cats* illustrate, the musical is still a medium that many filmmakers struggle with. But Jon M. Chu's version of *In the Heights* and Lin-Manuel Miranda's *Tick, Tick . . . Boom!* have proven what those with a love for the musical form can do. Perhaps too there's hope for another version of *Rent* down the line that might prove more successful in the eyes of fans.

It is of course difficult to create the film version of a much loved, and hugely successful, stage musical. Originally there was a five-year hold placed on *Rent*, a not unusual agreement to make sure that the show first got the very most out of the Broadway and touring versions before a film made it available to everyone. There's always been a bit of divide in opinion over the impact of film versions of stage productions on tickets: do they increase or decrease interest overall? Logic would say increase in the long term, with people who have seen the film wanting the "real thing" but there's also a fear from producers that people having seen the film won't bother with the real thing, and so often a hold is put on productions. Something less common in some instances, with more Recent movie musicals like *The Prom* (2020) and *Dear Evan Hansen* (2021), though, proved to be the exception, choosing to go into film production virtually straight away upon realizing they had a hit—perhaps an indicator of a faster-moving pop culture today, but also a heartening indication that appetite for movie musicals has at least continued to grow.

For *Rent* too there was a question of "just because we can doesn't mean we should" around it, and the notion, particularly from the producers that its power lay in being a live event. There is a broader element of this for movie musicals to be debated—some lend themselves perfectly to the screen—*Singin' in the Rain,* for example, is a movie musical about the movies and works perfectly. *The Sound of Music* is a beautifully shot screen musical that works impeccably as cinema. Others like *Cats* rely on the in-person experience and the suspension of disbelief, or at least an understanding of the musical format, to work properly. Was *Rent* more *Cats* than *The Sound of Music* (a sentence nobody should really have to contemplate)?

With such a hit, and to be honest a good story around it surrounding Larson's death, it's not surprising that studios were interested, and interested quickly. That it ultimately was such a long road to making the film is both testament to the difficulties of the film industry but also the manner in which Julie and everyone else involved was determined to protect Larson's work.

After some back-and-forth with different studios (Warner Brothers, Universal, Fox Searchlight, and others) the film landed with Miramax and Harvey and Bob Weinstein. Luckily perhaps in terms of that association, things didn't work out with that studio and after a number of years of development, the film moved to Warner Brothers instead.

By this time, director Chris Columbus was on board with the project. Initially, though, Spike Lee was slated to direct. The director, who had been hugely successful in the 1990s and yes, as all *Rent* fans know, is name-checked in "Light My Candle," spent the summer of 2001 working on the project with Stephen Chbosky, who had been hired to write the screenplay. Chbosky was known for his coming-of-age novel *The Perks of Being a Wallflower*, a film he would later direct himself and another "controversial" book about young people and something of a cult hit also. On paper then he was ideal. But the course of filming seldom runs smoothly, and by 2001 *Rent* was in development but stalling at the same time. Coupled with the fact that by then *Rent* was no longer the "next big thing"—the film was looking like a harder sell all round. Weinstein started pitching it to NBC as a TV adaptation—a curveball to many involved. Luckily the contract that the Larson family had gave them veto power. They remained firm it should be a film. (Interestingly, years later, they would sign over TV rights for both the Hollywood Bowl broadcast and the *Rent: Live* program but its unlikely they'd have done so if the film itself had not first been made.)

However, Rosenthal remained committed to the project and continued to work on finding a studio. Elsewhere Chris Columbus, as noted above, known for his 1990s hits with *Home Alone*, had formed his own production company—1492 Productions—and came on board as coproducer with Warner Brothers.

It might have ultimately been fortuitous that *Rent* took so long to make it to preproduction, because suddenly Hollywood and, perhaps audiences, had faith in the movie musical again, thanks to the success of the film version of *Chicago*. As noted, *Chicago* showed what film musicals could be. Fusing both stage and screen and making the best of both worlds, including casting dancers from the Broadway show, the film had something movie musicals had lacked: credibility. It also had immense crossover appeal, becoming hugely successful at the box office as well as winning the Academy Award for Best Picture.

The *Rent* film went into production with Columbus at the helm the following spring. Also on board were the original production team of Jeffrey Seller, Kevin McCollum, and Allan S. Gordon as executive producers and Julie Larson as coproducer—all acting as "guardians" of Larson's vision in his absence.

CREATING *RENT* ON FILM

There is always the danger when casting a movie musical that the extremes of what is known in theater as "stunt casting" will be embraced. So, for example, instead of Patti LuPone you get Madonna, or in the modern sense perhaps Ariana Grande instead of Kristen Chenowith. Indeed pop stars were in consideration for the film, with names like Justin Timberlake floated around. If unknowns had been cast that would have been in keeping with the original ethos but there was a sense that for the fans, one last reunion of the people who made the roles was what they wanted. Really, with time going on, this was also their last window of opportunity to do that before they all aged out of the roles.

Even so, most were pushing the upper limit of credibility when the film was made, but fans were likely to forgive that in favor of seeing them on screen. And everything else aside, it did feel right that these were the people to make the film.

Six of the original eight principals were back: Anthony Rapp (Mark), Adam Pascal (Roger), Idina Menzel (Maureen), Taye Diggs (Benny), Jesse L. Martin (Collins), and Wilson Jermaine Heredia (Angel). Fredi Walker agreed she was too old at that point, and bowed out of playing Joanne, while Daphne Rubin-Vega was also pregnant at the time so wasn't available to play Mimi, the role she originated on Broadway. Instead the part of Mimi went to Rosario Dawson, an actress who had gained early fame in the 1995 film *Kids* (which also touches on AIDS and its impact on New York). She had moved on to more commercial roles after studying at the Lee Strasberg Institute and was known for parts in films like *Josie and the Pussycats*, *Men in Black II*, *Ash Wednesday*, and *Shattered Glass*. She'd also appeared in music videos. She took on her first stage role months before *Rent* was released playing Julia in the Public Theater rock musical version of *Two Gentleman of Verona*. The role of Joanne went to Tracie Thoms, who ended up with the ultimate "Renthead" story: as a fan of the show she not only got in the show, but also in the movie (and later the closing cast). She had auditioned many times for the show—both Broadway and tour—but was rejected. But the show meant a lot to her, and she kept coming back. Three years after the film, she got her chance to play Joanne onstage. She joined the show for the final six weeks of the run and was part of the cast that filmed *Rent: Live on Broadway*, the recording of the show. She also reprised the role for the Hollywood Bowl production directed by Neil Patrick Harris.

Rent was a labor of love for all involved. Chris Columbus had no commercial or critical reason to be making this film, other than love of the content. Equally all the original cast had moved on in their careers and were doing well, their motivations for revisiting were again from a connection with the material. Columbus began his career in the film industry as a screenwriter before becoming a director. He worked for Steven Spielberg's company in the mid-eighties and worked on scripts for his big hits like *Gremlins* and *The Goonies*. He also worked as a writer and creative consultant on the animated TV series *Galaxy High School*. His first feature film was *Adventures in Babysitting* (1987), which happened to feature Anthony Rapp. He then moved on to writing and directing with *Heartbreak Hotel* and *Only the Lonely*. His most famous work probably remains the *Home Alone* films, written by John Hughes.

By the time Columbus was on board, there was a script written by Stephen Chbosky for the film version Spike Lee was going to make. This was, naturally, with a different director a different version to what was eventually in Columbus's film. Lee's take on the modern musical was to figure out situations in which the characters might naturally be singing or performing rather than it be integrated and accepted that this was (unapologetically) a musical. An element some might argue was the downfall of musicals for some time—an apologetic approach to the songs rather than fully owning their existence. The script largely went back to Larson's original in the eventual version that Columbus rewrote.

However, fans and critics still had trepidation over what would be cut and what would survive. The big hitters were always likely to say, but the full sung-through format was in danger from the start, with some elements replaced by dialogue, some gone entirely as well as a fear that favorite but lesser-known songs would be lost. Other fans feared who would be cast in the beloved roles.

Columbus was at least experienced at making movies with his Harry Potter legacy; no doubt the very worst of judgment on him as a director he'd already heard a thousand times over from the dedicated Potter following which was at its height in the early 2000s with the release of the first films and final books, and before its creator, J. K. Rowling, took a nosedive in public popularity thanks to her repeatedly expressing transphobic views on social media and in the press (Brendon Morrow, for *The Week* on February 13, 2023, compiled an article outlining Rowlings's transphobic tweets and quotes up to the time of writing). Columbus himself as with many associated with Rowling's work might find he is lumped in with her views. To that end Columbus has declined to comment. In an interview with *Variety* in 2021, he said, "I don't really have any comment on that. I don't want to get involved, sorry" (Rudin, Rebecca, *Variety*, 2021). While any creative declining to support the trans community in the wake of Rowling's comments is disappointing, it is particularly so from a director who also was at the helm of *Rent*. However, as Columbus has not expressed agreement with Rowling, *Rent* remains outside of the boycott of output many LGBTQ people and allies engage with over Rowling and her supporters work. Perhaps watching *Rent* directed by someone who worked on the Potterverse can also be considered an act of trans solidarity in retrospect. Columbus then no doubt came to *Rent* with thick skin but, more importantly, an understanding of a work that not just meant a lot but was truly formative for many people.

The movie begins in December 1989 as Mark and Roger are facing eviction (most of which was done with the visuals of the street at Christmas). Benny arrives in his Land Rover, dispensing with the original voice-overs that told this part of the story. The time lines shift a bit further with the events of Act 1 taking place over three days rather than one night, which does make more narrative sense, and a few slight lyric tweaks ("tomorrow" for "today," etc). We lose much of Mark as the narrator but in the slightly slowed down pace of the film, and with the visual storytelling added in the narrative, the story is easy enough to follow. Columbus also embellishes some of the narrative: Roger and April in flashbacks, showing them getting their test results, the aftermath of April's suicide. All of which rounds out the sparse details that might be easy to miss in the lyrics of the songs on first listen.

Other visual shifts were Mimi's "Out Tonight." As in the theater, it starts in the club before moving out onto the street, and, then, to her apartment. She mimics the famous balcony dance of the stage production on a real outdoor balcony before swinging into Roger's apartment. The whole number then becomes a means to "travel" Mimi both physically and in terms of the narrative to deliver her back to Roger for "Another Day." A beautiful visual sequence happens after she leaves, and ends up below Roger's apartment singing "Another Day" up at him before being joined by Mark, Collins, and Angel. It shifts the scene from being just a lovers' (or potential lovers') tiff to the group of friends pleading with Roger to shift his attitude and mindset. It's a simple element but one that showed Columbus's familiarity with the material and his determination to not just throw open the stage show onto film but really work with it. The visual, and the arrangement, work wonderfully and powerfully to deliver a nuanced bit of character development that we don't get to see in the stage version as clearly. Adding also to this moment is the dynamic with Mimi and Angel—where Angel hugs Mimi at the end of the number, consoling her over Roger. This was one of a number of visual moments that Columbus included to establish the relationship between Mimi and Angel since although in the stage version she's alluded to being friends with them at the funeral, we see little evidence of that beforehand. Luckily the film is able to insert some cinematic shorthand it with some visual clues.

Other visuals were shifted for sensitivity purposes; we no longer have a "chorus" of homeless people, for example. Understandably it was deemed to be insensitive: it was thought that on film with its more "real" look this would become and insulting addition. Instead any of the music usually "chorused" by the homeless people was shifted to other cast members.

The cast rehearsed for several months in San Francisco prior to actual filming: it's usual in feature films for that to happen, but less so for a musical that obviously needs time to get the musical elements right.

The cast also recorded the music, first to sing to but also for the film's accompanying album. Slightly different in tone and style to the original recording, Columbus said he wanted it to be more like the Green Day concept album *American Idiot* (ironically later made into a musical). Tim Weil returned to be musical director along with an eight-piece band. It benefited from the state-of-the-art facilities, and a film budget instead of an up-and-coming Broadway budget. In terms of music production it is undeniably superior in production values, with also the added years of experience in performing for the cast too, and the familiarity with the characters and songs by that point for most, there is a certain extra something in the performances too. The movie soundtrack will never replace the original for most fans, surely, but it is also a great record of a slightly different version of the show. It was released on CD originally with eight different sleeves featuring a particular character: another great collectable for fans obsessed with *Rent* merchandise.

The musical numbers are slightly altered in the movie—the phone messages became dialogue, and a few of the more "transition" numbers were lost, including "We're Okay" and "Christmas Bells." The songs "Halloween" and "Goodbye Love" were included in the recording but ultimately cut from the film. An additional song (usually an obligatory component for musical films to make them eligible for Original Song award categories) was "Love Heals," a song Jonathan originally wrote for an AIDS benefit.

Filming largely took place in Oakland, California. The need for locations big enough to accommodate film crews necessitated the change of locations. Also much of the actual East Village had drastically changed by this point; places like the Life Cafe were no longer there and New York regulations on filming meant it was difficult (not to mention expensive) to film on location for much of the shoot. The film did pick up some scenes on location, though, mostly for background. On other songs like "One Song Glory" the crew worked against the odds to lend the scene a "New York" feel.

There were, of course, changes to accommodate the visual language of film. There was also obviously a move away from the blatant theatricality discussed as central to the film version. In an act of meeting audiences halfway, Columbus kept the musical structure, the heart of the film, but dispensed with a few of the more "theatrical" musical devices. That meant that the sung-through parts like the phone messages, and other link scenes were cut. Some of these would have been awkward on film—it seems redundant in that medium to sing a line that could be achieved with a short line or even visual sequence. This did mean losing some of the more substantial numbers: "Halloween" and "Goodbye Love" are the most noticeable "victims," which left out narrative chunks in order to skip ahead. It worked in principle on film, and the cuts for brevity without an interval were understandable, but arguably the film lost a little something from them. "Halloween" in particular is one of the best pieces of musical storytelling that Larson wrote, and in a quietly understated way complements the raw emotion of "I'll Cover You" with Mark's quiet reflection and the cutting line "Perhaps its because I'm the one of us to survive." There were areas where we might critically question the artistic choices of the film, much like any reinterpretation. Columbus played with the structure and content. Probably the most striking (or certainly the first noticeable) is the shift of "Seasons of Love" to the start of the movie.

While purists might object to the move, it makes a lot of sense in the movie format. Firstly it sets out the parameters of how the film will function, in this case, as a musical and this is important for letting audiences know what they are "in for": we've all heard stories from musical doubters who go and see one and declare their horror that someone was singing in it. This at least leaves no doubt from the opening notes. It's also a nice moment, a nod to the original, and to the fans; the cast stands in that oh-so-familiar configuration, in a theater, singing the song that has become such an anthem. For fans it was a bit of signaling from Columbus: we get you, we understand you, we're making your story.

It's also undeniably a moment of emotional connection—seeing those people who brought the show to life, either for the first time in a while, or maybe for the first time "in person" performing that role. It's a moment to catch your breath as a fan, to settle into the world again.

Obviously some fans would argue with that sentiment, and that's fair. The film isn't the stage show, and it doesn't capture everything that fans wanted it to. For some it was too glossy, too shiny . . . it lacked the grit of the original. Some had very strong thoughts about cast members being recast, others had strong thoughts about original cast members being cast . . . others even had stronger opinions about Roger's hair. Big and small you can't please all the fans all the time, and arguably nor should you try.

RENT ON FILM

The film adaptation both attracted new fans and brought old ones back to *Rent* and curiously it did so before it even was finished. Such was the excitement about a filmed version, and a return of (most of) the original cast, that interest was piqued early. With the proliferation of the Internet in the interim, access to knowledge for fans and sharing of knowledge was far easier. Despite it being a decade after the original opening, enough of the fans were still engaged to want to be a part of it. Fans followed production news, which for location shoots took place in New York and relayed the information to those who couldn't be there. And then, when the promotional machine kicked in for the film, American fans shared information with international fans, and among themselves about appearances, where to read and where to watch. It very much felt like a coming together of the "original" fans, in what felt like "one last time" to see what the film would bring.

There was an almost halcyon moment of the early days of internet-fan-*Rent* with a new access to online content and communications.

During the filming fans could share filming tidbits—from locations to casting to sightings of the costumes—across both social media and message boards. The online message board community was very strong, and the threads about *Rent* were alight again in a way they hadn't been for many years. Once the promotional tour started, fans used YouTube (then in its infancy) to share clips of the cast on TV shows promoting the movie (as a aside, musical theater fans were early adopters of YouTube as a sharing platform for bootlegs). A particularly memorable moment occurred on *Today*, which held a concert series in Rockefeller Plaza every summer, and for which *Rent* was a featured show. The whole cast performed "Seasons of Love" and Anthony and Adam performed "What You Own" while the rest of the cast could be seen watching and cheering them on. This promotional tour was the last time the majority of the principle original cast (and the couple of new additions) would be together, and fans were conscious of that. For *Today*, fans camped overnight just to be in the audience.

Seeing the film was an act of sharing the show that fans loved with fellow fans one last time. It could also be a slightly odd isolating experience. Outside of North America the film's release was sporadic. Fans in larger US cities at least were able to go in groups, and in this way replicate that theatrical experience watching the film on the big screen. Either way it felt like something of another "goodbye love" to the original cast and to the original production that came shortly before the end of the Broadway run.

Was this nostalgic act a bad thing? Not really. *Rent* was not a groundbreaking film and couldn't match what happened onstage—very little could live up to those expectations. Instead the film was more like a conversation with the fans, a tribute to them, to the original theatrical production, and to Jonathan Larson himself. There has always been an element of sentimentality, and, yes, nostalgia, attached to *Rent*, and the film is part of that. It gave Larson part of the dreams he never got to see—a big-screen musical. It gave the original cast a chance to preserve their performances, as they existed onstage in an era before prolific pro-shoot musicals. And finally, most importantly, it gave the fans a chance to celebrate Jonathan Larson, to celebrate the musical, and to preserve the people who gave them that experience. It might not have done that as fans—or even general audiences—might have wished. But it's still important. In a way, *Rent* is still a little Off-Broadway musical, with themes that "shouldn't" have worked, and which somehow made it to the big screen. And that's something in itself.

Where does *Rent* sit in the history of musicals on film? Probably, sadly, it is largely forgotten. On the other hand, it is remembered fondly by those fans whose first encounter with the musical was the film. Even for other fans for whom it may not have been the same as the original they loved, but it does have the cast they loved, and they treasure it for that. But, unfortunately in style, form, and maybe content, it didn't hit the screen at the right time. Whether that was a sense of just old enough to be dated, but not old enough to be retro or perhaps today *Rent* has grown into its themes again in a way it hadn't in 2005. For when looking at 2021 productions its themes feel like they have resonated again. We understand the characters and their motivations, and look perhaps at the rest as history. Maybe 2005 was just not close enough to capture the original moment, and just that bit too close to be considered historic, or retro. Maybe even, in another ten years we'll see another remake.

Because *Rent* now sits in a landscape of renewed interest in—and perhaps hope for—the film musical given the success of the adaptation of *In the Heights* and its innovation and loyalty to the original source (and indeed the inclusion of *Rent* cast member Daphne Rubin-Vega). And with remakes of *West Side Story* (2021) and adaptation of newer musicals such as *The Prom* (2020) and finally the long-promised version of *Wicked* (Thanksgiving 2024), the movie musical is alive and actually thriving. And *Rent* is part of that conversation. The movie was imperfect—as was the original musical. But what has comes after is important.

Finally, *Rent* continues to lead us from one thing to another. *Tick, Tick . . . Boom!* itself was part of the bigger conversation. The film adaptation of Larson's autobiographical story came to Netflix in 2021, directed by Lin-Manuel Miranda. As we know, *Rent* and Larson inspired Miranda to pursue a career in musicals. Without Larson, we wouldn't have *In The Heights*, or the successful film version of it. We wouldn't have *Hamilton* and all it has done for the genre either, or the Disney television version either. Miranda made his film debut as a director with a film about Jonathan Larson, and that feels like an apt way to conclude a dialogue about *Rent* on film.

8

"GOODBYE LOVE"

Closing *Rent* on Broadway

As the Broadway run came to a close, a segment in both the fans' and the original cast/creative team's lives came to a close. It was an emotional moment for many. For both fans and the cast/creatives, *Rent* had been a formative experience, and the closure of the Broadway production was a milestone.

Rent was filmed as part of the closing process. This was a sign of an evolving Broadway—or indeed a show ahead of its time, as very few Broadway shows are still commercially filmed. This meant a filmed version joined the cast recording as a permanent reminder of the show. The cast recording had been, at the time, the fastest-selling Broadway cast recording of all time. The significance of this record passed among Broadway fans who did not have access to the "real thing" in New York but also had a kind of widespread appeal that was not seen before— other than the odd "breakout hit" such as "Memory" from *Cats*. That *Rent* was the last musical until *Hamilton*—whose creator is well documented in citing Larson and his music as inspiration—to be filmed was important since recorded versions of *Rent* could now transcend its "live" lifespan and spun it forward into a new era for the musical.

It felt like a conscious move regarding the importance of the show in its "pure" Broadway form that it needed to be preserved in this way. Like the film, the recording was an "event" in fans' lives. They were in the audience and were once again were able to participate in being part of a "history" of "their" show. Filmed with the closing show cast, which now included Tracie Thoms (also part of the film cast), there was a special additional finale with the original cast. All of this forms part of the history and "*Rent* lore" finally preserved on film, along with the little special details: Anthony Rapp doing what he did at the end of every show sending three "claps" up to Jonathan Larson; the original cast standing in the famous "Seasons of Love" line onstage one last time; and as the show ended, a pan across the audience to see the fans who were part of capturing this moment in history. The film or the later *Rent Live* would never capture or conclude a chapter in history in quite the same way.

There were, of course, many "finales" in the closing chapters on Broadway—for cast and fans. The last time cast members were there, some who left early, countless fan stories of their personal "lasts" and, of course, the final last show. The day that *Rent* left the Nederlander was a joint closing of theatrical history and personal history for so many people.

Parallel to this, becoming a global musical phenomenon altered what *Rent* was. You can't be bohemian on Broadway (as, twenty-five years later, *Moulin Rogue* the musical was perhaps proving). But is there a midpoint to be achieved, as the show moved toward closing—from the "message" of Larson's work being spread to more people—even if that

message was now mediated commercially? Tied up with these reinter-
pretations of various kinds, and as Broadway itself became "Disneyfied,"
how did *Rent* retain its bohemian spirit and not sell out to Broadway?

RENT LIVE ON BROADWAY

The closing night (or nights) of *Rent* were filmed for posterity by Sony
Pictures. At this point (2008) filming for archive purposes was a long-
established tradition on Broadway (and indeed *Rent* had already been
filmed for this purpose). But these recordings were from fixed cameras
at the back of the stalls or similar. They are also not generally accessible to the public but were housed by the New York Public Library in
their Theater on Film and Tape Archive. For preservation purposes the
archive must limit access to the recordings, many of which are delicate
and have not been, and possibly cannot be, digitized. As a result only a
limited number of people are able to access the recordings.

In 2008 the filmed theater and cinema broadcasts popularized by
Live from Lincoln Center and *NT Live* were in their infancy, and so a
recording like *Rent* of the actual stage production was a relative rarity.
It seemed fitting after the twelve-year run, however, to finally preserve
the original staging of this iconic show. Fitting too seemed the decision not to film it in an empty theater, making a composite of the real
thing, but to do it indeed "live" for the final show (it was in fact done
over two shows, much like the "live broadcasts" today usually record
a dress rehearsal in case of technical issues). In this instance too the
filming of the final show allowed the *Rent* team to capture the celebration at the end of the show, when *Rent* alumni joined in a version of
"Seasons of Love."

In terms of putting it together its obviously not as "orchestrated" in terms of filming as the actual movie, but still some planning into where to focus or edit the shots for different scenes. The result is perhaps a clearer version of the show than some might have experienced from the "cheap seats" or even in their first viewings—the cameras zoom in on individuals and help us follow the story as it unfolds, making a little more sense of the sometimes-chaotic moments of the narrative. What it also does is preserve that staging forever. Some scenes were filmed for perspective around the performances—in the empty theater—so that the full sweep of the stage could be seen, and viewers might experience an entirely different perspective on the show they know so well.

GOODBYE LOVE (EVENTUALLY)

Replacement Casts

The casts of the Broadway production inevitably moved on, and as documented with regard to the tours, the producers continued to source talent from unknown performers and nontraditional routes. However *Rent* wasn't immune to a bit of Broadway "stunt casting."

Firstly a caveat: "stunt casting" isn't always a bad thing. Many of the "famous" people who are derided as "stunt casting" often have a background in the theater. Ironically, Neil Patrick Harris, who often gets pigeonholed as "stunt casting," today following his TV success, has a solid background in theater, including Mark in the early *Rent* tours. Similarly many a contestant on *American Idol* or *The X Factor* (insert reality TV show of choice here) also spent a lot of time either training in musicals or performing in them—again ironically many a contestant gets booted from them for being "too musical theater." A couple of examples of casting that was more "legit" than it first appeared included Jai Rodriguez, who joined the show as Angel in 2004 and at that point was known for his role on *Queer Eye for the Straight Guy* (the first incarnation of the current Neflix offering *Queer Eye*). However Jai was also a fairly seasoned performer, including gigs with *Rent* six years earlier, as well as being a TV actor. Similarly, Tamyra Gray, who played Mimi during a lot of the last year of the run, had been on *American Idol* but had previously already made her Broadway debut in *Bombay Dreams*. Similarly Frenchie Davis came into the show as an ensemble member after her stint on *Idol*, proving that not all casting with "known" performers was without a basis in talent.

The show then did give into some "stunt casting" over the years, though, not quite like *Chicago*, which on both sides of the Atlantic became infamous for its questionable casting. Depending on your point of view, some of the higher profile or "selling out" examples included Melanie "Scary Spice" Brown who joined the company as Mimi in 2004. She did at least have the quality of being peak 1990s in her other career. Other pop stars included Joey Fatone of *NSYNC and Drew Lachey of 98 Degrees. Or in the UK, on the tour, Adam Rickitt, who had a questionable pop career following his stint in the popular and long-running soap opera *Coronation Street*.

The show plodded along just fine—by this point a Broadway staple—with steady enough ticket sales, and yes with the odd "famous face" in the show. However a couple of years previously, longtime supporter Anthony Tommasini returned to the show, and was prompted to write a column titled "Some Advice for *Rent* from a Friend," his long-term relationship with the show making this assessment of where *Rent* had gone wrong rather than a scathing critical review. He says: "The performance was not stale, but the opposite: pumped up with a rockish energy that seemed forced and generic, and blaringly loud. The cast looked great and was brimming with talent. But the young performers, it appeared, had been encouraged to play the show for raw power."

He goes on to ask:

> Does no one involved still trust in the subtlety of Larson's characterizations, the textured layers of his music and the impish and poignant lyrics? So much of the show's impact comes from the specificity in Larson's words and lyrics. But if this performance was indicative, specificity has been replaced by sonic wattage.

Wondering perhaps if the faith in the raw content of Larson's work had been lost to the "performance" of the rock musical element, Tomassini was left wondering if some of its heart therefore was lost on the way. Tomassini goes on to reflect on feeling a certain attachment to *Rent* due to his, as he puts it, "inadvertent role in Larson's life" after writing the last profile on the composer (in January 1996 the night before Larson died). But Tomassini's thoughts also echo that of the long-term *Rent* fans who did not want to see their beloved musical watered down or losing its impact.

Rent had not exactly "done a Chicago" and recruited every reality TV star and soap actor who was willing to get on a plane to New York, but it had obviously gone through its share of replacement casts, not all of them perhaps on par with the originals. There were fierce debates among fans over who was the "best" of them, and of course who was the worst. But all of them still were chasing a version of the original, something that was replicated one last time at the tenth-anniversary concert.

The year following the film's release was important for *Rent*—it was its tenth anniversary. Not many musicals make it that long in the dog-eat-dog economy, and reaching that milestone put it on a par with other famous long-runners like *Phantom* and *Les Mis*. Obviously not hitting their seemingly never-ending status yet, but a ten-year run was still an impressive achievement.

The show had also seen a natural boost in ticket sales following the film, which was assurance enough that it would be a success. For the anniversary a special reunion concert was organized with he original cast as a benefit to support the New York Theatre Workshop as well as the Jonathan Larson Foundation and Friends; indeed, all organizations closely associated with Jonathan and the show.

There was a concert version of the show where all the actors sat onstage and got up to perform their number. However, mirroring perhaps the performance after Larson's death, cast members integrated "performing" the key numbers: Daphne Rubin-Vega did manage most of the "Out Tonight" choreography, while Jesse L. Martin and Wilson Jermaine Heredia couldn't resist including Angel's twirls in "I'll Cover You" (the moment captured and uploaded to YouTube also features Jesse declaring "oh shit I forgot how fast you are"). At the same time, Wilson also demonstrated he hadn't lost the skill of backflipping off a table in "Today 4 You" (Wilson also did a quick change into full Angel drag for that number despite the rest of the concert not being in costume).

The show was a fitting full reunion for the cast—for the first and last time since the original cast members started to move away from the

Broadway production. The only missing member of the fifteen-member original cast was Gilles Chiasson, who had the very valid excuse that his wife had given birth that very morning!

The fitting conclusion to the event was the original cast being joined by an array of previous cast members for a finale of "Seasons of Love," a celebration of the previous decade. Good things don't last forever, however, and by 2008 the start of *Rent*'s long closing had begun.

For many fans it felt like the show was "closing" forever. In 2008 when the box office for the film had slowed, ticket sales slowed with it too. Jeffrey Seller made an official announcement that the show was closing on June 1. The response (and boost to ticket sales) meant this it was extended to September 7. There was a sense as it closed, of the importance of the moment, and of the show and what it had achieved over the previous decade. Bob Ickes in *POZ* magazine said, "But the show was remarkably prescient too. At a time when AIDS was primarily portrayed as a gay white man's disease, *Rent* dared to focus on gay men of color and heterosexual Latino woman, now two of the demographics affected by HIV. . . . *Rent*'s cast was also youthful, a reminder that many new infections occurred then—and continue to do so now in those younger than 30."

Charles Isherwood also wrote about the show in 2008 and revised his earlier stance on it. He said: "One of the weaknesses that bothered me a dozen years ago—the ending that finds the doomed Mimi springing back to life after appearing to expire—strikes me today as a flaw Larson may have recognized but could not bring himself to correct. The integrity of art must have seemed a less urgent priority than the dissemination of hope. The awkward affixing of a happy ending to a fundamentally tragic story was a form of prayer, a plea that life might imitate art. I probably rolled my eyes at this absurd resurrection in 1996; this time I fought back tears."

There was clearly a lot of love for the show, even as it closed. There is much to be said too for a show not outstaying its welcome on Broadway if we look at the examples of the big hitters that stayed a bit too long—*Phantom*, *Les Mis*, record breakers for perhaps the wrong reasons. Yes, *Phantom* continues to haunt Broadway, but is it at this point anything other than a museum piece? To a degree, no. In a continual revolving door of replacement casts but very little change, these shows end up a time capsule of a moment, offering little to audiences and performers alike. Every show too is a product of its time, and the nature of theater is that time passes. *Rent* and in particular the Broadway performance, incumbent at the "wrong" end of the Broadway map, was a product of a cultural moment, a theatrical moment, in the 1990s and that was enough. It lives on in revivals, in tours, and in school productions, and that is better than a stale and stilted version of the original. That surely is what Larson would have wanted.

The Broadway closing was an important moment. This ground-breaking, rule-breaking show was finally leaving New York. Much had changed in the time that *Rent* had been on Broadway; the wider world no longer looked like the one Larson had written about, Broadway was different from the one Larson was trying to break into. A whole generation of performers had come through the doors of the Nederlander—many of them onstage, many of them too in the audience. So many fans had sat in the audience and had their lives changed, so many had sat on the street outside too and made friends, fallen in love with musical theater (sometimes fallen in love with fellow fans). Fans had come and gone, found a love of other shows, followed actors to those shows, and returned to *Rent.*

One thing was certain that with *Rent* closing on Broadway it did feel like the end of an era. The Nederlander would be refurbished again, and no longer be a piece of downtown-uptown. The rush line would be no more (or, now, the daily lottery). The signatures on the walls would be painted over and the physical space would cease to be quite the same. It would be replaced by revivals (*Guys and Dolls*) and Disney shows (*Newsies*). But what would remain strong was the connection fans had to the show. Their stories are as integral to *Rent* as the story of Larson or any of the cast. And one fan, who was young at the time of the closing, remembers both the importance and urgency of the closing, and visiting the Broadway space:

> When I was 14 and had only recently fallen in love with *Rent,* the closing notice was posted and I felt the world collapse under me. I could not fathom the fact that I would never get to see it. I had only been to NYC once, in November of 2007— the closing notice was posted in January 2008 saying the show was closing in June, and I figured there was no way to make another trip happen so soon. I lucked out though—my junior high choir was chosen to perform at Carnegie Hall in April 2008. We had precisely one night off, because every other night was rehearsal, and naturally, that was my night to see *Rent.* I brought my best friend and another choir member, and my mom bought a single seat far away from us because we were 14 and too embarrassed to see a show like this next to my mom. It

was transcendent. I really felt like an adult (we'll ignore the fact that my mom was ten rows away). It was my second ever Broadway show, such a significant influence on musical theater, and I had squeezed in the impossible trip to see it before it closed. I literally still remember what I was wearing, where I sat, and what understudies were on, 13 years later—that performance will never leave me. Later that week, my mom and I snuck back to the white wall in the alley behind the theater and I scribbled, "Ali was here 4-21-08 I <3 *Rent*" with a giant Sharpie. I knew people signed the walls of the outside as well—I can't remember what drove this decision specifically, considering that the outside walls were so much easier to access, but it felt incredible to make my mark along with so many other people and commemorate this show that gave me so much.

Another fan remembered:

When *Rent* closed in September (bumped later from their previously announced June closing), I literally threw a funeral at my house where my friends and I wore all black and watched the movie. I made an invitation using the same stencil font that said something along the lines of 'dearly beloved, we gather here to say our goodbyes...' etc, and then 'in honor of the death of *Rent*, a not-so-impromptu salon will commence at Ali's house on September 7th, 2008.' We had uniforms, but we wore some kind of black accessory to school the next day, and I wore my *Rent* dog tag as well."

The closing—and the physical space—were hugely important then to fans of the show. The loss of the show meant a great deal to them. Those fans too had been the heart of the show for the previous twelve years, and would continue to be as *Rent* moved beyond Broadway. The closing on Broadway had a similar effect on fan engagement but in a much broader sense. Now in the twelve years since opening, *Rent* had multiple "generations" of fans, all of whom felt like they had an investment in this, the end of the run. That feeling like it was the end of an era, and the need to mark it by fans, became apparent. And once again the demand for on-the-day tickets—now a lottery as the original queue got too out of hand—spiked again, as did a discussion of the musical online as the final cast was put in place.

The closing of a show is an emotional moment for fans, whether it's been in their life for a few months, a few years, or even decades. It becomes a part of life, and there is something comforting, even when you as a fan aren't in attendance, to know it is out there happening regardless. Every night. Somewhere. Rather than "fear of missing out" there's a sense of comfort in knowing the show does indeed continue to go on. For fans then contemplating a Broadway landscape without *Rent* at the Nederlander was a profound and powerful moment. Post-closing it feels almost like "graduation" day as *Rent* ends and fans move on.

9

"HAPPY NEW YEAR"

Rent Beyond Rent

REVIVALS

Rent has never truly closed with the proliferation of touring productions and international productions. The Broadway production closing was never going to be the end of the line for *Rent*. Soon after, it was back in New York, if not on Broadway, then back on off-Broadway once again. A tour shortly after a show being closed on Broadway isn't unusual, but an off-Broadway revival is. In 2011, three years after it closed on Broadway, it was back at New World Stages, a relatively new theater complex on 50th Street. The complex, which has five theater spaces, hosts a variety of work, including circus shows, plays, and small-scale musicals. Before *Rent* made its way there, *Avenue Q* also performed here. *Rent* played the 499-seat house, the size of the audience for the New York Theatre Workshop (NYTW) run.

Revivals can potentially be a problematic theatrical endeavor. They run the risk of being considered inferior to the original production. In staging a revival, there is also the risk that an audience's appetite for seeing the same show again has been overestimated and, thus, the potential for revivals to fail commercially is very real. However, without the revival, the theater would arguably be quieter and less financially stable. There is a kind of "safety net" associated with a revival: the material is a proven commodity. In taking existing or known theatrical stories and restaging them as revivals, productions also reappropriate a familiar performance story for a new audience. Producers and theater companies rely on revivals of proven commodities to bring financial rewards.

REVIVING TEXTS ON AIDS

There had been a cultural shift in the political and social status of people with AIDS and gay people in the intervening years. The impact of AIDS had also shifted by 2006 as effective drugs lengthened life. In Britain, they were available through the National Health Service (NHS).

The media and cultural representations of gay people, on the whole, have also shifted since the early 1990s and are wider-ranging. The portrayal of gay and lesbian characters in film and television had proliferated since 1992–1993 when *Angels in America* and *Rent* were developed and first performed. Imported American television, like imported plays, also evolved to depict AIDS and gay and lesbian characters. Two American dramas in the early 2000s broke new ground. *The L Word* and the American adaptation of the British drama *Queer as Folk* both centered on lesbian and gay characters. This premise would have been unheard of on mainstream television a decade earlier. In addition, gay characters became integrated into American drama. The critically acclaimed *Six Feet Under* alongside teen drama *Gossip Girl* and popular series like *Grey's Anatomy* have all successfully depicted contemporary gay and lesbian characters, and all have been shown on British television.

In British-made television, there was also a proliferation of gay characters. Soap operas regularly included gay characters, both male and female, while throughout television, incidental gay characters appeared regularly.

The depiction of AIDS in popular culture, in contrast to the developing inclusion of gay characters, was not as common. Again, in soap operas as in real life, characters were tested for HIV. American dramas that depicted AIDS have been limited; examples include the character of Saul Holden in *Brothers and Sisters,* characters in *ER* such as Jeanie Boulet, and the superhero "Speedy" in the Superman prequel series *Smallville.* In a reversal of the theatrical response to AIDS, which had been quicker and more developed in America, the intervening years on television had been far more conservative. It was also notable that work by gay writers such as screenwriter Russell T. Davies, seemed to shy away from dealing with AIDS altogether post-2000, possibly in a move to no longer have gay men reduced simply to a disease. In the groundbreaking *Queer as Folk*, which was in many aspects a more explicit approach to gay life, AIDS features minimally, indicating a desire to move beyond the associations with the condition and onto a more rounded approach to depicting gay characters. In Britain, at the point at which *Angels in America* and *Rent* were initially staged, depictions of gay people onstage and on-screen were developing (albeit slowly); and they continued to grow in the intervening years.

The context of television is significant in considering the wider cultural backdrop relating to depictions of gay people and AIDS. In theater, the more progressive work seen after the repeal of censorship continued. Directly following *Angels in America*, the most famous gay theater piece was Mark Ravenhill's *Shopping and Fucking*, staged at the Royal Court in 1996. Ravenhill's controversial piece marked out the playwright as a confrontational playwright; his play *Some Explicit Polaroids* (1999) included a character with AIDS, while *Mother Clapp's Molly House* (2000) depicted a diverse exploration of sexuality. In fact, Ravenhill is heralded was the leading gay playwright of the late 1990s and early 2000s. His work was mainly presented at the Royal Court and other fringe venues. Gay theater in Britain continued to multiply while the repeal of censorship allowed for more explicit depictions onstage.

In this later period, there was less focus on the early 1990s gay plays and AIDS plays. Still, gay characters, just as in television and film, were beginning to become integrated into the theatrical landscape. In *The History Boys* (2004) and—shortly after the revivals of *Angels in America* and *Rent*—in *The Habit of Art* (2009), Alan Bennett integrated tales of gay life into his plays. These works from one of Britain's leading playwrights and performed at the National Theatre indicate the integration and developing acceptance of gay characters onstage. Tom Stoppard with *The Invention of Love* (1997) and David Hare with *The Judas Kiss* (1998) also showed that British establishment playwrights were now more comfortable than ever presenting gay characters in their work.

This sociohistorical background is important in considering the revivals. As Carlson states, theater is "The repository of cultural memory'"(2003, p. 2). Their personal experience also modifies how an audience experiences these theater texts. Carlson also notes: "Always ghosted by previous experiences and associations." By this, he means previous cultural and theatrical encounters brought in by audience members. As

Roland Barthes argued, the focus should shift to the reader's interpretation and the "intertexual network" in which that reader is situated" (pp. 142–48). The reader is influenced by the wider cultural elements outlined here; for a revival, these experiences include experiences or expectations based on the original production.

REVIVING MUSICALS

Revivals of musicals are more common than new musicals due to the expense involved in mounting new productions. In his work on corporate influence on Broadway, Steven Adler notes that a revival of a musical is now more likely than a new musical. The "proven commodity" element of the musical is a more secure bet than a new, expensive, risky musical (2004). Adler also noted that more straight plays are restaged for the same reason: the risk involved in financing them. As with musicals, revivals of "classic" plays are reliant on the perception of the audience's appetite for revisiting these plays; and there appears to be a continual appetite for this in the West End. J. Hillis Miller states, "We need the 'same' stories over and over, then as one of the most powerful, perhaps the most powerful, of ways to assert the basic ideology of our culture" (1995). This can apply to plays in general and, more specifically, to the texts on AIDS examined here. In the retelling, these dramatic stories—like any other stories—reassert basic cultural ideologies. In that reasserting, the ideology in these narratives on AIDS becomes a part of a wider cultural ideology.

There is an appetite for revival among the theatergoing public. But, as noted, the continuous stream of revivals is not without its problems. There is a financial danger in staging the same material time and time again in that this may create audience fatigue. Audiences will undoubtedly pay to see a favorite actor perform a much-loved role, as indicated by decades of repeated Hamlets and Lears with various star turns in the leading role. However, reviving texts can also lead to fatigue with the plays themselves or frustration with the lack of newer work.

Concerning the revival of musicals, American critic Ben Brantley provides some interesting critiques in his review of the 2006 *Les Misérables* revival. Comparatively, little has been written academically on theatrical revivals. However, Brantley, an eminent American theater critic, articulates clearly some of the issues in his theater review, "Didn't We Just See This Revolution?" (*New York Times*, November 10, 2006), and he likens the reviving of *Les Misérables* here to a father tiredly repeating the same bedtime story night after night. In this instance, because *Les Misérables* ran for so long on Broadway (1987–2003) and had been closed for a comparatively short period of three years, Brantley felt the revival was, at best, a poor copy of the original. He describes it as "functioning in a mild state of sedation." Although unimpressed by this particular revival, Brantley raises interesting points about the nature of revival itself. "The new 'Les Miserables,' he wrote, "belongs to a trend that might be described as revival by Xerox. In many ways it is a facsimile of its prototype. But its colors look less sharp and the humanizing textures of the original are almost entirely absent."

Brantley suggests that restaging is an attempt to create carbon copies of earlier productions onstage. What this does not show, however, is that perhaps they also provide what audiences are looking for—a copy of a much-loved original or a production they missed. Brantley's review echoes Jacques Derrida's work on texts being "haunted" by other texts. In *Specters of Marx*, Derrida explores how the identity of things are marked by our interactions with that thing (1994). As Carlson argues, drama has relied on retelling stories already known to the public. Carlson concludes that this means, "[A] narrative that is haunted in almost every aspect—its names, its character relationships, the structure of its action, even small physical or linguistic details—by a specific previous narrative" (2003).

Carlson refers to all theatrical production; however, this is particularly true of revivals. Fitting with Brantley's reflections on revivals, audiences are always working with texts haunted by past productions and other expectations of the stories being told. These expectations draw on various cultural influences and are taken into any production. However, when that production is a revival, these expectations are multiplied.

What Brantley highlights in the quotation above, however, is that these revivals, in trying to re-create exactly what the original was, will inevitably fall short. In the examples Brantley discusses, revivals were trying to replicate the original production; the examples of *Rent* and *Angels in America* considered here differ in that they were both revivals that sought to stage, in some respects, a different version of the text to the original. They perhaps are thus able to avoid some of the "Xerox" pitfalls that Brantley describes; however, there is still, in any revival of a text, the danger that the new version will be considered an inferior copy of the original. This consideration will be incorporated into evaluating the depiction of AIDS in these revivals alongside the wider artistic impact or merit.

REVIVING *RENT* OFF-BROADWAY

When asked to remount it off-Broadway, Michael Greif decided to scale down the Broadway production for the new space and to redirect it.

The move from off-Broadway to Broadway had been so fast that Greif did not have time to rework the piece, tweak the direction, and improve on his "vision." With over a decade to reflect, it wasn't surprising Greif decided to make those changes.

For the set, Greif worked with designer Mark Wendland and included scaffolding and different "levels" like the original. However, it wasn't as fixed, allowing it to be adapted to create the street or the apartment as needed. He also added the use of projection throughout—not just during Mark's film screening at the end. He included a montage of images from the era, including footage of ACT UP demonstrations. He also clarified the story with his direction. Greif made the references to AIDS more overt. He showed Roger in a hospital bed in "Without You," reminding us that he also is suffering the effects of his illness— just not to the extent of Mimi and Angel. This is a needed reminder that all of them are in real danger of not surviving. Greif leaned into the AIDS legacy in his rehearsal process, encouraging the cast to seek out other texts about AIDS and having them watch films of *Angels in America* and documentaries like *How to Survive a Plague*.

The casting process sought to find fresh talent. They ran an online contest where anyone could submit a self-tape audition and win the chance to be auditioned in person by the producers. This generated interest and created publicity for the show and. Winner Jessie Hooker received 12,945 votes and had the chance to audition in person. Jessie continues to perform and has been in the Broadway tour of *Waitress* as ensemble and understudy for Dawn, and a swing in *Beautiful: The Carole King Musical*. A variety of "new faces" were cast in *Rent* along with experienced actors. This formula had worked previously, and in an ensemble company it helps to have experienced actors support

Jesse L Martin, Anthony Rapp and Wilson Jermaine Herdia are filmed in NYTW for the transfer to Broadway ZUMA PRESS, INC. / ALAMY STOCK PHOTO

1995—Anthony Rapp, Adam Pascal, Jesse L. Martin, and Wilson Jermaine Herdia
ZUMA PRESS, INC. / ALAMY STOCK PHOTO

Exterior of the Nederlander Theatre RICHARD LEVINE / ALAMY STOCK PHOTO

Anthony Rapp and the original Cast of *Rent* at the Nederlander Theatre, 1995.
JOAN MARCUS PHOTOGRAPHY

"La Vie Bohème," Original Broadway Cast, Nedelander Theatre, 1995.
JOAN MARCUS PHOTOGRAPHY

Mark and Roger (Anthony Rapp and Adam Pascal) Original Broadway Production
JOAN MARCUS PHOTOGRAPHY

Angel and Collins (Wilson Jermaine Heredia and Jesse L Martin) Original Broadway
Cast JOAN MARCUS PHOTOGRAPHY

The cast of *Rent: Live* (2019) including Jordan Fisher, Brandon Victor Dixon, Brennin Hunt, and Valentina. AUTHOR'S COLLECTION

Adam Pascal and Rosario Dawson perform 'Light My Candle' in the *Rent* film— dir. Chris Columbus AUTHOR'S COLLECTION

"Tango Maureen" Anthony Rapp and Tracie Thoms from the *Rent* film dir Chris Columbus AUTHOR'S COLLECTION

"La Vie Bohème" from the *Rent* film—dir Chris Columbus AUTHOR'S COLLECTION

Cast of *Rent* renunited at the 2008 Tony Awards REUTERS / ALAMY STOCK PHOTO

The cast of the 2011 Off-Broadway revival with Larry Keigwin and Michael Greif
New World Stages. New York. WENN RIGHTS LTD / ALAMY STOCK PHOTO

Billy Cullum with the cast of *Rent*—St James Theatre London 2017

Layton Williams as Angel Schunard. *Rent*—St James Theatre London 2017

(Above and below): Lauren Marcus and Nick Blaemire sing at The Jonathan Larson Project CD Release Celebration held at Barnes and Noble bookstore on July 29, 2019.

Cast of *Rent: Live* (2019) ZUMA PRESS/ALAMY STOCK PHOTO

Al Larson, Nan Larson, and Julie Larson at the *Tick, Tick . . . Boom!* Opening Night Party 2021. WENN RIGHTS LTD / ALAMY STOCK PHOTO

(Above and below): Andrew Garfield as Jonathan Larson, *Tick, Tick . . . Boom!*
Film dir Lin Manuel Miranda AUTHOR'S COLLECTION

Andrew Garfield as Jonathan Larson, *Tick, Tick . . . Boom!* Film dir Lin Manuel Miranda

Roger and Mimi *Rent* Fan Art BARREL OF SCREAMING ALOE VERA (TUMBLR)

Fanart—"Seasons of Love" in Binary JON RAINFORD

Angel Fan Art GOGGLE MCGEE

Mark Fan Art VINIRLO

newer performers. *Rent* alumni, including Marcus Paul James (ensemble) and Arianda Fernandez (Mimi), who had done the tour, were included. The Mark for this version had performed in *Next to Normal*, directed by Greif, and unlike previous incarnations of Mark, he looked like Jonathan Larson. Greif adapted his costume accordingly to give him more of Jonathan's "look." *Rent* fans and performers have always known that the character Mark is based on Jonathan, but it had never been directly signaled. The production also included notable breakout stars, echoing *Rent*'s ongoing performer legacy. Annaleigh Ashford, who played Joanne, would go on to be a big Broadway star within a few years. Already on that trajectory pre-*Rent*, she had originated roles in *Legally Blonde*, and was part of the *Hair* revival in 2010. She has since mixed TV roles with returns to Broadway in plays and musicals, most recently in the New York City Center's *Sunday in the Park with George*, which was also headed to London in 2020, but sadly was canceled due to COVID-19.

Michaela Jae Rodriguez played Angel. She is known now for her role in FX's AIDS-era drama *Pose*. Michaela Jae was nominated for an Emmy for *Pose*, a show that made history for its representation of trans women of color. She has talked about how playing Angel in *Rent* influenced her own journey with gender identity. She said in an interview with *Playbill* in 2016, "Just living me onstage," she recalls. "It wasn't like being a character. I was in character, of course, but I was also living me and telling my story through Angel." From being able to wear "feminine" clothing to being addressed as "her" onstage, Rodriguez has talked about viewing Angel as genderfluid or genderqueer, not just the drag queen people previously labeled her as. Rodriguez went on to tell Playbill of the personal impact stepping out as Angel every night had: "When that gate got lifted up and everyone saw me as Angel dressed up, I was like, 'This is me. Now I'm about to serve y'all, so get ready! It's going to be a ride!'" *Rent* was also part of her musical theater coming-of-age. For Rodriguez, it happened first at the New Jersey Performing Arts Center, where *Rent* original cast alumnus Freddie Walker-Browne saw her perform and told her she needed to be in the upcoming off-Broadway production.

The revival opened on August 10, 2011, and ran for a year—a respectable run. It is difficult to make a profit in a small off-Broadway house with a large cast, and sustaining it much longer wouldn't have been possible. A critical and commercial success, it introduced countless new audiences to *Rent* who had missed it the first time around, and it provided a chance for those who had long loved the show to return to it.

Critical response was strong, suggesting that New York had not forgotten its love affair with *Rent* just yet. Steve Suskin told Variety, "It's already back, and the news is all to the good. *Rent* is not so provocative as it was back in 1996, but even so, the tuner is plenty effective in its new Off-Broadway guise." Suskin went on to remind readers that "the original 1996 cast . . . created their parts so memorably that the new crop can't be expected to compete." A reminder that with such an iconic first run, any follow-up will inevitably pale in comparison. It also wasn't long enough between the runs to erase most of the original versions from audience memory either, but the off-Broadway production proved that you can now start to reinvent.

The notoriously difficult-to-please *Times* critic Ben Brantley said, "To me this *Rent* feels neither close enough to nor different enough from the original to warrant revisiting." This is fair, given the short window between the two. Still, it is important to remember the

strength of the musical. Matthew Murray of Talkin' Broadway (www
.talkinbroadway.com) commented, "It all works not just because it's
all real and all unique, but because Larson was a true theater artist, the
kind of writer who knew—and cared—about what was necessary to
properly tell a story. . . . *Rent* is at once a lush emotional spectacle in
the Golden Age tradition and a pulsating New Idea, one with a core of
intelligence and strength that will allow it to thrive in productions at
all levels for decades to come."

Whether critics loved the new production or not, the core takeaway
from *Rent*'s return is that it had the strength to do so. The material
stood up to revival away from the Nederlander, the original cast, and
the legend of Larson. The original was so embodied with the ghosts of
those early days, the off-Broadway production marks a moment of transition away from what *Rent* was and toward what it could be.

WITHOUT YOU

While not strictly part of *Rent*, it's impossible to talk about the musical's
expanding influence without considering the impact of Anthony Rapp's
Without You. Rapp's 2006 memoir details his history with the show and
the impact it had on him during a turbulent time in his life—his mother
died and he experienced a variety of mental health and relationship issues.

After the release of his book, Rapp decided to make a stage version
of the show set to music and a script. His one-man show, written and
performed by Rapp, gives the audience a visual depiction of his memoir.
The stage show has played in Boston, Edinburgh, London, Toronto, and
Tracy, California. The stage adaptation features songs from *Rent*, covers of songs, and Rapp's original music. Rapp recorded the soundtrack

for *Without You* in London on September 17, 2012. The recording was released on December 11, 2012. The five-piece band was under the musical direction of Dan Weiss with arrangements written by Tom Kitt (*Next to Normal*). The show's format was a series of songs interspersed by adapted extracts from the book and additional scenes written by Rapp.

Rapp received mixed reviews for the show. The *National Post* claims that Rapp's staged production is an extension of a memorial for his mother: "Basing a public performance on private grief is a dodgy proposition, worsened in this case by the fact that Rapp has nothing to say about either person that can make them matter to anyone but him" (Cushman 2012). In the *Huffington Post*, Chris Cox wrote "The pace, writing and sheer passion behind this show instantly push it from your mind as you find yourself at ease with Rapp's delivery and impressive vocals as he's backed by a tight five-piece band" (2012).

THE JONATHAN LARSON PROJECT

The Jonathan Larson Project is based on a concert originally presented at Feinstein's/54 Below, directed and conceived by Jennifer Ashley Tepper (*Be More Chill*). After spending time in the Jonathan Larson archives, she conceived the idea, looking through files of drafted and never-used songs. The piece was created with music supervision, orchestrations, and arrangements by Charlie Rosen (*Be More Chill, Prince of Broadway, Honeymoon in Vegas, Charlie Rosen's Broadway Big Band*). The five-piece band includes musical director Natalie Tenenbaum, Charlie Rosen, Cody Owen Stine, Megan Talay, and Marques Walls, with Danielle Gimbal as copyist. The album is produced by Jennifer Ashley Tepper, Charlie Rosen, and Kurt Deutsch.

When the Jonathan Larson Project premiered at Feinstein's/54 Below, it was hailed as "a treasure trove of unperformed, unrecorded, and unheard material" by DC Metro Theater Arts and "One of the Top 10 Broadway special events of 2018" by Asbury Park Press. According to TheaterMania.com, "this show seems destined for a future life onstage and on disc. His songs simply deserve to be heard."

Performed in October 2018, each night featured a different special guest in addition to the cast of Nick Blaemire (*Tick, Tick . . . Boom!, Found, Godspell*), Lauren Marcus (*Be More Chill, Beatsville, Company*), Andy Mientus (NBC's *Smash, Spring Awakening, Les Misérables*), Krysta Rodriguez (*Spring Awakening, First Date, The Addams Family*), and George Salazar (*Be More Chill, The Lightning Thief, Tick, Tick . . . Boom!*). The guests included Harrison Chad, Daphne Rubin-Vega, Will Roland and Julia Mattison, Caissie Levy, Matthew McCollum, and a group of Jonathan Larson Grant award winners. The venue agreed to release a number of $20 rush tickets for each performance via the TodayTix app (an app that might well not exist if it weren't for *Rent*) to ensure accessibility to the concerts.

The concert tracks were released as recordings by Ghostlight Records, an independent label specializing in smaller-scale cast recordings and albums of Broadway artists. They started back in 2002 as an imprint of Sh-K-Boom Records, cofounded by Kurt Deutch and Sherie Rene Scott. Today they are a leading producer of Broadway cast recordings, having recently been responsible for the recordings of *Beetlejuice* and *Be More Chill*.

The importance of the Jonathan Larson project sits alongside *Tick, Tick . . . Boom!* It was a way for the world to see more of Larson's work. As the *British Theatre* review said of the recording, "Twenty plus years after his death, Jonathan has a new show. It's one that I'm sure will be performed all over the world with this recording as its single most valuable calling card" (Mayo 2019). The review continues, reflecting on the resonance the recording/project: "There's much to recommend this recording, but what strikes me most is that you can hear the heartbeat of this amazing writer in the melodies and at moments throughout." The project acted as an archival work, allowing Larson's unheard work to be heard and saved, rather than languishing in an archive for decades. It's a tricky balance to be struck not knowing what Larson would want of his "unfinished" work to be shared. However, we know he was fiercely ambitious and wanted his voice to be heard, so his music finding new life twenty years after his death is a good thing.

RENT: LIVE

In 2019, *Rent* became the latest of the Fox network's "Live" musical broadcasts. The network has been producing a variety of live musicals including *Hairspray*, *Grease*, and *The Wiz*. These involved several celebrity performers alongside an ensemble/supporting cast of Broadway actors. They have received mixed reviews with 2013's *The Sound of Music* having the biggest ratings with 19 million views and a decent critical reception. The second-highest rating was for *Grease* in 2016, which was well received critically and had 12 million views. *Rent* unfortunately had the lowest viewing figures with only 3.4 million viewers, and Fox pulled the plug on the next planned musical, *Hair*, shortly after. With the COVID-19 shutdowns, it remains unlikely there would have been further shows.

Rent had a variety of young stars, as is the trend for the live broadcasts: Jordan Fisher as Mark, Brennin Hunt as Roger Davis, Tinashe as Mimi Marquez, Brandon Victor Dixon as Tom Collins, Valentina (a drag artist who has appeared on *RuPaul's Drag Race*) as Angel Dumott Schunard, Vanessa Hudgens as Maureen, Kiersey Clemons as Joanne, and Keala Settle as Cy (a gender-flipped version of Paul from the original, also combined with soloist 1). Marc Platt, Adam Siegel, Julie and Al Larson (Jonathan's sister and father, respectively), Vince Totino, Scott Hemming, and Marla Levine are credited as executive producers. On January 26, 2019, during the Saturday dress rehearsal, Brennin Hunt, who plays Roger, broke his foot. Fox announced in an official statement that despite his injury, the show would air as planned, using both prerecorded footage from a previous dress rehearsal and live footage. On January 27, the show was performed in its entirety with limited physical activity before a studio audience as scheduled, with Hunt performing in a wheelchair. The simultaneous telecast consisted almost entirely of the prerecorded dress rehearsal from the prior night; only the final fifteen minutes of the program, which consisted of the songs "Finale," "Your Eyes," and "Finale B," and an encore performance of "Seasons of Love" featuring the original 1996 Broadway cast, was broadcast live. The choreography of the final act was modified to accommodate Hunt being in a wheelchair.

The special received mixed to negative reviews from critics. On Rotten Tomatoes, it holds a 27 percent approval rating from twenty-two reviews, with an average score of 5.8/10. The critical consensus reads, "Despite the show's earnest intentions, *Rent Live*'s clumsy production and pre-recorded broadcast render it an underwhelming 'live' musical event." On Metacritic, which calculates a weighted average of review scores, the special holds a score of 49 out of 100 based on twelve reviews, indicating a "mixed or average" reception.

Much of the criticism focused on the production's failure to hire understudies for the main cast in reference to Hunt's injury, as well as the decision to broadcast a prerecorded performance for a program marketed as live television. Daniel Fienberg wrote in *The Hollywood Reporter* that the network "could have quickly strategized a live concert setting with a limited staging around Hunt and then aired the dress rehearsal at some point during the week" (2019). Aisha Harris, reviewing for the *New York Times*, echoed these sentiments, writing, "How do you measure three hours of chaotic visuals and middling audio most of us were never meant to see and hear?" called the camerawork "overwrought" (Harris 2019). Extensive edits to profanity and sexual references in the musical's lyrical content, made to meet network broadcasting standards, was also the subject of criticism. *Variety* critic Caroline Framke questioned if a broadcast network was an appropriate outlet for a production of the show in the first place.

However, the cast's performances (particularly Fisher, Dixon, Tinashe, and Hudgens) were generally praised, and the production design of the program was also well received. In a mostly positive review for The A.V. Club, Caroline Siede wrote that the special "did what these live musicals are supposed to do—reimagine a beloved musical with a new aesthetic, new performers, and new staging choices" (Siede 2019) and praised the show's finale featuring the 1996 Broadway cast.

The telecast received a 1.4 rating among adults eighteen to forty-nine and 3.42 million total viewers, making it the lowest-rated live musical broadcast as of its airdate. In markets where ratings were available segment by segment viewership fell dramatically after the opening segment. It was, however, critically well received with a handful of Emmy nominations for make-up and design categories, along with Outstanding Variety Special.

It seems *Rent: Live* fell afoul of an unfortunate version of "the show must go on." Despite the corporate overlay, it's a very *Rent* sentiment to make it happen regardless of the circumstances. Because the show was produced by Fox, a notoriously right-wing and conservative broadcasting network known for its conservative news bias and its support of conservative values, it is an interesting choice. The Larson estate guards the production of the show, so the bigger question is why they allowed Fox to use the show. There is an argument to be made for infiltrating the establishment that stands against the values *Rent* supports. If Fox enabled the work to be seen by as many people as possible, then maybe a "deal with the devil" is worth it. Fox didn't censor the piece, and the creative team was of the caliber and background that we'd expect for *Rent*. Given the impact of the day itself, perhaps *Rent: Live* is best chalked up alongside *Rent: Remixed* as an experiment with mixed results.

ORIGINAL CAST BEYOND THE SHOW

The original cast has had universal success. Adam Pascal has had steady work appearing in Broadway shows—from *Cabaret* to *Chess* (in London's Albert Hall) as well as in a music career that has seen several albums released. Anthony Rapp steadily worked in theater post-*Rent* for many years before shifting to TV work. He wrote his book and created his one-man show/album that toured internationally. Rapp has not left *Rent* behind, also touring and doing regular gigs with Pascal. In the last few years, he has starred in the newest *Star Trek* franchise *Star*

Trek: Discovery on Paramount Plus—he now has Trekkers following his career. Jesse L. Martin has carved out a niche for himself in TV with his long-term role on *Law & Order* and is possibly better known for that role than his role in *Rent*. Similarly, Taye Diggs moved into TV work with roles in *Private Practice* and films like *How Stella Got Her Groove Back*. He also returned to musical theater in 2015, taking over the role of Hedwig in *Hedwig and the Angry Inch*. He's also the author of several children's books. Of the male principals, Wilson Jermaine Herdia has had a less high-profile career following *Rent*, but he continued to perform in musicals including productions of *La Cage Aux Folles* and *A Little Princess* (in San Francisco where he now lives).

Of the female principals in the original cast, Fredi Walker continued to work in theater; she is now teaching and running her own production company, Big Spoon Productions. Daphne Rubin-Vega continued to work in theater, moving between plays and musicals. She earned another Tony nomination for her performance in Anna in the *Tropics* in 2003. She worked steadily post-*Rent* across a range of productions including *The Rocky Horror Picture Show*, *Wild Things* (with Kevin Bacon), *The House of Bernard Alba*, and *Les Mis*. She has gathered an array of film and TV credits, including the role of Daniela in the film adaptation of *In the Heights* (2021).

Idina Menzel did not immediately find a niche in theater or elsewhere post-*Rent*. However, in 2003, she had a second "breakout" performance as Elphaba in *Wicked*, the worldwide musical juggernaut by Stephen Schwartz that tells the "untold tales" of the witches from *The Wizard of Oz*. A second flagship musical cemented Menzel's career, and she moved on to appear in smaller-scale musicals like *See What I Wanna*

See at the Public Theater, and later joined Pascal and Josh Groban at the Albert Hall version of *Chess*. After moving into more theater and film work, and producing several albums, Menzel was cast in a variety of projects from *Enchanted* (2007) to *Glee*. In 2013, Menzel voiced a Disney queen in what would become the biggest Disney animated film in many years. Her role as Elsa in *Frozen*, and the ubiquitous song "Let It Go," introduced her to a new generation. Menzel is known as Maureen, Elphaba, and Elsa to different demographics, and she has had a fascinating career from East Village performer to Disney queen.

As a *Rent* fan, it is an emotional experience to sit on a ride at Disneyland and hear Maureen singing "Let It Go" or to see "her" in a thousand merchandise tie-ins or to find younger musicals fan discovering *Rent* because "Did you know Elphaba was in it?" This is the same for all the cast—Rapp's new *Star Trek* fans have discovered his musical theater past through his book and in *Rent* clips on YouTube. Those who grew up watching *Law & Order*, and maybe had a crush on Jesse (as well they should), discover he was one of the first gay principal characters in a Broadway musical. In all these ways, the original cast leads fans back to *Rent*; they have become inseparable from it. They've embraced that legacy by being part of *Rent* reunions, talking about *Rent*, and singing songs from *Rent* in their concerts. They are creating a symbiotic relationship that exists with what they do now and what they will do next, confirming that the show was a tipping point in their careers.

10

"ONE SONG GLORY"

Rent: Remixed

In 2006, *Rent* was revived in a radically different format in London's West End. Billed as *Rent: Remixed,* the version was drastically altered in both staging and musical arrangement from previous versions. *Rent* was still running on Broadway, and a film version had been made and was released in the UK later that year. There had been skepticism about the success of the original London production. Still, the booking in a West End theater illustrated a vote of confidence by producers that *Rent: Remixed* was a marketable commodity. What the producers also sought to do was to update or, as they put it, "remix" the original production for a contemporary audience. In the context of *Rent: Remixed*, the term takes on two meanings: remixing the existing music and in the broader culture in changes made to the text.

THE PRODUCTION

Rent: Remixed was directed and conceived by William Baker, most well known for being Kylie Minogue's concert director, and designed by

Mark Bailey, known for his theatrical work in opera, ballet, and various plays and musicals in the West End. The piece was drastically altered from Larson's original, with changes to set, character, and orchestration that rendered parts unrecognizable. Baker includes a "Then and Now" section in the program to explain the rationale for the update. He focuses on AIDS, saying: "*Rent* was unique in its frankness in dealing with the AIDS epidemic." "There's no question that the AIDS issue has changed." Baker's reasoning is sound. AIDS as an issue had changed dramatically since *Rent* was first staged. He then asked: "But has our awareness of it stagnated so much that we are not shocked by it but have become numb to it?" These points are valid questions and a good reason for any revival of *Rent*. They also perhaps present a basis for some alterations to make certain aspects of the text more accessible. Baker was not the first to make minor changes to the production. However, most productions followed the set and costumes of the original Broadway/London productions. Few can replicate this exactly; many original costumes for Off-Broadway/Broadway were unique.

The set had previously been a slightly scruffy representation of the East Village loft in which Mark and Roger live, both in the original Broadway production and, subsequently, the London production. This was made with a series of gray metallic poles and ledges reminiscent of scaffolding or the bare steel girders of a building. The loft and the surrounding areas were created with minimal furniture, mostly two large metal tables, a couple of chairs, and a Christmas tree made of scrap metal. In Baker's version, however, Mark Bailey's set was stark white with a raised platform in the center to represent the apartment, furnished with stylish contemporary-looking furniture. Sets were moved into the space to represent venues such as the Life Café, which in the original was created out of the existing set pieces and/or props brought on by cast members. The original design's only similarity was the band situated onstage alongside the actors.

Stage design can have a marked effect on a production. In *Rent,* the original sparse set and the slightly grubby air it lent the production was a deliberate attempt to re-create the East Village setting. The new design was criticized by many reviewers, including several who felt it did not reflect the ethos of *Rent.* As noted by one: "inhabitants of this Alphabet City are hardly slumming it, on a chic white multi-leveled set by Mark Bailey." Changes to the set immediately alter an audience's perception and interaction with a production.

Baker appeared to be situating *Rent* in an indeterminate location, which also fueled his direction and characterization across the play. He allowed actors, notably Mimi and Maureen, to keep their English and Irish accents, while others seemed to attempt something in between. Perhaps Baker was attempting to replicate Larson's multicultural approach. However, in a show so overtly set in New York, this style confused the matter. Arguing in favor of Baker, it can be suggested that this allowed a British audience to connect with *Rent,* feeling that through the characters' accents, there was a direct line to the locality. It is also feasible that the young, trendy East Village, of a seemingly indeterminable point in time that Baker depicts could have British or Irish inhabitants.

Baker's casting was far less diverse than the original cast. While he could not have been expected to cast to the original's exact specifications, the changes he made were significant by altering the diversity that had been a major factor in *Rent's* significance and appeal. The original Broadway cast had become iconic. Carlson talks of the problems in competing with an actor who has put their mark upon a role (Carlson, p. 96). This is to be expected in a revival, and a successful production or talented actor will succeed in putting their mark upon the role. Many actors had, of course, stepped into these, as Carlson refers to them, "ghosted" roles but within the same production (be it Broadway or the original London production). These new actors were invariably physically and vocally similar to the original cast. In replacing cast members within a long-running show, there is generally a desire to mimic the original actor; in revival, this can be altered so that a new interpretation of the character can be depicted. But in Baker's production the replacements weren't strong enough to eclipse the originals. Nor were they able to put their own "stamp" on the roles.

The changes to the set and cast raise questions of authenticity: should the "real" *Rent* adhere to the same principles of design and casting as the original? If it does not, is it "really" *Rent* or is it a different text? In reviving a text, there is always scope for reinvention and alteration to fit changing needs in a practical sense, for example, scaling down production to fit a smaller venue. Likewise, in terms of demographics, international productions may not have the diversity of actors available to fill these roles (for example, a South American production of *Rent* may struggle to fulfill the diverse ethnicities of the original cast). However, in the British revival, none of these were factors. This returns then to the question of "authenticity." Does a production of *Rent* need to adhere to certain principles of production to be considered authentic? In the largest sense, *Rent* is not defined by its set, casting, or costume. However, certain facets, including music and narrative clarity, are required to produce a version of *Rent* that is true to the original. It is in these areas that *Rent: Remixed* became problematic. While there is room for alteration and even updating, Baker's alterations undeniably and substantially affected the presentation of *Rent* and its depiction of AIDS.

DEPICTIONS OF AIDS IN THE REVIVALS

Baker's production did not drastically alter the text in this sense as much as Kramer's production of *Angels in America* did. *Rent*'s content was identical in terms of narrative content; the essential story remained untouched. However, the substantial changes to staging and, most significantly, the musical arrangement meant that the depiction of AIDS in *Rent: Remixed* was altered.

Baker included a "Then and Now" section in the program to explain the rationale for the update. He focused on AIDS, saying: "*Rent* was unique in its frankness in dealing with the AIDS epidemic." Baker is correct to some degree. *Rent*'s approach, its way of dealing with AIDS, was unique—and remains so in theater. He says: "There's no question that the AIDS issue has changed." The comment is sound; however, it was his execution of this idea in the play that was perhaps questionable. We live in a very different world today: young people aren't afraid of AIDS as Larson's generation or the next generation who queued for *Rent*. Baker then asks: "But has our awareness of it stagnated so much that we are not shocked by it but have become numb to it?" Again it is possible to acknowledge that he has a point: AIDS has become—to borrow Crimps's word—"normalized," meaning that young people do not necessarily understand the seriousness of the condition. These points are valid considerations for any revival of *Rent* and perhaps present a basis for some alterations to make certain aspects of the text more accessible. In terms of staging and reorchestration, Baker muted the existing depictions of AIDS within *Rent*.

The element of the physical depiction of AIDS in *Rent* is useful in revival, allowing for minimal alienation or confusion of an audience when confronting them with outdated medical information. As noted, when he wrote *Angels in America*, Kushner deliberately kept his play a few years before the present day. This writing back allowed the depiction of medical elements to be kept at a fixed point in time, which was not subject to question or change about medical advances. In *Rent*, audiences may assume a similar effect: Larson began the production years earlier and set the musical several years earlier than its performance.

The remixed version seems to "gloss over" the effects of AIDS as a medical condition. To quote Billington's review: "But, instead of focusing on Mimi's and Angel's condition, the show has a newsreel ticker-tape that catalogs some of the famous victims of Aids: Freddie Mercury, Derek Jarman, Kenny Everett and many more" (2007).

Billington referred to the artistic choice of projecting the names of those who had died from AIDS above the set. It seemed, as Billington makes clear, that these aesthetic choices and broader statements were prioritized over the characterization and depictions of AIDS within the plot. That is, the depiction of the personal impact of AIDS within the play was, like much of the "remix" in Baker's version, glossed over. Baker's version's overall polished and glossy look seems incongruous with a detailed or hard-hitting depiction of AIDS.

Larson's use of an emotional connection to characters in *Rent* for an audience rather than an informative one means references and details were in less danger of becoming outdated, unlike in the more medically detailed *Angels in America*. Detailed references to AIDS in *Rent* are limited anyway, so the revival and altered form did little to diminish the effectiveness of the text about its informative value. The only point at which a reference to AIDS is problematic in *Rent* is the reference to "AZT," which was outdated by the time *Rent* was first staged in Britain. With this distance, however, the piece transitions: like *Angels in America*, it becomes a historicized piece on AIDS rather than a contemporary commentary. Nevertheless, this historicizing of the piece did not make the broader message or depictions of AIDS less valid or powerful.

Despite highlighting it in his program notes, the depiction of AIDS seemed to be an aspect Baker was less concerned about. The reorchestration mentioned, along with the staging, all contributed to this. The crucial aspect of Baker's failings in depicting AIDS lies in these twin aspects. For *Rent*, its music was key to its communication with audiences about AIDS (along with every other issue). In addition, the changes in design removed the piece from the particular time and place of the original set. These aspects contribute to communication with the audience but *Rent: Remixed* created confusion or disengagement with the audience.

Ian Shuttleworth summarizes well the feeling Baker's production induced while referring to Baker's professional background: "This is pop-concert staging: get your stars moving across the front so the crowd can see them. When Baker tries to use the depth of the stage, he does so by layering flat two-dimensional compositions one behind another" (2007).

Comments were also made about Baker's choice of casting and the direction of his cast. Pop star Siobhan Donaghy's Mimi is described as "strangely sung," according to Paul Taylor's review (2007). Although Sam Marlowe refers to the cast as "sexy," (2007), there is little in the way of praise for the performances. These press responses support the earlier analysis that the substantial changes made by Baker directly and negatively impacted the portrayal of the characters written by Larson.

Some critics also felt that there was a loss of identity in the new version. Billington called it "a grisly synthetic, pseudo-pop concert with no particular roots or identity" (2007). Those aspects that were altered—music, costume, set, and characterization—leads to *Rent*'s distinctly American identity to be lost, according to Billington, and also causes the text to lose its focus. Billington ends his review by saying: "But the show is not so much a carbon copy of the original as a reductive rehash of a show that caught something of the flavour of 1990s New York." What Billington highlights here is that *Rent* was a success because of, not despite, the distinctly 1990s New York identity. For audiences in Britain and New York, *Rent* captured a time and place, which helped it communicate its message of AIDS awareness and activism.

The revival muted the depiction of AIDS. The anachronistic and confusing setting made engagement with the characters and subsequent depiction of AIDS problematic. If the format had been untouched, *Rent,* although set in another era, would have retained an authenticity of performance that is lost by altering the form and mode of delivery. The critics went further, drawing attention to what they perceived as a subpar production. Those who were never enthusiastic about *Rent* to begin with, such as Charles Spencer, highlighted the production's shortcomings. A vitriolic Spencer called "*Rent* drastically reduced," while those who were fond of the original, such as Nicholas de Jongh, found it simply "strangely disappointing" (2007). This indicates that the production rather than the revival in and of itself was problematic. In depicting AIDS, the new production fell far short of the original.

CHARACTERS WITH AIDS

The overt medical references being few, the text of *Rent* relies on a mixture of music and characterization to communicate the impact of AIDS. While Larson's text gives little detail, Michael Greif's original direction and the performances from his cast—particularly Daphne Louise-Vega as Mimi and Wilson Jermaine Heredia as Angel—strongly impacted the text. In *Rent: Remixed*, the combination of alterations to characterization, as outlined above, and the casting decisions left the depiction of AIDS' impact somewhat diminished from the original.

Certain aspects of the original productions of *Rent*, such as costume and staging, have become synonymous with the text. Although unlike *Angels in America*, there are no strict guidelines for a set, *Rent* productions usually copied the original's approach. This meant that productions mimicked the minimalist, industrial-looking set of the original Broadway production. Certain costume choices for characters also are seen across nearly all productions: Mark's combination of glasses and a scarf, Mimi's leopard-print coat, and Angel's "Santa" outfit. These costume choices, set by the original production and replicated by the London production, have become iconic costume pieces. Baker's production was, however, the first to be granted permission to make extensive changes. Previously it had been accepted that although changes within reasonable limits of artistic license would be made, on the whole, and particularly about music, *Rent* was expected to follow the original production closely. This was written into the terms of its license. In *Rent: Remixed*, however, the depiction of the characters' costumes was altered dramatically. While a change to some degree marks an evolution of a work, the costumes also root the characters in the time and place of the action. In the case of some characters, such as Angel and Mimi, costumes also form an integral part of their identity. In altering these, the central characters in *Rent* shift in identity.

Baker also made significant alterations to the ethnicity of key characters, notably Joanne and Mimi. In the original, Joanne is Black, and Mimi is Hispanic; in Baker's production, both are Caucasian, and Mimi is specifically Irish. In the case of Mimi, it might be questioned whether the casting of "celebrity" former pop star Siobhan Donaghy motivated this rather than any artistic element. Her Irish accent also may have been more practical based on her acting abilities rather than a deliberate choice by Baker. In the case of Joanne, however, the highly competent theater actress Francesca Jackson took the role. Although she used an American accent, the original was altered drastically by the change in her ethnicity.

Larson and director Greif chose the mix and dynamics of ethnicities in an extensive casting process for the original production. The musical was then workshopped and rewritten further with the specific ethnic identities of the performers in mind. In the New York production, the tours, and the original London production, the ethnicities of the main characters have always followed the blueprint of the original cast. In changing this, without apparent artistic motivation, Baker radically alters and, it is argued, weakens the text. In Baker's cast, only three of the fifteen members are of non-Caucasian origins; Larson's cast was designed to reflect the multiethnic East Village, and only three were Caucasian.

According to original cast member Jesse L. Martin, *Rent* was "minority heaven" (quoted in McDonnell and Silberger, p. 35). As David Savran notes, the largely non-white cast of *Rent* was significant.

In the original casting, although *Rent* was not explicitly "about" race, the racial elements of the text play an important part in communicating with an audience. For example, Savran notes that casting Benny, the "yuppie scum," as African American (his description) plays against expected stereotypes (2002). If Baker had been updated to reflect the ethnic diversity in present-day London, his cast should have been far more diverse. Larson, of course, did reflect the ethnic diversity of the city where he set *Rent*. Baker's changes to the characters' ethnicity feel like a reduction rather than an addition.

The recasting in the remix impacted the depiction of characters with AIDS. In addition, the most puzzling and troublesome aspect of the redesign, which also impacted the deception of characters in *Rent: Remixed*, was the use of a projection of names of those who had died from AIDS-related diseases, including Rock Hudson, Freddie Mercury, Rudolph Nureyev. This was also anachronistic or, at best, troubling since including these figures takes *Rent* out of its time and place, confusing the audiences. What this effect also does is detract from the narrative of *Rent*. As discussed previously, one of the text's greatest strengths was the power and emotional impact of the narrative. The projection of real-life celebrities' names detracts from audience engagement with the characters onstage and, therefore, from the depiction of AIDS. This effect was included, it appears, as a means of education, or to make the text more relevant to younger audiences.

The characters in the text themselves become altered by Baker's catalog of changes. In so doing, the depiction of AIDS they serve as a conduit. Although characters can evolve with each production, as each director and actor develops their own interpretation of the characters, the essence of the narrative must remain. To take Mimi as an example, in changing her ethnicity, the style of dancing she does in the club is less meaningful as it appears less a part of Mimi's character and story.

With the overt medical references in the text being minimal, *Rent* relies on a mixture of music and characterization to communicate the impact of AIDS. The impact is almost purely emotional, with only two real instances of physical impact—Angel's death and Mimi's almost death—being depicted, If the audience struggles to connect emotionally to the characters, the impact of the characters' battle with AIDS is lost.

MUSIC IN THE REVIVALS

The most drastic change Baker made to *Rent*, which is largely unprecedented, was the remixing of the musical score. Total reorchestration of a musical is rare, but composers occasionally revisit a score, or older works may be reorchestrated for revival. The Larson estate granted permission for Baker to do so in 2006. Although previously, they had not granted a license to make major changes to Jonathan Larson's work, it is understandable that they gave it in this case, given what appeared to be Baker's sound reasoning. Baker proposed updating the score in keeping with contemporary music like Larson's was when he wrote it. However, as with the direction and design, the drastic change to the music was not successful. Baker's reorchestrations, carried out with sound designer Steve Anderson, drastically altered key songs from the musical, including central characters' songs such as Roger's "One Song Glory" and Mimi's "Out Tonight."

The song "One Song Glory" was slowed down and softened, losing the more authentic rock feel that had grown organically out of the original Roger, Adam Pascal's rock background. In Baker's version, the tempo and style gave "One Song Glory" a ballad feel that was incongruous with the music as written and the style in which it was originally intended. The song is an angry cry against the injustice of Roger's condition. Roger is a struggling musician; we're told he has had gigs at the New York club CBGB, which indicates to an audience the kind of musician he is. Baker's altering of the musical style of Roger's key song confuses depictions of the character. This level of change alters the audience's perception of the character and brings into question the artistic integrity and relation with the original version that Baker is trying to create. With the change in his music, Roger changes from a particular kind of rock musician into someone else. For the kind of musician, and therefore the kind of person he is, Roger's style of music, as much as the words he sings, are important. These changes dramatically alter the meaning or effect of the music, which becomes problematic.

The music changes did not only affect this character. Mimi's "Out Tonight" also changed from the high-tempo declaration of life in defiance of illness to a more somber number that once again alters an audience's interpretation of Mimi's character. The song changes Mimi from the "S&M dancer" she was originally described since the original orchestration's hard rock tempo is also changed. Sam Marlowe describes the new version as "the slinky burlesque number that replaces Larson's original shouty song of seduction." Marlowe's less-than-flattering account continues: "Siobhan Donaghy's strangely sung Mimi (a smack head dancer at the Cat Scratch Club—think Miss Adelaide with a syringe and no sense of humor)" (2007). Although this is a critique of the performance, both comments illustrate the impact of changing the musical approach to Mimi, particularly her key song.

In Baker's version, the song becomes "Burlesque," and her job/identity alters with it. The change is significant. S&M dancing indicates a certain identity: edgy, away from mainstream culture, deviant, and associated with sexual encounters still considered taboo. Burlesque dancing and culture had by 2006, through prominent figures like Dita Von Teese, become seen as acceptable, almost mainstream. Mimi's song "Out Tonight" indicates her employment. In the original, she is a stripper in an underground, deviant setting—one that would be not, as Larson's later lyrics suggest, "in the mainstream." In Baker's version, the more socially acceptable version of stripping, her music, and her style now suggests dramatically altering the character. In altering how Mimi presents her sexuality and attitude toward AIDS in her song, her character is altered. She is softened and appears weaker. In Larson's original, the loud, aggressive music of Mimi's anthem demonstrated her personality and attitude toward AIDS. She was attacking life—attacking her AIDS diagnosis—and her subversive use of sexuality, being subversive about the dominant culture. In Baker's version, all of this—and Mimi's personality—is muted. The songs in a musical are integral in creating a character. The original characterization and identity are lost in drastically altering both musical numbers.

Rent's relationship to *La bohème* is a question posed since the musical's inception and is important in considering the musical changes. Peter Royston created *Rent—A Study Guide* (published by the New York Theatre Workshop, where *Rent* was staged in 1996). In it, he asks questions about Larson's integration of Puccini's score. Royston quotes Larson as saying, "I analysed the libretto, broke it down beat by beat." It is clear from an analysis of the libretto that Larson took more than just his story from *La bohème*. Ian Nisbet's "Transposition in Jonathan

Larson's *Rent"* (*Musical Theatre* 5, no. 3, 2011) explores this in detail, reading Puccini and Larson's scores side by side at key moments in the story. This continuity with *La bohème* is significant in considering *Rent: Remixed*. In the original, a certain continuity was running through that marked out the pieces as part of the same body of music. Nisbet explores how Larson draws on the musical facets of Puccini's score, transposing it to his own modern score. Larson used Puccini's score, making his adaptation directly related to the source material. In Baker's changes to the score, *Rent* becomes further removed from the source material. Because Larson was influenced directly by *La bohème*, the adherence to his adaptation or transposing of Puccini's music is an integral part of *Rent*. Altering this changes Larson's intent with the music and alters *Rent* considerably.

The music of *Rent* is integral to its narrative and depictions of AIDS. The musical, as mentioned, is sung through, with all the distinct songs linked by short pieces of dialogue also set to music. The overall similarities in the style of the original orchestrations mean a continuous flow to the piece that is absent in Baker's version. The marked stylistic differences in each major musical number result in a discordant feel to the piece. The alterations to the character's key musical numbers drastically alter an audience member's interpretation of the characters and the piece.

PRESS RESPONSE

In considering the impact and success of *Rent: Remixed,* it is pertinent to consider the ongoing perception of *Rent*'s initial failure in London. Much was made of the perceived lack of success from the original

London production as a preordained indicator of the failure of *Rent: Remixed*. Some critics used this as a focal point of their reviews. Ian Shuttleworth comments that while the New York production had been "a Broadway fixture," the show was "unable to duplicate its success in the West End" (2007). This is, if taken literally, a fair analysis: *Rent* in London or anywhere else could not hope to duplicate the success of the Broadway run. Sam Marlowe offered a similar sentiment: "In London, it was a different story. *Rent* hit the West End in 1998 and flopped, with British audiences and critics failing to respond to its blend of bombast and sentiment" (2007). Compared with the critical response to *Angels in America*, which heaped praise upon the original while being wary of a revival, the critics had been wary of *Rent* from the days of the original production. In reviewing the "remixed" version, the dislike critics had shown of the original production, coupled with the almost universally agreed "failure" they concluded it had been, did little to support *Rent's* critical reception in Britain.

Nevertheless, there were those who, perhaps due to a dislike of the original, did support Baker's reworking. Sam Marlowe felt that if anyone could, in his words, "give Larson's musical a hip replacement," it was Baker (2007). Marlowe goes on to be one of the minorities who felt the "makeover" was an improvement, going as far as to say: "I suspect Larson wouldn't have been displeased with the makeover. And a flawed production stylishly repackaged." Marlowe here reflects Baker's motivation for "remixing" *Rent*. As outlined in the introduction to this section, reworking, including the reorchestration of musical theater pieces, is fairly common with or without the composer's input. It is neither unheard of nor necessarily a bad thing. However, the reorchestration is problematic for the audience, particularly those familiar with the original. With established musicals like *Rent* with an available cast recording, the likelihood that audience members have heard the original arrangements increases. This creates a preemptive impression of the music and, by association, the characters. Changing this expectation, or challenging it, can be a good thing or an interesting artistic choice, but in this case, for reasons already explored, it was not. For audiences expecting something similar to the original, this would have lead to a frustrating experience. In diverging from the original sound so dramatically, *Rent: Remixed* lost the musical identity influenced by the time and place Larson set it.

The center of critical problems with the production lies in a stylistic approach that detracts from the intention of Michael Greif's original production. This attempt at updating appears at its core misguided, as *Rent* was in its staging originally about encapsulating a specific time and place. Critics showed that they felt this in their responses. One review summarized *Rent*: "You could say *Rent* is a Nineties musical for the Generation X-ers" (Butler 1998). This comment indicates that the show appealed to a particular demographic, and in altering the original—indeed, in seeming to alter the time it was set in as Baker did—this appeal was lost even to the demographic to whom it should have most appealed.

Many musicals and plays speak to a particular time, place, or demographic but retain an appeal and significance beyond this. *Hair*, to which *Rent* is so often compared, while being a "voice" and "depiction" of the generation it represents, has endurance and appeal beyond its original target audience. It is significant, as noted earlier that Larson himself was rewriting or perhaps "remixing" an existing text, one that itself was of a specific time and place. The conclusions drawn about *Rent: Remixed* by critics like de Jongh and Billington, who liked and respected the approach of Larson's original, are that it is worryingly anachronistic and confusing. It would be particularly so to an audience not familiar with the original. As Billington also said, "it is all as misguided as a recent attempt to yank *Hair* out of its 1960s world and treat it as a modern protest musical" (2007). In the eyes of the critics, the updating of *Rent* that Baker envisaged would clarify the communication of its message to a new audience had the opposite effect. Summed up effectively: "Larson wanted nothing like this. His original, dazzling idea was to recreate the world of Puccini's *La Boheme* . . . Baker's *Rent* -resisting bohemians are not so much drop-outs as chic society people" (Billington 2007).

Drawing on the links to Puccini's opera, de Jongh points out the slightly vacuous or hypocritical feeling that Baker's direction or "remixing" left critics and audiences with. These specific faults found with *Rent: Remixed* builds to an overall sense of disappointment and a feeling that such revisions were unnecessary.

REVIVING *RENT* IN 2007

The changes Baker made to *Rent* made the piece lose clarity. Overall the plot became muddled, and thus so did the depiction of AIDS. Logically, directors desire to change, to revive a text to put their mark upon it, and Baker seems to have had sound motivation aside from artistic vanity. However, Baker's approach is misguided as in the alterations, it loses much of the existing text's musical, emotional, and artistic integrity.

The text lost much of its identity and, as a result, alienated existing fans and gained few new ones. For the existing fans, the changes to the music they loved were too great to reconcile. Musical theater fans often indulge in repeat viewings, so the need to replicate some element of the original is often quite strong. Carlson uses the original *Rent* as an example of a show where, on a revisit, "Everything—costumes, scenery, lighting, even basic blocking and gestures has remained essentially the same but with a totally new set of bodies in place" (Carlson 2003, p. 98). This is not a phenomenon unique to *Rent* but rather more a symptom of contemporary musical theater production. However, in terms of reviving *Rent*, the element of "ghosting" was particularly strong. Through the recorded versions of *Rent* and their own experience, fans had very particular expectations. They were expecting the kind of revival that Brantley's review critiqued. For *Rent* fans and any major musical, recapturing the original production is often a significant element of the experience. Productions may slightly alter elements of the production; they may even restage and redesign it, but if it loses the essence of what that musical originally was, fans lose interest.

This element—the lack of theatrical ghosting—explains why fans of *Rent*, perhaps even including the most casual of fans, were left disenchanted and disillusioned by the revival. The motivation behind the reinvention of *Rent* by Baker and his team was sound. To further adapt *Rent* for new audiences and to bring a new artistic take to the material is the basis for all theatrical revival. However, the adaptation must also work alongside the original. As Linda Hutcheon says of adaptation, "It is repetition but without replication, bringing together the comfort of ritual and recognition with the delight of surprise and novelty" (1988, p. 173). *Rent: Remixed* failed to retain that which was "comforting" about the original and also failed to replace this with anything of "novelty" to audiences. Overall, the effect of *Rent* appears diminished by Baker's changes. As Carlson puts it, "One of the most important effects of drama's recycling of material is that it encourages audiences to compare varying versions of the same story" (Carlson 2003, p. 27). What Baker's production managed to do was to make audiences wish for a return to the original version. For *Rent* to be effective as a theatrical work and as a depiction of AIDS, it needs to connect with an audience emotionally. The original production transposed effectively to Britain because this emotional connection overrode any cultural dissonance about AIDS. As illustrated, the changes Baker made alienated audiences and severed the emotional connection with *Rent*.

Baker's production also diminished the effect of *Rent* in the changes to the music and style of the piece that he made. The importance of *Rent* stems as much from its theatrical style as its content or depiction of AIDS. While not unique as a rock musical or a musical that used contemporary musical influences, *Rent* was markedly different from the offerings of the London theatrical landscape. Baker's musical and stylistic changes to the text were anachronistic, discordant, and, ultimately, alienating to audiences. The effect they had was to take an innovative musical theater text and change the music and the content beyond recognition. The *Rent* Baker presented in 2007 was too far removed from the original, and its effectiveness in depicting AIDS on the British stage was severely diminished.

Clearly, Baker's remixing of *Rent* in 2007 did not prove successful. In terms of critical response, in part, this is a remnant of the original resistance to *Rent*—but it is more a reaction to changes that simply did not work. Baker's changes hurt the narrative as well as the depiction of AIDS. The British experience of AIDS—certainly that of *Rent*'s target audience's experience of AIDS—had been profoundly different from that in the generation and country Larson was part of and writing about. The fact that "remixing" the play failed illustrates something inherently powerful in Larson's writing that connected audiences to his depictions of AIDS despite a disparate experience.

11

"CONNECTION IN AN ISOLATING AGE"

Rentheads

RENT FANS ACROSS THE DECADES

Rent is a story of a loyal fanbase. It was the first show on Broadway to have the now commonplace "rush tickets," tickets that could be bought on the day of the show for a fraction of the usual price. For this, producers got a line outside their theater every morning, indicating to the casual passerby that this show was a "hot ticket." For *Rent*, this also ensured that the audience would look like the people onstage. They also got an enthusiastic front row and an endlessly returning group. The fans got to see their show over and over.

Beyond the initial hype, there was a quiet revolution happening in the Nederlander—a closeness between fans and a show, the stories of the people who loved the show, and the people in the show being intertwined like few had before. We can see the engagement of fans by looking at the ephemera from that era—remaining websites, discussion, fan fiction, fan art, and interviews with fans from the original era.

A living, breathing element of *Rent* and its fan story is the rush line. This was where *Rent* community was born. Fans returned time and again to see "their" show, and the hours waiting outside with like-minded fans forged connections and friendships. There is something about then experiencing the show with those people you have sat side by side with and cementing that "shared experience" of the show. They laughed and cried at the same moments alongside like-minded friends, and this is unique to theater fans. Created initially as a marketing gimmick and to ensure the demographic of *Rent* could still see the show uptown, the rush line became the hub of the fan community.

Rent fans managed to create and gather in friendship groups. No doubt there were clashes and arguments between fans, as any large group will encounter. But *Rent* created a large group of fans who became friends around the show. Coinciding with many people's teens/early twenties, *Rent* fandom was a period when young people were looking for acceptance, and the show offered that on- and offstage.

PERFORMERS AS FANS

Following performers from *Rent* was often a huge part of being a "Rent-head." Several fans say that being part of the fandom continued their engagement with musical theater. One fan put it bluntly: "I stan the original cast. I'm also very into Broadway replacements and tracking their careers. I'd say that I will generally see anything with the original cast in it—especially Daphne Rubin-Vega." Others have been more selective in their followings, which led them to new things; "I've honestly only followed Anthony Rapp. I've seen *If/Then* despite not really being a fan of Idina because of him. He's a sweet man and meeting him was a highlight of my life. My queer journey involves his influence and writings. I got into the whole Star Trek franchise because I wanted to watch him on [Star Trek] Discovery." For others, it's been a slightly territorial experience as the cast's fame has grown: "Idina Menzel definitely was frustrating to see people 'discover' this talent because of *Frozen*, when she'd been around for ages because of RENT (and later *Wicked*)." Many a *Rent* fan can sympathize with the idea that Menzel is "Elsa" when to a generation she is forever Maureen.

Rent shaped people's careers and influenced their connection with theater:

> *Rent* massively shaped my views on musical theatre dramaturgy. To this day, I prefer something that's messy but reaching for something over a show that has been crafted to a formulaic structure. I still get hyper defensive whenever another theatre person criticizes the show, because it is an unfinished work!!! Jonathan died before finishing it. It simply cannot be judged as a polished piece, and he cannot be judged as a mature writer/composer because he never got the chance to become one.

Rent also inspired fans to follow their dreams:

> I saw the original cast shortly after it opened on Broadway when I was fifteen or so. I was already heavily into theater and knew by then I wanted to be an actor and move to New York, but these characters gave me something concrete to hang those dreams on.

ONLINE FANDOM

The emerging world of online fandom was led by *Rent* fans. They were the perfect intersection of worlds—theater fans and the first generation to embrace the internet. With the advent of fan forums (such as All That Chat and Broadway World) alongside personal fan websites, *Rent* fans found ways to meet, share information, and form an online community. Gradually, these worlds would blur with fans who met at the show moving online to discuss the show, and fans who met online making plans to see the show together.

For Rentheads, attending the musical was key in the early days. Theater fan engagement naturally centers on the act of going to a performance, and for Rentheads, queuing for rush tickets and stage dooring were central, performative acts of fandom. Before the cast recording was available and in the era of limited internet access, attendance at the theater was the only way to experience *Rent*, so in the early months and years, the experience entirely depended on attendance at the theater.

There was, however, even early on, an element of online fandom involving *Rent* that was highly unusual in theater fandom at the time. *Rent* fans operated in the early world of internet fan culture. Their engagement with the show went online in a way other Broadway shows at this point hadn't. Fans made websites dedicated to their show and cataloged lyrics (important in an era when CD liner notes were the only other way to know lyrics) and collated press coverage. Fans began a digital archive for the show to an extent no other Broadway musical had seen. *Rent* fans borrowed from fans in other media and became the first fandom to create fan works for their show online. While fan art— specifically mock posters and portraits of leading actors—had been made for decades by devoted fans either for their own enjoyment or as gifts for actors, *Rent* borrowed from the sci-fi fan community by creating fan art to share with one another. This art, often with a pop art style that reflected the ethos and style of the show, was shared among themselves. Likewise, a small, but still noticeable, contingent created fan fiction for *Rent*. This was unlikely the first theater work to inspire fan fiction, but *Rent* was certainly the first to show up in digital archives and on fan sites. Quietly existing alongside the louder voices of media fandom, *Rent* carved out a niche of theater fan works.

The largest online engagement for *Rent* fans was in discussion forums. These were, and remain to this day, the focal point for theater fans to gather and talk about their shows. While social media has now carved out areas for fan discussion—theater Twitter is an active and vocal area of discussion, and Facebook groups for specific shows offer fans a place to trade information—it is the forum that still reigns supreme in theater fans' eyes. The long-form discussion and the corralling of multiple shows in one site appeals to the theater fan mentality. The largest and most active across *Rent*'s original lifespan was the American-based Broadway World and All That Chat board. Periodically, a discussion on the text will occur on one of the major theater discussion sites that cater to both the United States and the UK such as Broadway. com, Broadway World, and What's on Stage. These discussions illustrate an ongoing engagement with *Rent*.

The use of online engagement by theater fans is an area that has grown alongside *Rent*. Across the run on Broadway and the subsequent productions, spin-offs, and all manner of connections to the show, theater fans developed their use of the internet to engage with favorite shows and performers. *Rent* appealed to the young people who were gaining access to and developing an interest in the internet as a social and fandom tool. Online fandom and discussion have become important aspects of theater engagement for *Rent* fans and all theater fans since then.

COMING OF AGE WITH *RENT*

Being a *Rent* fan was to grow up in an era of theater fandom where "fandom" wasn't a "thing" in theater. It is only in recent years that the terminology has leaked in from other areas. Theater fans never used to describe themselves as "in [title of show] fandom" they were just "fans of [title of show]" or "Rentheads." Likewise, to be fans of a person was not to be in the "Adam Pascal fandom" but to be "an Adam Pascal fan." A small semantic distinction, but one that emphasizes the different and separate nature of theater fan engagement compared to other forms of media.

The fan interest and interaction with *Rent* ebbed and flowed as all things do. Over twelve years of a Broadway run, it would be very unusual for even a core group of fans to remain consistent. Unlike film or TV fandom, theater fandom requires direct access—particularly without the internet access of present-day fandom. The demographic appeal of *Rent* also has a natural shelf life for some fans. Many came to the show while in high school or college, once life took them away from New York City itself in some cases, or just away from that period where travel and time to see/camp out/hang out with their fellow *Rent* fans wasn't as available, some would naturally drift away. As they outgrew the period in their lives they might only return periodically to "check in" with the fandom and the show. As digital engagement grew, it became a continuous way to keep in touch with the show.

As one fan looks back on having been a fan since his early twenties:

> I would have been twenty-two [when I first saw it]. And I
> think, you know, that that early twenties is the period for you.
> I stopped feeling quite as invincible as I had done from the
> eighteen to twenty-one period when I first went to university
> and traveled and did all those sorts of things. I look back on
> that now and think why did I do any of those things? Why
> would any sensible person go and do these crazy things? But
> I think in your early twenties, you start to become a bit more
> aware. Not so much of mortality, but it's a bit more compli-
> cated. And it's not all in your control.

Rent fans can be roughly divided into a series of chronological categories. There are the "originals" who saw either the downtown production or the early days of the original Broadway run. If you saw Anthony Rapp and Adam Pascal the first time around, you can be counted in this. "Second generation" fans found it in the middle years. They might have been familiar with the cast recording before but saw it mid-Broadway run, with any number of replacement casts, or saw the first tours. Then there are the fans who came to it around the time of the film or with the closing cast. Finally, there's the brand-new generation who discovered it post-Broadway. These younger millennials never knew the early days of *Rent* but still discovered it along the way. The original Broadway production closing allowed for a gradual reinterpretation of *Rent* and fans having to deal with different versions of "their" show. Larson's musical was a strange beast, being both unfinished and enshrined. Larson's death meant that the creative process of rewriting and restaging through rehearsals and previews was halted, stuck in a moment and trying to fill in the gaps the composer had left unfinished. When people argue *Rent*'s flaws, it's hard not to wonder what might have been if Larson had the chance to sit in the room and bring it fully to life with his director. Instead, Michael Greif was left to guess—and looked to honor Larson's memory. *Rent* was enshrined in that first production. It seemed every director and company sought to replicate the original and only the original. Greif's original was the only way *Rent* was "allowed" to be produced.

Rent is part of a journey—a personal, musical, and cultural one. It is a moment in time and a continuous part of the fans. They never claimed that the characters were perfect—in fact, that was part of the appeal, an imperfect group of twentysomethings making mistakes. Fans never said *Rent* or the characters were perfect. That's why they loved them. As they grow up, looking back feels reassuring.

> I think it's really interesting that you come back to it with different eyes in different years. There's that cliche that you can always remember where you were when you heard something else. But there are certain songs on that soundtracks that transport you back to another place. And it's formative, when you see something in your twenties, and it lives with you.

FAN CONNECTION TO THE SHOW

There are many ways to go about considering what *Rent* means to fans, but really, the best way is to ask them. So, twenty-five years on, I asked *Rent* fans to simply tell me. In a series of questions, I asked them to reflect on the show and its part in their life. Their stories are anonymized, partly for those who didn't wish to be named but also because *Rent* is a community, and each individual story represents dozens more over the decades.

The connection to seeing the show at the Nederlander was important, and even romantic: "[I saw it] at Nederlander, six-plus times, including one Christmas performance with it snowing outside." Others also went to locations associated with the show: "I've seen it at Nederlander and made a bunch of my friends go to the Life Cafe when I went in 2008. They didn't understand why we were there, but it was so special to get to be there. The idea too that it is the space in which you connect with other fans, and perhaps stake a claim to your own fandom in doing so." "I saw *Rent* at the Nederlander about six times, including its final weekend of performances there when I won a contest for the top-fifty Rentheads to come to see it and other locations (such as the Life Cafe) that weekend."

Fans talk about how the connection to the wider locations of *Rent* were a big part of fan tourism: "I went to the East Village and had lunch in the Life Cafe and chatted with the owners who knew JL personally. They showed me where he used to sit and write—a bench was named in his honor, so of course I sat there!"

And this: "I saw *Rent* several times at the Nederlander, and we used to bar hop in St. Marks place, which dead ends into Tompkins Square Park. We once had brunch at Life Cafe. I also spent a summer living in the East Village with a friend—there were five of us in a one-bedroom apartment—we often joked about it being *Rent*, but with electricity."

For some, the importance endures today:

> When I was in high school and college, my friends and I
> spent a lot of time trying to win the pre-show lottery. It's hard
> to describe how connected I feel to that theater, even from
> outside. I spent so much time on that sidewalk—waiting in
> line, hoping to hear one of our names called, taking photos
> of each other or the exterior . . . sometimes we would just
> hang out there. I STILL, to this day, will cut through 41st
> Street so I can pass by whenever I'm in that area, mostly just
> out of habit. I've never seen another show in that theater even
> though there have been a few since. It's hard to think of it as
> anything other than "The *Rent* Theater." As for the "real life"
> locations of the show—yes, I've also visited many of those
> but not necessarily because of *Rent*. That being said, the first
> time I went to the Life Cafe was because of the show, and I
> always still think briefly of the show any time I pass through
> Tompkins Square Park."

The connection isn't erased by the show leaving, because the strength
of the memories and the emotional attachment to the space is strong. For
many, the sense of connection to that real time and place was important:

> I saw *Rent* at the Nederlander about two months after they
> had opened. I had only been in NYC since February I had
> never seen or heard anything like it before. It was raw, honest,
> moving, and touched me. It was like the whole show and cast
> brought you with them, as if you were part of the show. I

felt like it presented a true sense of what it was like to live in Alphabet City in NYC in the nineties and the struggle trying to survive and trying to find love and also living with a disease and addiction. It affected me profoundly.

Of course for many, being a Renthead was part of a particular period in their lives—often their teens and twenties. The memories associated with it coincide with formative periods in their lives, often reflecting times of great personal loss or upheaval:

From when I first saw the show at the Sydney Festival in 1999 I *desperately* wanted to be *in* RENT, #dreamrolez, and my sister and I obsessively listened to the cast album (double disc cd!). During college, I worked the lighting board for a local production, and one of the cast member's mom's died from a brain tumor. After college, I was cast in the ensemble in a community production, which was a dream come true. During the rehearsals, my dad was diagnosed with prostate cancer. Several years later I was working as a vocal coach at a summer camp, and we were *finally* doing RENT. I was excited. The kids were excited! During casting, I felt like I had the worst flu ever invented. Two days later I was diagnosed with acute myeloid leukemia and spent a month in hospital. I missed out on doing the production and working with my kids. I was so devastated! #YourOwnBloodCellsBetray

For many too it was a part of a certain part of their lives, giving them comfort, solace in times of difficulty:

Rent was there for me at a time in my life where I needed a place to escape. It was also there for me at a time when I was trying to find where my story (my uncle's story) fit in this world. I often go back to the soundtrack when I need to feel a certain way, when I need to give my mind an escape for a while, or when I'm looking to reconnect with my uncle. The songs bring peace to me. But I don't have the urge to run and see the show like I used to. It's coming back to Boston on tour, and I didn't even get tickets this time around.

It's absolutely a part of who I am, very formative, key in consolidating my oldest friendship. We were so lucky to be the people we were, non-straight teenagers, in London, right then, with that cast, who were so kind to us when we ran up to them at the stage door back in 1998—it felt like a total encapsulation of things that were and weren't us, things that were universal and things that were specific. It was very enabling, and it meant so much, I could never leave that behind; it's elemental.

Rent is most strongly associated with my teenage years—specifically 2007–2009, when I was in junior high and transitioning to high school. It's not a dominating force in my life anymore, like when I was thirteen and wearing a *Rent* dog tag necklace to school every day. I still love it unabashedly and sporadically will go on a *Rent* binge where I just listen to it on loop for a day, but it's a little bit more nostalgic now.

Of course there are always complications with how we look back at our younger selves, and younger obsessions:

> It's complicated—I still have a deep love for the show and would see it if given the chance, but I would say I have a healthy amount of shame around how much I loved it when I was younger. I think that as an adult, it's hard to engage with anything as earnestly as you did when you were a teenager and it seemed like this incredibly edgy and groundbreaking thing.

And equally for those more deeply embedded in the "fandom" side of things there were toxic elements that perhaps tarnish some of the memories: "It was unreal what a wonderful, but toxic, fandom that was. The New York Line Queens and the subsequent line/list queens on the tours were generally terrible and mean. But it still was the absolute best time of my life for many, many years."

It could be an overall toxic environment due to the dynamics of fandom: "For those of us who that was important to, but who weren't in the popular kids' club . . . [One fan was] not all about a starving artist group mentality, she was interested in being 'in' with the cast, showing how 'in' she was, and making sure the rest of us mortals knew it."

But, outweighing that for the most part was a culture of fans who did try and embody the ethos of the show: "There were multiple times I gave up my rush seat because there was someone who hadn't seen the show and couldn't afford to get regular seats, and I had seen it so many times—and I am definitely not the only one who did that. THAT is the culture that RENT was, and that is the culture you don't really see!"

But even for the fans who had some toxic experiences, the show remains a hugely formative and important part of their lives:

> RENT is not just a show to me, it is a significant part of my life. I don't think I can adequately put into words everything it meant to me. The thing I cannot emphasize enough, though, is how incredibly toxic the culture could be, when the whole point was supposed to be about friends and acceptance—for a lot of people, it was about who the actors paid the most attention to, and who "knew" the most insider stuff.

Beyond the potentially problematic elements, the show was part of a very specific time and place in their lives and remains there from both a personal and broader fan-engagement point of view:

> I definitely associate the show with a specific period of time, but I do also still consider myself a Renthead. I don't think that's something you lose. I don't actively engage in the fandom anymore, but when *Rent* or *Rent*-adjacent things pop up, my heart and mind are right back in it. For example, I didn't know that Daphne Rubin-Vega was going to be in the *In The Heights* movie, but I instantly felt so much love for her when I first saw her in the trailer. The same thing happened when I heard "Let It Go" for the first time—I recognized Idina's voice immediately and made a mental note to find and watch the movie. The show, and the people attached to it, impacted me so deeply and for so long that I'm not sure those connections can fade. They take up a lot less of my time

and brain space these days, but are no less intense when they make an appearance.

It also aligns with an investment in the performers, both at that very specific moment in *Rent* and beyond.

As one fan remembered:

> During my Renthead era, I fully invested in the fan culture surrounding the show. During the peak of this, I consumed as much of the other work that the OBC actors were attached to as I could. I followed them to other plays/musicals, TV shows, movies, etc. I bought Anthony Rapp's memoir and read a play his brother wrote. I was really into seeing live music at that time and followed some actors from the show into their music careers—specifically Adam Pascal, Matt Caplan, and Manley Pope. I remember even getting attached to some people from the touring companies even though I never saw any of their shows live—the actors and their music/other projects would get discussed in online fan groups I was in, and I'd dive in from there. I think that this all shaped how I later interacted in fandoms in general . . . like creating a blueprint for behavior.

For many it remains an important part of their continued connection to the show, even in the most casual ways:

> Since then, I have of course followed Idina's career closely, and I've seen Adam and Anthony both when they returned to *Rent* around the time of the movie and in concert several

times (individually and together). I bought Anthony's book and went to his book signing and saw the one-man show he developed from it. I'm always happy to see another show that a *Rent* cast member I saw is doing and I get excited and nostalgic whenever a name or face pops up that I know because of *Rent*.

The involvement of *Rent* alumni has shaped their pop culture and theatergoing tastes:

> I still scan cast lists to look for former *Rent* cast members. There are some cast members who I will consume media solely because they were in it. When I was a teenager, I watched everything I could get my hands on involving the OBC. I've been exposed to many shows (theater) that I wouldn't otherwise have paid attention to if it wasn't for *Rent*.

Or similarly, "I've also watched many TV shows and films that I wouldn't have watched if it weren't for *Rent* alumni, and there's also some musicals that I only listened to or saw because of *Rent* alumni involvement (e.g., *The Wild Party, See What I Wanna See, Aida*)."

None of this is unique to *Rent*—the nature of fandom and media consumption is that fans will follow people from one project to another. But for theater fans of the *Rent* generation, the alumni of the show have also been the actors they grew up with in theater. Starting as young actors in *Rent*, the original cast and replacements like Matt Caplan and actors in the off-Broadway production like Annaleigh Ashford became the next generation of Broadway stars. Long-term fans could say, "I saw them back when."

Whether it's following the stars or awaiting the *Tick, Tick . . . Boom!* film with anticipation in 2021, it's clear that *Rent* lives on beyond the original format for a lot of fans. Many of them are following not just the original cast, but also their favorite replacement casts, "their" Roger or Mimi, or even that guy who was in the ensemble once and is now a leading Broadway actor or a favorite on a TV show. Or it's reconnecting with Jonathan at the Jonathan Larson Project—or in spirit of the original, international fans anxiously trying to get hold of the recording (or bootlegs). It's meeting Anthony Rapp as he toured his show, it's doing a group watch of *Rent: Live* even though you're all now a decade older, and it's the friends made through *Rent* or the moments in life it reminds you of. It has been the fans that made all these spin-offs possible.

Finally, and most importantly I asked, "What does *Rent* mean to you?" For many fans, there was a huge element of *Rent* being formative for them as members of the LGBTQ community. Or even as allies to that community seeing a different representation to what they had been given at home or by mainstream media.

> It feels sort of dumb to say this now but . . . I was brought up by my mom and dad who always instilled in me that it didn't matter who someone loved. I saw my uncle and his boyfriend many times as a child. But for most of my childhood and teen hood, the world around me didn't really reflect that. *Rent* was, for me, the first time I really saw that love displayed openly in front of me. The music from *Rent* had already made a huge impact in my life. But seeing it on a stage was so impactful for me in so many ways.

Or this: "I think *Rent* was quite ahead of its time, and it addressed topics and conversations that weren't taking place in the open. I think it would be interesting to see how it would have been received now, in a world where LGBTQ relationships are generally treated with more respect in general."

"There's no way to say this without it sounding cheesy, but bear with me—I don't think I would have been homophobic, but I did grow up in an environment where I didn't even know you could be gay until I saw *Rent*. It immediately made me an impassioned 'ally' at a time when that was still a difficult thing to be."

And of course, there are those who felt a powerful connection to the stories in the show:

> My uncle, who was gay, died of AIDS when I was ten years old. He was one of the best people I have ever known. When he came out, my mom's whole family rejected him, and he fled to California, where he lived until he died. My mom was the only one who supported him and stayed connected to him. We spent my childhood traveling to California multiple times a year to see him. He was the first person I would call with good news. He supported all my crazy performances and sewed me costumes to match my songs. I loved him so much and his death affected me greatly.
>
> When he died, AIDS was still such a taboo subject. I was told by my family not to say he died of AIDS; tell people he died of cancer. It felt like I was hiding a piece of him. Everything around me was telling me I should be ashamed of his story, even though I knew that wasn't the case. Back then,

relationships between two men or two woman were not often depicted on TV or movies. It wasn't until I saw *Rent* for the first time that I saw a story that reflected my uncle's life, and it wasn't in a negative way. It was beautiful. There was love and light and friendship and joy with the sadness. I can't even pinpoint an exact thing, but *Rent* became a place where I felt close to him, connected to him. Going to see the show was like reconnecting with him every time.

Beyond the show, the idea of community comes up time and time again:

To me personally, *Rent* opened up my teenage mind to so many new things and altered the way in which I understood myself. The show, and the community of fans I found around it, was my first queer safe space. And even though I'm not as engaged as I once was, that still means everything to me. Thinking back about the show and that time in my life is like reminiscing about an old love who changed me for the better It's sad that we drifted apart, but we still love each other very much.

For anyone who was part of that community, the show shaped them and their way of seeing the world (and themselves):

Rent is a big part of my past and of who I am. It was the first time I was told it was okay to be gay. It was a celebration of differences at a time when I was under pressure to conform (middle school, ugh!). Now I still appreciate the messages: love, acceptance, No Day But Today. And, again, I still get warm feelings inside when I see the show. I still cry my eyes out and end up smiling until my face hurts.

Theater influences also play a huge part in the passion for *Rent* and how they regard it:

> It's the musical I recommend to people who don't really have much experience of musicals; it's the musical soundtrack I put on if I fancy listening to a musical; it was an early point of connection with my wife; its probably the musical I quote like an oaf most regularly; it was a DVD I watched about three times a week through my three times of Uni. I think *Rent*, really, is a rallying call to the "island of misfit toys" which makes up the theater community I don't think I've ever met anyone (outside of academic circles) who doesn't love *Rent*, or at the very least has a fondness of it. If you gather a group of theater people together and play the open chords of "Seasons of Love" the whole room lifts. It's a shortcut for "Are you one of my people?"

There is a fondness for the things *Rent* stands for, and encapsulated: "As a work of art, I see *Rent* as a celebration of love—on romantic, friendly, family, and community levels. It's an exploration of how those different types of love can define a life, with 'measure your life in love' as a powerful directive."

Sometimes it's as simple as the impact of a piece of theater, and how it makes you see the world: "For me, *Rent* will always be my first

Broadway experience (it was the first show I saw on Broadway), my favorite soundtrack, and the first experience I had with the world outside of my immediate environment."

It's also the places those feelings meet:

> *Rent* is a story about self-discovery, about community, and about love. As a queer performer myself, it has always held an important place in terms of my own journey of figuring out who I am. Whether I was feeling like a Mark, a Maureen, a Joanne, or any of the other character archetypes, it's a touch point to go back to and a way to connect with others who have been like-minded. It's a beautiful story, and though it doesn't resonate like it used to, it'll never leave my heart!

And sometimes it's just about what it makes you feel, a familiarity, a time in your life, or just something you love:

> If I may be so cheesy as to quote *Rent* in this survey about what *Rent* means to me, "Connection in an isolating age." For me I do love the music and performance of *Rent*, but I really love the community of Rentheads. I know that some aspects of the show are dated and haven't aged very well, but I really love that at its heart it's a show about the power of community and love/friendship.
>
> It's like an old sweater. I'm old enough now that I do wonder why they don't just go get jobs because you can't just not pay the rent. But. . . that musical was my everything during a time of personal confusion.

It's so hard to articulate this, but I'll try. *Rent* is love, it's living for today, it's friendship, it's struggle, it's solidarity, it's making the best of what you have, it's sticking it to the man, and so much more. It's helped me find who I am and how I want to live my life. It's given me perspective, friendships, and hope.

Sometimes it's funny or a little bit silly when you hear it back: "Just because it's quite a funny anecdote—I discovered *Rent* through reading a *High School Musical* fan fiction where they were putting on a production. I first listened to the cast recording, and then watched the film. I actually think I managed to buy the DVD from our local Tesco."

Sometimes it's about the connections and the memories you never thought the show would make for you: "I took my dad to New York once to play the *Rent* lottery. We were rough and tumble working class people, not fancy rich people. He hadn't been to NYC in many years and thought it was a dangerous and awful place. We won and sat front row center. He loved it so much. He definitely mooed. <3"

This collection of memories is important, because even today, twenty-five years on, these memories mean a great deal in the lives of the fans. The show is part of them, their lives and who they are. The good, the bad, the weird, the funny, and the emotional. In any account of this show, the stories of fans should be part of that narrative, because as the show continues to have a life in the world beyond Broadway, the fans keep the show alive.

12

"CAGES OR WINGS"

Tick, Tick . . . Boom! and Jonathan Larson's Legacy

How Larson was remembered is as much part of *Rent*'s legacy as the show itself, and the day of his death is a story well-known to many *Rent* fans but also a testament to the power of theatre. Ultimately, he is remembered through his work, *Rent* primarily, of course, but also *Tick Tick . . . Boom!* Which is his autobiographical story and one that has enjoyed a resurgence with the release of the film version in 2021. The story of Larson's life—at least the version he decided to tell in that musical—was being shared. But also with fans, over the preceding decades, the folklore of Larson's life is part of the fabric of *Rent* and its story. Before looking at *Tick Tick . . . Boom!* And it's impact in curating and continuing Jonathan's story, a reminder of that story is appropriate.

Jonathan Larson was involved in theatre from a young age. He was in *West Side Story* in school—a musical that made it into *Tick Tick... Boom!* At the time, Larson's sights were set on a career as an actor. He built up a repertoire of performances from high school shows to community theatre and studied piano and singing in school choirs.

Jonathan Larson was born in Mount Vernon, New York, on February 4, 1960. He died in February 1994, the night of *Rent*'s final dress rehearsal. His death and the final days working on *Rent* have passed somewhat into theatrical legend. Often the story is told that he went from working at the Moondance Diner, where he famously hung up his battered Converse shoes when *Rent* went into production. Of course, the story is slightly more than that. Larson had spent over a decade post-college working on his craft, developing his work as a composer.

Larson told John Istel of American Theatre; "Adelphi was a lousy place to go to school in the sense that it's in suburbia and that's where I grew up. But it was run by a disciple of Robert Brustein's named Jacques Burdick, who basically made an undergraduate version of Yale Drama School. And I was mature enough coming out of high school to appreciate it."

Burdick would become a mentor to Larson: he developed his composing skills under his tuition by first composing a score for a play he wrote called *Libro de Buen Amor.* While at the university Sacarimmoralinority, Larson would also write a Brechtian satire on the Moral Majority written with fellow student David Glenn Armstrong and produced in the winter of 1981.

Larson moved to New York after college. He spent the summer working in summer stock theatre in the Barn Theatre in Augusta, Michigan, which earned him his Equity card (the Equity set up in the US being a catch-22 of many shows since actors require an Equity card even to audition, but to get an Equity card you have to have performed/worked in a professional theatre company). In his early years in New York, Larson continued to audition for many shows—plays and musicals—but still considering performing more as a pathway to the industry. He didn't fit the "mold" casting directors wanted. Meanwhile, he continued to perform with friends from the Barn Theatre, including actor Marin Mazzie, who would go on to be a Broadway performer before tragically dying young in 2018, and singer/songwriter Scott Burkell. They called themselves J. Glitz and performed in open mic and cabarets around the city. Burkell recalled to James Sanford in the *Lansing City Pulse,* "Our opening number—without a hint of irony—was a medley of "Fame," "Downtown," and "On Broadway…", showing that the musical theater and popular/populist music roots were firmly there from early on in Larson's career.

While he auditioned, Larson started a series of "survival" jobs, including the (no longer with us but immortalized in many films) Moondance Diner in New York's Soho. The diner also has a long film and TV history—it's featured in *Friends* as one of the places Monica worked (but not filmed in the actual diner) and appeared in *Sex and the City, Miami Vice, Spider-Man,* and in an ah-ha music video. Until it was sold, it was also a place of pilgrimage for many *Rent* fans. Renthead fans will gladly remind us that Jesse L. Martin also worked there. And it has since, of course, been immortalized in *Tick, Tick…Boom!* and Lin-Manuel Miranda's iconic reimagining of Larson's reimagining of Sunday set in the Moondance Diner . . . theatrical meta layer on metalayer (or to keep a Spider-Man reference, the metaverse is real).

This period in Larson's life mirrored what he eventually wrote in *Rent*—much of the experiences, from the illegal stove to being hassled for the actual rent and, ultimately, the loss of friends—all grounded in Larson's time in New York as a young creative. In "Why" from *Tick,*

Tick . . . Boom!, a song that is about discovering a love for theatre, Larson wrote:

> *Hey, what a way to spend a day*
> *I make a vow, right here and now*
> *I'm gonna spend my time this way.*

That reflected how he did indeed spend his time. As in the song's lyrics where he asks, "Am I cut out to spend my time this way" and "I'm afraid it might be time to give in," Larson was living out his imagined life by spending time on his craft and making musicals. He rejected the 9–5 that many of his friends fell into epitomized by Michael in *Tick, Tick . . . Boom!* and Benny in Rent. Larson did live out that bohemian lifestyle he wrote about. In *Tick Tick . . . Boom!* The Jonathan character questions whether he can continue with his dream and ultimately decides he can. The real Jonathan also went through several periods of trial and error before *Rent* gained attention.

Rent fans have taken inspiration from his life. In the years before *Rent,* Larson was indeed living the *Rent* lifestyle, specifically, most of all, Mark's lifestyle. As a writer, he was consciously trying to work on projects true to his heart and artistic morality rather than (as he saw it) "selling out" to TV, writing for hire, or other commercial projects (though ultimately, he did do a few of these). He worked his "survival job" schedule to accommodate his writing, not the other way around. He also sought to write a song per day, a technique he adopted from classical composer Franz Schubert. He was contradictory: living a bohemian, somewhat exciting social life and was incredibly disciplined about his work.

Friends were important to Larson. His collective of friends reflects the notion of "chosen family" adopted by many queer people—the idea of forming a friendship group that becomes a new version of family. Used by many queer people when rejected by their "real" families, it also became a popular notion for young twenty-somethings living away from home and trying to make it in the world. And while Jonathan had a good relationship with his family back in the suburbs, the family he made in the city with friends also became family. Larson was more an observer of the more "gritty" side of *Rent*; his friends were largely middle-class college graduates, and while they weren't on the whole wealthy, they weren't the kinds of struggling homeless people or drug addicts that form the backdrop of *Rent*. They were the Mark, Roger, Collins, and occasional Benny of the story—figuring out where they fit in. The question of who Jonathan was often comes up, and really like any writer, he was part of all of them. He was Mark, the observer and filmmaker (admittedly getting dumped for a woman as Larson did). He was Roger, the songwriter struggling to find that "One Song Glory" (which he did, albeit tragically without seeing it). He was Collins, the philosopher asking for another way of doing things, and Angel's heart was open to love so constantly despite life's setbacks. Many people, after his death, of course, speculated Larson had AIDS as well and was gay; in fact, he was a serial dater in his life, having an easy way with women, and it seemed also managing to stay friends with many of them. Janet Charleston, one of his ex-girlfriends, said of the relationship, "Part of Jonathan is in Angel—the romantic part, that belief in love in an idealistic way." And that shines through in his story.

On January 21, 1996, the cast of *Rent* were in technical rehearsals when Jonathan said he felt dizzy and mentioned chest pains. He thought he had a heart attack at one point. Someone called 911, but he collapsed before the ambulance arrived. The last thing he heard beforehand was—suitably ironic—the lyrics "dying in America." Jonathan was taken to Cabrini Medical Center, where he was diagnosed with pleuritic chest pain, a pain made worse by breathing. The doctors took X-rays and he also took an electrocardiogram test; later, food poisoning was suspected, and his stomach was pumped. He was given painkillers and sent home.

Larson went back to work on Wednesday for the final dress rehearsal—the first full run for an invited audience and the only time Larson saw the show with an audience. Also in attendance was Anthony Tommasini from the *New York Times*. As the opera and classical music critic, he had gone because, through sheer coincidence, *Rent* was set to open exactly 100 years after *La bohème* (a total unplanned coincidence it seemed nobody involved was aware of). Tommasini hoped to interview Larson post-performance. His *Times* profile would end up being delayed after Larson's death and taking on a far greater poignancy than the critic intended. Tommasini's piece has become iconic, tragically so, as the last interview Larson would give: the idea of "making it, then compounded by the tragic circumstances when the piece was finally published. In particular, Larson talked of his career as being on track: "I'm happy to say that other commissions are coming up, and I think I may have a life as a composer." A final quote from the interview has additional resonance when viewed in the context of what was to come: "It's not how many years you live," Larson said, "but how you fulfill the time you spend here. That's sort of the point of the show."

Larson's work is limited to what he could produce in his lifetime. Two musicals that continued his legacy in Britain are Larson's own,

Tick, Tick . . . Boom! (2001) and Anthony Rapp's *Without You* (2010) use many of Larson's songs. *Tick, Tick . . . Boom!* and its eventual move to film became an important part of Larson's legend and mythology and the inspiration for *Rent.* That the productions of *Tick, Tick . . . Boom!* and *Without You* were years apart from *Rent* itself and each other illustrates a continued audience for material related to Larson and his work. Much of this has been sustained by fan engagement online. Online fandom, of course, became such an important part of *Rent's* legacy.

TICK, TICK . . . BOOM!

Tick, Tick . . . Boom! is one of Larson's full-length works for which we have audio recordings and performances. Originally known as his one-man show, *Boho Days,* its existence is owed to Victoria Leacock Hoffman, who believed the world deserved to see more of Larson's work. With the release of the film, directed by Lin-Manuel Miranda, it has become the most important part of Larson's legacies beyond *Rent* and a way to celebrate his life and impact. First performed in off-Broadway in 2001, it went on to several productions worldwide—including London runs. The film is Lin-Manuel Miranda's directorial debut and stars Andrew Garfield as Larson. This is an ode to Miranda's love for Larson and his impact on his career. Meanwhile, Garfield strongly connected to the AIDS angle with his part in the National Theatre's revival of *Angels in America* in 2017.

The journey to *Tick, Tick . . . Boom!* onstage began with Victoria Leacock Hoffman, who had started her own production company. She contacted Robyn Goodman, the co-founder of Second Stage Theater. The piece had morphed from *30/90* to *Tick, Tick . . . Boom!* in the final incarnation, which Jonathan had performed himself. This was the one stumbling block: Do you take something Larson performed himself, adapt it, change it, and make it into something new? Or should it just be left as it was?

The Larson family agreed to the adaptation—most likely thinking it was a chance for Larson's unheard work to be produced. It had been a solo piece with five different "finished" scripts, and Scott Schwartz was chosen to direct and adapt them into a workable performance piece.

The piece deals with Jonathan's struggle to get a foot in the door as a composer. It centers on his trying to get his musical *Superbia* made. Alongside the professional aspects of his life, it also reflects on his relationship with his dancer girlfriend and learning that his best friend (based on Larson's friend Matt O'Grady) had been diagnosed with AIDS. It was an intensely personal story for Larson.

The challenge for Schwartz was adapting it for multiple voices and structuring the monologue into a full musical. They enlisted playwright David Auburn to help rework the story. Auburn was an up-and-coming playwright whose play *Proof* had gone from the Manhattan Theatre Club to Broadway, where it won a Pulitzer Prize. (*Proof* later was adapted into a film starring Gwyneth Paltrow). A writer like Auburn, who had gone from the world of small-scale off-Broadway to accolades, was the best fit for Larson's story. Auburn was familiar with Larson's attitudes. He represents what could have been for Larson. With this understanding, he brought certain sensitivity to it. He told TheaterMania, "I liked how kind of brutal he was about his own feelings and how he didn't shirk from portraying himself as being sometimes arrogant, a little irritated. He put all of his warts on display as well as all his incredible gifts" (Rickwald, 2016).

Taking elements from the previous drafts, the show reframed the story to end with Larson's birthday party. Following in the footsteps of Sondheim, there are elements of *Company* in the framing of Jonathan's thirtieth birthday standing in for Bobby's thirty-fifth. In Larson's case, he focuses on career angst over romantic angst, but the parallels and tribute to Sondheim's *Sunday* remain. In Auburn's version, he shifted the birthday element to the end, so we see that even after Larson's professional struggles, he's still loved and celebrated by his friends. He comes through it with the resilience to carry on. Auburn said, "I felt that you needed to see him anticipating it and looking forward to it and having hopes invested in it and then share his disappointment when it didn't turn into what he wanted and then watch him come out of that" (Rickwald, 2016).

The restaging also allowed us to see more of Larson's story and work. The framing of *Tick, Tick . . . Boom!* around the workshop of *Superbia* resurrected one of the songs from the tapes and sheet music Larson had written for it. "Come to Your Senses" is the perfect addition to Larson's journey, as he questions what he is doing and providing insight into the show we will never see.

The show ends with two emotive pieces, "Why" and "Louder than Words." In "Why," Jonathan looks back on his journey with the theatrical life. We see him at nine making a vow to spend his life in the theater; we see him with Michael forging their friendship and cultivating a love for theater. Then we sit with Larson at twenty-nine, wondering if he's cut out for the life he's tried to create. With prescient lyrics that reflect on the transience of life and not wanting to waste the time we're given, it walks the line between wanting to give up and knowing when to. The song concludes on an uplifting note: "What a way to spend a day." Jon ends the song, vowing, "I'm gonna spend my time this way."

The final number, "Louder than Words," is an affirmation of that sentiment. It asks the characters—and the audience—a series of questions: Why do we carry on when we know we're in for pain? Why does it take an accident to get through to us? Why should we keep trying when we can just get by? Jonathan then asks, "Cages or wings, what do you prefer?" This line turns the song into an anthem for change, for fighting for what you want. The call to arms echoes "La Vie Bohème" and "What You Own" from *Rent*. The phrase "what does it take to wake up a generation?" foreshadows Larson's impact. The words he wrote before *Rent* was a fully realized dream makes an audience want to say, "Actually, Jonathan, you do."

Tick, Tick . . . Boom! is a bittersweet piece. It feels like being invited into the mind of an old friend or like getting to spend time with someone we've lost because, for *Rent* fans and Jonathan's friends and family, it was. It brought his work to life and is a memorial to him.

The show opened in 2001 with Raúl Esparza as Jonathan. A relatively new actor to New York, he had mostly performed in plays, but he'd recently been in *The Rocky Horror Picture Show*. (Later, he would make his mark on Broadway playing Bobby in John Doyle's 2006 production of *Company*.) *Tick, Tick . . . Boom!* was staged in the Jane Street Theater in the West Village, where *Hedwig and the Angry Inch* originally had its run. Even though the show wasn't a runaway commercial hit, it ran for a respectable 215 performances. Like much of New York theater, 9/11 affected ticket sales. The title of the show—*Tick, Tick . . . Boom!*—was also unfortunate in its timing.

But critics warmed to it. Ben Brantley called it "sweet, simple, and hopeful," while Charles Isherwood said you could hear the influence of

Sondheim and "Billy Joel with an angry edge" (2001). It gave the world a glimpse into Larson's bigger picture and, as Brantley added, "reminded us of what an infectiously tuneful composer Larson could be."

The small scale of *Tick, Tick . . . Boom!* makes it incredibly popular for small theater companies, amateur companies, and colleges to produce. It's had a healthy and prolonged life with new productions. In 2014, the New York City Center's Encores! The off-Center series had a production in which Lin-Manuel Miranda played Jon. Having had success with *In the Heights* before he turned thirty, Miranda knew the struggles of the young artist; he also felt a huge connection with the work. This affinity with Larson's story led him to direct *Tick, Tick . . . Boom!*

The film was released in theaters in November 2021, as a limited run before streaming on Netflix. Because the streaming service doesn't release viewing figures, there's no way to rank the film's success in viewership. Still, critical response has been largely positive, culminating with an Academy Award nomination for Garfield. While the film may not have won, Larson's story of making it to the Oscars would surely have fulfilled his ambition to be "the future of musical theater." The film also adds to our understanding of Larson and the *Rent* universe. As it says, "all of it is true. . . except the bits that Jonathan made up." Larson was a master at adapting his life for his stories, occasionally romanticizing, but what's a good musical without a bit of romanticizing? *Tick, Tick . . . Boom!* gave us the missing puzzle pieces of Larson's life, and the film version put those pieces together. The original play returned to the roots of *Rent,* a small-scale production with three performers and a band (Larson would be relieved it wasn't just the piano player). The original was also a throwback to the New York Theatre Workshop—stripped back and rough around the edges. The film version is the future of musical theater film and what the *Rent* film should have been (Lin-Manuel Miranda for a *Rent* remake, anyone?).

The beauty of *Tick, Tick . . . Boom!* is its ability to make a musical about making a musical. It is a love letter to Larson and musical theater. For the original version, it was a hard line to walk because it was relatively soon after Larson's death. Twenty-five years later, it is the perfect way to celebrate his legacy with the benefit of knowing all that it entails. In the film, Larson declares, "I'm the future of musical theater," something he would say in life. And he was—not just in the way he imagined by writing a game-changing musical but also in the people he changed along the way.

The film also expands the world of *Rent* by highlighting the impact of AIDS. We spend so much time thinking about lovers and family left behind during the AIDS crisis that we forget the friends who lost people too. We see this in Jonathan and Carolyn, scared for their friend Simon who ends up in the hospital, and in Jonathan's vow to be there for Michael, "whatever happens next." We see a much-needed friendship between a straight man and his gay friends. Their powerful friendship speaks to the theme of chosen family that is so integral to *Rent*. We understand from Miranda's retelling of *Tick, Tick . . . Boom!* why *Rent* mattered so much to Larson and, by extension, why it came to mean so much to the audiences who had gone through what he had.

We also understand Larson more as a writer, which is a fascinating exercise in film biography and a brilliant act of nostalgia. *Rent* fans have survived on grainy video recordings and in a handful of interviews. The real triumph of *Tick, Tick . . . Boom!* was feeling that Larson was here again, if just for a moment.

Garfield and Miranda manage to do the near impossible by creating a version of Larson that is both a character but also authentically him. Because Garfield is playing Larson when he performs, Garfield can impersonate him as he is onstage, which we can see in clips that show them performing side by side. When Garfield, like Larson, is in the "real" world of the film, he can step away from mirroring Larson's exact mannerisms and create a character that's still him.

In "Sunday," Miranda creates the biggest gathering of musical theater—with Joel Grey and Bernadette Peters, the original cast members of *Rent* (Daphne Rubin-Vega, Adam Pascal, and Wilson Jermaine Heredia), and Michaela Jae Rodriguez, as well as appearances by Phillipa Soo and Renée Elise Goldsberry. It wouldn't be a Lin-Manuel Miranda musical without a cameo from the man himself. Miranda appreciates and integrates the legacy of *Rent* in all its multitudes.

He also incorporates wonderful "Easter egg" references. The visual of Larson riding his bike echoes Mark in the film version of *Rent*. The answering machine references the iconic "speeeaaak" greeting, and Michael calling Jon "pookie" are just a few. There's more to be found on repeat watches, solidifying this as a film for musical theater lovers. The most moving reference is the close-up of Jonathan putting a kettle on to make tea. This is a clear depiction of the moment before his death. The film avoids dwelling on this part of the story, but this nod is powerful. His death forms a shadow throughout the film, especially for those who grew up in Larson's mythology; it ends in victory and tragedy. There also came a bittersweet moment, weeks after the film's release, when Stephen Sondheim died at the age of ninety-one. In the film we hear Sondheim's voice on Larson's answering machine—itself a reference to *Rent*. The unintentional parallel of both Larson and his mentor passing away added another layer to the film's message of creating while you can.

Lin-Manuel Miranda's hugely creative film adaptation of *Tick, Tick . . . Boom!* was a huge success. Fittingly for the story of Jonathan Larson, a man who referred to himself as "the future of musical theater," it is an inventive movie musical that shows what the genre can be and has the potential to reinvent it.

Tick, Tick . . . Boom! is more than just a very good movie musical; it is part of the legacy of a man who steered musical theater in a new direction. It's the story of the man whose work and life inspired a generation of musical theater artists and fans, including director Lin-Manuel Miranda. Without Larson, there might not have been a *Hamilton*; without Larson, many of today's musical theater fans might not even be fans.

Tick, Tick . . . Boom! expands the world of *Rent*. We get to see Jonathan telling his own story, and the beauty of Miranda's *Tick, Tick . . . Boom!* is its ability to make a musical about making a musical and, in the process, create a love letter to Larson and musical theater. With the stage version that was a hard line to walk, still relatively soon after Larson's death, a life story that was so concerned with "would he manage to succeed?" Now, twenty-five years after his death, it feels as it always was, the perfect way to celebrate his legacy, with the benefit of knowing all that entails.

Tick, Tick . . . Boom! expands the world of *Rent*. We get to see Jonathan telling his own story.

Both *Tick, Tick . . . Boom!* and *Rent* also, and crucially, illuminate a much-overlooked element; the friendships and the impact of AIDS. One of the most heart-wrenching lines in *Rent* is from Mark, when he says to Roger, "Maybe it's because I'm the one of us to survive." We spend so long thinking about lovers and blood family members left behind during the AIDS crisis that we often forget the friends who lost people too, who were family to them. In Miranda's *Tick, Tick . . . Boom!* we see this addressed in Jonathan and Carolyn's fear for their friend Freddy who ends up in the hospital, and in Jonathan's moving vow to be there for Michael, "Whatever happens next." We see an often overlooked dynamic—not just in stories about AIDS but more broadly—close friendships between straight and gay men, just existing in the world of the film unquestioned. It's a powerful friendship, sexuality aside, that speaks to the idea that would become integral to *Rent*, that of chosen family. From Miranda's *Tick, Tick . . . Boom!* we also come to understand why *Rent* mattered so much to Larson, and by extension, why it came to mean so much to the audiences who had also gone through what he had.

It's become trendy among some of the younger musical theater fans to bash *Rent*, to tell us the characters are all terrible people, and even to tell us that the music is terrible. Perhaps Miranda's *Tick, Tick . . . Boom!* will shed light on the fact that the story was Jonathan's truth; it was his life, including the funerals he attended and the friends he lost.

Tick, Tick . . . Boom! feels like being invited into the mind of an old friend. Like getting to spend time with someone we've lost, and in essence for *Rent* fans, and poignantly Jonathan's friends and family, that is exactly what the original stage production was; a way to bring more of his work to life and in doing so allowing us to spend more time with him. *Rent* and Larson's other work remain a kind of memorial to him, but *Tick, Tick . . . Boom!* particularly so.

It matters that this was the theatrical backdrop to Miranda's new film version because it is rooted in theater and in musical theater mythology now too, but crucially *Tick, Tick . . . Boom!* embodies Larson before he was mythologized. Yes, the words of the musical's script (and the film's screenplay) were written after the fact, but the songs are unfiltered by Larson. It brings to mind "They are your words, George," the showstopping number from Sondheim's *Sunday in the Park with George*. Larson's "Sunday" in a *Tick, Tick . . . Boom!* is a musical tribute to the song.

It's his Sunday, as the film points out clearly with the characters watching the Bernadette Peters/Mandy Patinkin version as Larson wrestles with how to be an artist and how to maintain his life but is also filled with the kind of existential dread of "finding your voice" that haunts every artist. Fusing that with the perhaps less than subtle are the parallels with Sondheim's *Company*, following in the footsteps of his mentor in framing Jonathan's thirtieth birthday much as Bobby's thirty-fifty is in *Company*. In Larson's case, too, he focuses on career angst over romantic angst, but the parallels, along with, his tribute to Sondheim's Sunday, are still there. In David Auburn's version, he shifted the birthday element to the end, so we see after all of Larson's professional struggles, he's still loved and celebrated by his friends. We see him come through it; if not renewed, then resilient to carry on. For theater nerds, too, that the original production of *Tick, Tick . . . Boom!* starred Raul Esparza, who went on to Broadway acclaim in John Doyle's production of *Company* a few years later, is a pleasing, neat parallel.

Speaking of theater nerds, the whole film is a love letter to the theater Larson adored. It is filled with visual references, jokes—"Cats auditions this way," a series of parody theater posters in Schubert Alley—and what might be the biggest gathering of musical theater legend in film history. This is all there for the reading for theater nerds because Larson was musical theater to his core, and Miranda manages to weave that into the film by making it a love letter to the theater of today that Larson helped to create. Because Miranda is that theater nerd that Larson *helped* to create. Without *Rent*, we likely wouldn't have Lin-Manuel Miranda. He's said repeatedly that *Rent* and Larson inspired him to write, and you can't help but think of the Tony Award opening in 2013 that Miranda wrote for Neil Patrick Harris with the lyrics that made every theater kid cry in recognition:

> There's a kid in the middle of nowhere who's sitting there, living for Tony performances singin' and flippin' along with the Pippins and Wickeds and Kinkys, Matildas and Mormonses. So we might reassure that kid and do something to spur that kid, 'cause I promise you all of us up here tonight, We were that kid.

It's always felt like a certain generation of theater kids—Miranda's generation—was that kid, looking specifically at *Rent*, including, of course, Neil Patrick Harris, who played Mark on tour. There's a generation that *Rent* raised, and it's part of the through line of musical theater. Miranda incorporates this in his film. In *Sunday*, in particular, he manages to integrate generations of musical theater, from Joel Grey and Bernadette Peters, through to the original cast members of *Rent* (Daphne Rubin-Vega, Adam Pascal, and Wilson Jermaine Heredia) to "second generation" *Rent* star Michaela Jae Rodriguez, to the performers and shows that came after *Rent*, with original *Hamilton* cast members, Philipa Soo and Renée Elise Goldsberry (who was in the closing cast of *Rent*). Other cameos that weave the web of links across musical theater include Joel Grey, the original cast of *Wicked* with none other than Idina Menzel, the original Maureen or André De Shields, part of the original cast of *Hadestown* produced by NYTW, part of the *Rent* legacy in creating new musicals there . . . we could go on and on). It's a meta, spider diagram leading back to *Rent*, including a cameo from Miranda himself. Miranda appreciates and integrates the legacy of *Rent* in all its multitudes.

While Miranda not only expands the world of *Rent,* he gives us the context for Larson's writing and the roads that led there as well as those meta nods to the world of musicals it fits into.

The final number, "Louder than Words," acts as an affirmation of this. It asks the characters—and the audience—a series of questions: Why do we carry on when we know we're in for pain? Why does it take some kind of tragedy to get through to us? Why should we keep trying hard when we can just get by? Sung as a trio, the piece's essence is why we should try so hard for our dreams when we could just coast along. Jonathan then asked, "Cages or wings, which do you prefer?" Evolving it into an anthem for change, for keeping fighting for whatever it is you want. A kind of call to arms that echoes "La Vie Bohème" and "What You Own" from *Rent.* The phrase "What does it take to wake up a generation?" could almost foreshadow Larson's impact. The words he wrote before *Rent* were a fully realized dream, which makes an audience want to say, "actually Jonathan you will." Because, of course, if not 'the next one' that he sits down to write in the film, but the one after that, becomes the show that shaped the future of musical theater and the show that shaped a generation of musical theater lovers, performers, and of course, writers, like Miranda, who would follow.

13

"THE END OF THE MILLENNIUM"

Back to *Rent* in 2021

MEASURE IN LOVE, TWENTY-FIVE YEARS OF *RENT*

As the show moves toward its twenty-fifth anniversary, how do we measure its impact? Put simply, in its enduring importance to those who love it. Larson, and indeed the Larson family, could scarcely have imagined they'd be maintaining *Rent*'s legacy twenty-five years on. Fans who went to the early shows also never imagined it would be part of their lives over two decades later.

Rent as a live show lives on. The Farewell Tour in the United States is reflective of the first national tour in size and locations. It is the final tour to use the original Broadway staging to mark the twenty-fifth anniversary. There has been a sense for some time—since the closing of Broadway and the film—that the original staging should be an archival piece. Most musicals, when restaged, exported, and toured, change their shape and look. Tied to Larson's legacy and to preserve the show,

Rent has not changed much in the last twenty-five years. Being released from this obligation is a sign of a paradigm shift and another phase in the show's life.

The tour began in Chicago in October 2021. It was the first show back in Chicago's "Broadway in Chicago"—the collaboration of theaters that host the touring productions. It was likely many audiences' first show back at the theater when it began in late 2021. The tour took short stops in multiple US cities and ended in March 2022. The non-Equity tour is making short stops in multiple cities rather than longer sit-down runs.

The production uses Michael Greif's original staging, along with the original orchestrations. The set was adapted by Matthew Maraffi with choreography by Owen Johnson. Evan Ensign, a veteran of Broadway tours, is the director. As with other tours, the production is as similar as possible to the original with a variety of changes in costume and staging, which allows individual performers to interpret the show. While the *Rent* tours tend to stick to the original ethnicity of the characters, they don't stick to a certain "look" for the cast of actors. This means, across the years, and in this incarnation, *Rent* has retained a freshness with their casting.

The casting of the tour reflects the ethos of previous tours/productions by finding new talent for the show. Performers like Aiyana Smith, who plays Mimi, are making their professional debut. Others, like Mackenzie Rivera (ensemble), are on their first national tour. Returning veterans include Javon King, who plays Angel and was originally in the twentieth-anniversary tour, and James Schoppe (ensemble), who is in his third year with a show. The tour has curated an ensemble of returning and veteran cast members with new performers, which is tradition by now.

Rent was the first big Broadway show back post-COVID-19, which generated excitement. Actor Cody Jenkins told the *Chicago Tribune*, "It's a really cool feeling knowing that we're going to help bring life back to the city in terms of live performance and arts and music and theater" (Pierce 2021). In the same interview, Jenkins said he looks forward to being able to share the story and message of *Rent*, especially after the difficulties brought about by the pandemic. Jenkins said that the world is in a place where people need to come together more after so long feeling detached and separated.

Javron King, who plays Angel in the tour, also reflected on the continued universal appeal of the show: "Every person, no matter who you are, no matter what walk of life you come from, there's someone on that stage that you can relate to in some capacity, even if it's in the smallest way" (Pierce 2021).

The cast feels the weight of the "farewell" tour. Javon King comments, "We don't know the next time we're ever going to see *Rent* again. Who knows what the future holds. It's really a gentle reminder just to love everyone the way you want to be loved. If you just pick love first and kindness first, there's always hope for a better tomorrow" (Pierce 2021).

The show is a triumphant return to theater and an act of nostalgia. Two audience members for opening night in Chicago were first-timers to *Rent* in person. Beatrice, who is twenty-seven, had seen the recording of *Rent: Live* on TV and knew the music. Ben had never seen the show or heard it—a cellist, he's performed in *La bohème*. For both of them, there was a familiarity but not an in-depth knowledge of the piece.

Seeing the opening night and return to theater in Chicago also influenced their feelings about the performance. Beatrice was conscious of the difference between how people thought of the two pandemics: "The people in the US currently being affected the most are people who are actively resisting help/vaccines/etc., which feels very different to what was happening during the AIDS crisis." Beatrice was struck by how "the show does a very good job of depicting the homeless and also humanizing the tragedy of the AIDS crisis and putting faces to the illness." As younger audience members who were too young to see the original, Ben and Beatrice considered how the show is and isn't dated through contemporary eyes, especially with the original staging. Beatrice was struck by the contemporary feel of the conversations and themes: "I think the themes of *Rent* always resonate, which is why it's stayed in the collective consciousness for so long. But I do think that the theme of trying your best to survive in a society with huge class differences definitely hits very hard in 2021. Social justice, while different now than when the play was created, still feels much the same."

The US and UK return of *Rent* post-pandemic was hugely significant for audiences and casts alike. There are clear reasons for the show to endure, but how do we also read *Rent* in 2021?

This aligns with the fans, who are well into different phases of their lives. They might reject the new versions of *Rent* to spring up in the following years, but in the interim, they get to revisit that old friend once more. The farewell tour is a bookend in their lives, a chance to memorialize and bid farewell to their show before they move on.

We look to the future of *Rent* and a new generation of bohemians to adopt it. *Rent* has been set free in the wild for younger audiences to take as their own. As younger fans pop up, producing YouTube covers of the music and sharing their own school and college productions, *Rent* becomes what every theatrical production should be—ever evolving.

Rent never stands still for long. At the time of this writing, the Broadway tour is out across America welcoming audiences back to the theater. The show is being reimagined by the Signature Theatre Company in Arlington, Virginia, and the UK's Hope Mill Theatre production might make its way to London for the first West End run since the original.

ONLINE TRIBUTE

March 2021 should have been the twenty-fifth anniversary celebrations for *Rent* at the New York Theatre Workshop (NYTW). However, history had other ideas and at the time, the New York theater was closed due to COVID-19. In the typical *Rent* spirit of determination to mark the occasion, the theater took the event online.

NYTW described the event as follows:

> On March 2, 2021, we held our biggest fundraising event of the year, 25 YEARS OF RENT: MEASURED IN LOVE. This virtual celebration of RENT and its impact on the collective cultural consciousness featured a selection of iconic songs by some of today's most beloved recording and theater artists, exclusive content uncovering how RENT came to life, and reflections on the driving force of Jonathan's legacy in the American theatre.

Because the event streamed online and was not confined to the space of NYTW, a few thousand people were able to watch live or see the recording afterward. COVID-19 forced the theater community to adapt toward streaming. Perhaps in 2026 they'll hold a streamed concert so Rentheads the world over can share.

The evening, hosted by Olivia Lux, a drag queen known for her appearance on *RuPaul's Drag Race*, displayed a range of prerecorded performances from *Rent* alumni and Broadway stars. NYTW interspersed this with a new documentary and interviews from Jonathan's friends, family, and creatives who have been influenced by him over the years. They also talked extensively about how *Rent* is a legacy piece and influences the way the theater conducts its work.

The celebration of NYTW was a fundraiser and a pertinent reminder of the precariousness of art. Despite the financial rewards that *Rent* brought NYTW over the years, it still exists on a relatively low budget. Producing musicals is a risky and costly endeavor—even in a normal year, the theater requires generous support to get by; in the year of COVID-19, even more so. The theater's fundraiser emphasized the need for funds to continue after a year (and more) of no ticketing income. *Rent* resonates with the collective experience of living through a pandemic mismanaged by the government and rife with negligence. But through the despair, the themes of the show are a poignant reminder of community and love after a period of isolation. It is fitting, then that *Rent* was the first show back in the United States and the UK after the 2020 shutdown.

HOPE MILL THEATRE PRODUCTION— CHANGES FOR THE FUTURE

In 2020, a new voice in musical theater put on a new production of *Rent* in the United Kingdom. The Hope Mill Theatre opened in 2015 in an old mill space in Manchester. Inspired by the West End theaters that allow small productions and musicals to flourish, they set out to create something similar in Manchester.

In the summer of 2021, with the world looking like it might begin to get back to normal, Hope Mill announced the return of *Rent*. The show was slated to begin in August, when theoretically COVID-19 restrictions could be lifted for performances at full capacity. In the summer of 2021, *Rent* was back on British stages once again.

Joseph Houston, coproducer of the Hope Mill Theatre in Manchester who staged this British revival of *Rent* in 2020/2021, spoke in a recent interview on the striking resemblance of Manchester to the backdrop against which Larson first wrote the show. He says, "Manchester is going through such a surge, and regeneration, and hope now that we're based, by buildings that are completely owned and taken over by artists. So it now has graphic designers, photographers, DJs and paint painters" (Joseph Housten, interview at the Hope Mill Theatre, September 2021). A space for art was a driving factor in bringing *Rent* back: "To be able to bring back the show that is about artists struggling to survive, wanting to be creative, wanting to do what their passion is, but yet being affected by AIDS . . . parallel living through COVID."

This production instead retained a good deal of the rawness and integrity of the original. There was an element of consciously remaking the show in spirit, but not to the letter. They didn't want it to be "a bog-standard revival." The diversity of the production reflected the original intentions of the piece. While other productions, such as the 2017 tour/Other Palace production, mixed up and changed the ethnicities of characters, this production returned to the ethos of diversity among the cast.

It does not necessarily go against the ethos of *Rent* to have, for example, a white Benny or Collins, as neither of the ethnicities are written explicitly into the text. However, in 2021, casting the Benny and Collins characters as Black men was especially important in the wake of the Black Lives Matter movement. Benny, a "yuppie" businessman, portrayed as a Black man in 2021 matters. The discussion encompasses what Benny would have been up against. We can imagine whether his wife is white or Black? And how does this impact his reception in the business world? How does it impact her father's business that he's now part of? When we look at Collins, a rebellious college professor, and wonder how much harder he would have had to work to achieve an impressive status for not only a young man, but also a young Black man at this time. Adding Collins's illegal activities, hacking, and other protests, and contextualized as a Black man, the implications become even greater. This has always been so, but in 2021, the lens through which an audience understands this is amplified. Parallel to this, Joanne being played by a Black woman is also important. A qualified, successful lawyer from a middle-class Black family celebrates Joanne as a Black woman. Seeing a successful, happy Black woman in a musical story is formative for audiences who saw and will see *Rent*.

Another significant casting decision was casting Alex Thomas-Smith as Angel, who is a nonbinary performer (pronouns *they/he/she*). Alongside Alex, Isaac Hesketh, who understudied the role of Roger, is also nonbinary. They posted a few tweets on Twitter during the run that illustrate how important this was to them. Isaac said of playing Roger, "Last night a Leading 'Man' was simply just a Leading Actor. . . "Who says Roger can't be played by a Non-binary actor with a fresh set of nude acrylics?" (Twitter, August 25, 2021).

This moment helps shift how we think about casting. We can respect all gender identities and embrace them within casting decisions. Later, Isaac shared their elation: "I'm Angel. 13 year old me is beaming with pride. Angel played such a huge part in me discovering my queer identity in my early teens so this truly is a dream come true. Thank you so much to my amazingly supportive cast/team at *Rent* for helping me take over this weekend" (Isaac Hesketh, Twitter, September 6, 2021).

The beauty of theater is that it evolves, and in casting a nonbinary actor in the role, we can see Angel as they were perhaps intended all along. Performers like Isaac can step into the shoes (in this case, impressive platform heels) of the characters that inspired and helped them on their personal journeys. In turn, Isaac and Alex are doing the same for the next generation. The lived experience of that performer supports how we understand Angel. Without speculating about Larson's intentions, there is no reason a nonbinary actor cannot play Angel, in the same way they can play any role.

The production pares back some elements of the show while introducing/expanding on others. In short it does what revivals—particularly those so many years after the original—should do.

One notable feature is that the actors don't touch. Yes, a reflection of COVID-19-safe productions (by the time the second production came around, regulations were relaxed slightly in the UK, but a playing-it-safe mentality would still have been prevalent for the producing team). But instead of being a barrier, director Shepherd integrates it as a feature.

So we see a group of people desperately trying to connect (in an isolating age, if you will), while the physical staging reflects that. The idea of a community and friendship group trying to connect but physically remaining apart adds a powerful dimension to *Rent*, one that's subtle and easy to miss, but if you notice it, adds a powerful underscoring to the piece.

The staging also offers a suitable commentary on the show's ideas of community and distance. In this production, the ensemble sits around the square stage on three sides, always surrounding and observing the action—in a parallel to not touching—again ideas of what community and what connection might be in that "isolating age" brought home further by the external circumstances.

This element aligns with the choreography, which is, in some ways, a departure for *Rent*. Anyone familiar with the original production knows that for the first couple of numbers *Rent* used choreographed movement over outright choreography. The choreographed dance moves and movements feel a little jarring, especially in such a small space. Eventually, the choreography becomes part of the visual storytelling that enhances the piece. It's not to say that the original always needed it—far from it; in its original format, it worked perfectly although not for everyone. *Attitude* magazine's review commented that "There are also odd underwhelming moments, such as an AIDS demo which feels and looks more like a supermarket opening than a dangerous piece of street activism."

However, in this restaging, this choreographed movement, combined with physical distancing, enhances elements already there. We get a sense of the bigger world of New York around us in a different way. The ensemble never leaves the stage; they don't come on and off as different characters in the same way, so we need that communicated differently. But we don't lose any of the bigger picture that is written into the script.

There's something that feels like a return to *Rent*'s roots in this production. Maybe it's something in the memory of that first NYTW performance when the cast sat on chairs, singing Larson's songs that is evoked by the staging. But also, sitting the ensemble and observing the action is a really powerful staging choice. We get an image of community, watching love and loss unfold in front of them, watching their world shift and change too—through disease, through art and commercialization, through all those elements in the show.

There are slight changes to the show—twelve members in the company, reduced from fifteen in the original cast. But only the most hardened of *Rent* fans would notice. Integrated into into the production is one particularly brilliant shift in which a woman plays the drug dealer—probably not the only time among many a school or amateur production, but certainly the first in a major production. It's an interesting play with expectations for both those who know the show and on our societal expectations as well.

Where do we put *Rent* in the 21st century? It's always been an element that productions have struggled with as years go by as it threatens to become a period piece. However, these last couple of years have surely shown us that not just the obvious themes of *Rent* (pandemic) still resonate, but that there's a lot in it's very human stories that feel now more powerful than ever.

After *Rent*'s spotty record in Britain, the Hope Mill's production is a new chapter. As British Theatre Guide summed up in their review, "I first discovered this show when I found the double CD of the original cast recording in Vinyl Exchange in Manchester for a fiver Luke Sheppard's production for Hope Mill has all of the joy I heard in that original recording" (Chadderton 2021).

Sometimes you must rework the familiar to get back to the essence of the original. Sheppard looked at the component parts, considered what they meant, and put them back together again. The press response to the Hope Mill's production showed that—perhaps unlike previous productions—there was a British theater enthusiasm for *Rent*. Joseph Houston noted that the audiences were a younger crowd who were engaging with the show afresh. He added that this felt like being part of a larger conversation in musical theater:

> Musical theater has evolved. And we have, you know, the new smash hits that have come through. But they wouldn't be here if it weren't for shows like *Rent*. Being able to bring those younger audiences back to a show that was written in the '90s when they were not even born is absolutely amazing. (Joseph Housten, interviewed September 2021)

Speaking with the audience clearly shows that this production had an impact. Martyn was an unusual audience member in that he managed to get this far in musical theater life without knowing anything much about the show. As a gay man of forty, the show had a particular resonance when considering the piece in a British context. He explains: "[I knew] very little apart from it being about AIDS and the pandemic. I don't know whether my lack of knowledge about it stems from me being a late starter to musical theatre and therefore I wouldn't have heard about it as there wasn't a production running when I became obsessed, or because of Section 28 and it wouldn't have been allowed to be discussed or taught while I was at school. It was probably a bit of both."

In the UK, there is a whole generation of people, not just queer people, who are ignorant of aspects of queer life because the government decided they couldn't teach about gay people in schools and other settings. For Janine, in her twenties, seeing the show live was incredibly powerful: "The cast for this production was one of the strongest I've seen for any show in recent years and having such powerful performances in such a small performance space felt really intimate and added to the experience."

Martyn, who saw the show for the first time at the Hope Mill, comments on its resonance and the simple importance of being able to share the stories in the show: "As a gay man, [the themes] resonated incredibly hard. I can't comprehend how people went through that period in time of uncertainty and death. There's been a renaissance of sorts in recent times. For my first introduction to AIDs onstage the themes hit as hard."

Martyn also commented on how the show doesn't feel dated, perhaps in the context of a rejuvenated need to "know our history" as a queer community and rectify the lack of stories told about it. For Janine, the additional framing reflected a more inclusive approach and lead the way for other shows to follow. She was struck by this and said, "I also appreciated the show program including each performer's pronouns, which I felt was not only very in keeping with the LGBTQ inclusive message of *Rent* but also a lovely step forward in terms of inclusivity within theatre in today's modern world."

Rent connects with audiences, and this snapshot of responses illustrates the show's ability to resonate with audiences old and new in 2021. Press response to the Hope Mill's production was largely positive. *Attitude* magazine picked up on the parallels as central to their review, saying, "At the heart of this musical, though, are the timeless themes of love, illness, death, loss, self-expression and chosen family. And that's why it still works 25 years on. Indeed in the year of COVID, the viral elements to the story have a new resonance that freshens the whole piece." The reviews were also conscious of the show's legacy, with several referencing Larson's death—an indication that the stories are forever intertwined. It is comforting that twenty-five year on, those writing about *Rent* see Larson as integral to the story. "The play's haunted by a fear of dying and confronting this reality. The advent of Christmas is marked by cynical interludes, as the passing of time means the running out of time" (Barton 2021).

And then there is this:

> The show's own message of hope and friendship—woven into Larson's songs and characters with a great deal of wit and warmth and undimmed by 25 years of incarnations—and the confidence with which this young cast delivers now just has the added benefit of making this feel like the perfect production to welcome full capacity audiences back into theatres." (*Musical Theatre Review* 2021)

The reviews couldn't help but comment on both the parallels with another pandemic and the themes that resonate with audiences in a COVID-19 world. It's probably inevitable now that anyone who sees *Rent* will feel the parallels with that experience, making the show newly relevant in ways nobody foresaw and certainly, nobody would wish. Beyond the pandemic, the idea of community triumph in Larson's writing resonated with reviewers and audiences alike.

There's something too in the idea that this production resets *Rent* for many. It has not, as explored in this book, had the easiest history in British theater. While the original London production did well enough, it was resolutely an okay chapter in the show's history. Since then the production of *Rent: Remixed* rendered the show either one London audiences were loath to resist, or simply a chapter we do not speak of as fans of the show. And yes, the 2017 tour took the show back to the one fans remember, or casual audiences might have been familiar of from the film or recording. But the Hope Mill production felt like a new chapter. As British Theatre Guide summed up: "I first discovered this show when I found the double CD of the original cast recording in Vinyl Exchange in Manchester for a fiver. I loved most of the songs, but when I saw one of the early UK performances at the Shaftesbury Theatre in London in 1998, I was disappointed with the production itself and some of the performances (I've been told it got much better). The terrible Chris Columbus film version didn't help, but I did get hold of a DVD of the stage production that is pretty good. Luke Sheppard's production for Hope Mill has all of the joy I heard in that original recording."

Sometimes you have to rework the familiar to get back to its essence and that's what Sheppard did. It's not so much *Rent* from the ground up, its also (thankfully) not *Rent: Remixed* again . . . it's somewhere in between. It feels like Sheppard really looked at the component parts, considered what they meant, and put them back together again.

Rent shouldn't be impervious to criticism—especially twenty-five years on. The distance of time reveals elements that may no longer sit right, or that went unnoticed before, that are highlighted by new staging and performers. Even so, the core of the show continues to have power.

14

"WHAT YOU OWN"

Rent and Legacy

HOW DO YOU MEASURE IN LOVE? *RENT* ASKS.
HOW DO YOU MEASURE *RENT* IN 2021 TOO?

With every popular thing, there is an element of backlash. *Rent* was no different: even in its heyday there were detractors, from critics to theater fans, who didn't enjoy its style, subject matter, or actors. Some of those critiques are valid—no show is perfect, and fans don't claim *Rent* to be. Being part of a new generation of "internet musicals" with discussion online, *Rent* was no stranger to a slight—or even severe—tearing apart. Around 2016, a slew of articles started popping up to take down *Rent*. Starting with BuzzFeed—admittedly not known for journalistic rigor, but certainly for clickability, their January 2016 article "Don't Watch *Rent* as an Adult or You'll Realize How Annoying It Is" is a series of subheadings and pictures with short sentences (Golder 2016). The crux of their "takedown" is that Mark and Roger "thought they could live for free." This is hardly a deep dive into the musical as it circles around this "fact" and little else.

The critique that Mark and Roger were "entitled" and "spoiled" and should "just get a job" has always been present. The show omits the jobs both characters had in Larson's original draft, and being jobless makes them look like they're living—not unlike the TV show *Friends*—an impossible life. Similarly, by today's standards, their apartment seems impossible, but much like *Friends*, it can be explained by context. In *Friends*, the apartment was rent controlled, which meant Monica and Rachel were paying lower rates for the apartment. Similarly, Roger and Mark's apartment is huge by New York standards, but pre-gentrification, such loft spaces weren't uncommon. The East Village was also not a trendy place like it is now. Again, context is key.

Logistics aside, there has been a shift in understanding Roger and Mark. While in 2018 there was a sense of "just grow up and get a job," there's now a greater understanding of following your dreams and your heart.

Living in the context of "dying in America at the end of the millennium," Roger's limited lifespan, and Mark watching the ones he loves disappear, gave a sense of urgency. In a post-COVID-19 world, younger people, and the generation to which *Rent* fans belong, are also coming into this urgency. The idea of needing to write "one song" before you go, to have something to leave behind, doesn't seem so distant an idea now. The need to document life and leave a mark doesn't seem ridiculous either.

In the last decade, jobs have been shifting. The idea of a job for life went away some time ago. But in between, for those who grew up in the 1990s and graduated in the 2000s, there was still the possibility of a linear career: get a job, get promoted, buy material things, and live your life. After the 2008 crash and the post-COVID-19 pandemic, the notion of what constitutes a normal job has changed. The type of jobs available, working patterns, and the rise of freelancing has changed employment. Coming out of a pandemic, mass unemployment has also introduced the idea of living a bohemian life, and chasing dreams is on the rise again. These factors show Mark and Roger were not selfish or self-involved and that the dream is possible.

The BuzzFeed article was one of a collection around this time and since that have picked apart *Rent* and declared it "problematic." This is part of a wider trend of revisiting older popular cultural works—particularly from the 1990s—and demonstrating how they don't measure up to current standards. The same happened when *Friends* moved to Netflix in 2019, and again with *Seinfeld* in 2021. This journalistic trend tries to "take down" the shows/people/cultural events that are held fondly. Everyone accepts older texts from the 1970s or 1960s as "dated," but the 1990s are not yet exempt. This is part of the bigger idea that "millennials" are inherently "problematic" as a generation. The truth is more nuanced, because millennial and Gen Z folks who grew up with *Rent* are more than capable of seeing the problems and dated elements without the help of a BuzzFeed article.

A few articles took a curated, analytical approach that addresses how *Rent* sits in today's viewing. In April 2016, *Vox* ran two articles on *Rent*: "How Do You Measure 20 Years of *Rent* Backlash" (Romano 2016) and "Why *Rent* Feels So Outdated 20 Years After Its Debut" (Framke 2016). The two articles offer a balanced look at how we view the musical with some distance, and what it means for other musicals like *Hamilton*.

Framke sums it up in a balanced way: "*Rent* is neither as great a musical as many people originally thought, nor quite as bad as its most fervent detractors would rant about to you now."

That might seem like a too commonsense approach for the click-bait articles, but it's also the truth, as is Framke's argument that *Rent* is simply of its time. It's natural it would feel dated ten, fifteen, or twenty-five years on.

Framke's article spends time on the rock-pop sensibilities of Larson's work and how (in her opinion) it never worked. The dating of musical styles is inevitable, and the adaptation and adoption of them into musical theater is as much hit and miss as it is highly subjective. Did *Rent*'s rock-pop work? It depends on who you ask—if you're a musical theater purist possibly not; if you're a devotee of grunge from the nineties, also likely not. But it did work as an introduction to musical theater. We might look at *Hamilton* in twenty-five years and question how much it serves the hip-hop genre and the musical theater genre as things evolve in both. Like *Rent*, this won't invalidate what *Hamilton* has achieved in the here and now.

The article adds, "Jonathan Larson intentionally wrote a musical that mostly sounded like what you could hear on pop music radio, as a means of making the story of *La Bohème* and his beloved, endangered East Village even more relevant to the era in which he was living."

Larson was writing the music that sounded relevant to him to convey a story of his time. Framke says the issue is that pop culture moves on, as do the issues addressed. That shouldn't mean that a musical is entirely irrelevant—after all, we revive far more dated and problematic musicals all the time. We just do so with an awareness that they are of their time, as were the people who made them.

We can look at the show with new sensibilities today—Larson was from a privileged, middle-class, white background. His ability to get his writing seen and produced reflects this. We must acknowledge his privilege when we talk about Larson writing about Black experience, the LGBTQ experience, and the Latino experience. While he struggled in his career, he didn't face the same barriers that people of color, women, and the LGBTQ community faced. His middle-class standing also provided a safety net—Larson always had a family home to which he could return and a family with means to support him.

Of course, within the context, we can and should address things that do not sit quite right with our contemporary reading. Some of these are to be expected in how we read historical pieces on how information on HIV/AIDS is not to be taken as medical or current advice. The moment Larson was writing about (which was historic even as he wrote) has thankfully passed. Treatments, life expectancy, and prevention are much better informed and communicated and a world away from *Rent*. Similarly, attitudes to drug use or the depiction of it in *Rent* are perhaps slightly, if not glamourized, then glossed over.

The valid criticisms of the show include that Benny wasn't the villain we all were led to believe—he was a man doing his job, a man who made different life choices, and that's fine. There are gray areas in Angel's character and how today they would (should) have been better addressed. The queer characters aren't as robust and innovative as we would hope for today, from the "slutty bisexual" trope of Maureen to the fact the character who dies from AIDS is trans.

When we read this historic piece, the information on HIV/AIDS is not to be taken as medical or current advice. The moment Larson was writing about has thankfully passed, and treatments, life expectancy, and prevention is a world away from *Rent*. Attitudes toward drug use have also evolved. *Rent* is not a hard-hitting documentary on addiction. We see a very surface-level account of the impact on Roger and Mimi, but we don't see the medical, psychological, financial, or personal impact on others. All of these factors are glossed over when we look back from our contemporary view.

Rent seeks to represent a cross section of society in its cast, but does the show interrogate what this means? With our increased awareness of intersectionality, *Rent* does not measure up to a critical contemporary interrogation. We can clearly see that Larson wrote from the point of view of a white man. Like much of the show, it is well intentioned and informed, but we cannot neglect that it falls slightly short when we consider it now.

For all the non-white characters in the show, *Rent* glosses over the reality of 1990s New York for these characters. The everyday racism the characters would have been subject to isn't addressed in the show. Similarly, racism within the LGBTQ community is ignored—a phenomenon that Larson likely wouldn't have been aware of.

In 2021, of rebelling against society's expectations, as Collins does, is a contemporary idea. Collins's anarchy from within, his computer sabotage, and his use of education for anarchy could take place today. *Rent* rebels against the capitalist politics that have led to a particular situation. In the post-Trump America, or in a post-Brexit UK, Collins's anarchist politics at a grass roots level are current.

As we read *Rent* in its original form, Collins, who references AIDS activism group ACT UP, would have been one of the original members of the organization. It would be no surprise to see him in 2021 as one of the members. ACT UP actively supports those with HIV/AIDS and campaigns for various political causes. In 2020, ACT UP campaigned for action and research around COVID-19. It addressed government inaction and the disproportional impact on Black and other minority groups. Collins's alignment with ACT UP could be a chapter from contemporary history as much as 1990s politics.

More threads of the story continue to shift, but still resonate. Mark decides he cannot work for tabloid TV because he wants to make authentic work. The battle against tabloid press certainly hasn't gone away. If anything, it has amplified. The proliferation of clickbait articles and websites that rely on sensational stories has increased tenfold. As the Trump campaign in America illustrated, the "mainstream" media, sensationalism, and politics all have a lot to answer for. The idea of selling your soul when signing up for a job in media seems much more a reality today than in the nineties. With the proliferation of YouTubers, Instragrammers, and all-round digital influencers, we could see Mark choosing to make content his own way, sitting outside the mainstream and making a living that way. On one level, an "influencer" is possibly not quite what Larson envisioned for his rebellious filmmaker, but Mark was ahead of the curve with controlling his own voice and making his own films. The judgment on sensationalist media versus real stories is a very contemporary concern. How Mark remedies it—documentary filmmaker or YouTuber—is up for debate.

That said, Maureen would be very at home in "influencer" culture. Seeing her performance art via YouTube or Instagram, or even as a breakout TikTok star is apt for a version of Maureen in 2021. It's also a valuable lesson in the evolution of platforms for activism and art. Maureen's 1990s performance art, and what social media creators have done today, aren't that far apart. In 2020, art of all kinds went online, spurring innovation (and some disaster). If she wasn't already an online artist and influencer, a post-2020 Maureen would surely have pivoted to make best use of the largest audience.

Angel would also make use of social media, perhaps streaming their performances. With the shift toward mainstream with the rise of *RuPaul's Drag Race* and new platforms for drag artists, Angel was ahead of their time in their choice of bohemian performance—and imagine their embracing the benefits of the new world.

While these are simply speculations, we can read these characters in alignment with our contemporary ideas and situations and find a place they would fit into society and culture today. Nineties politics and attitudes toward work, capitalism, and art are part of how we get to where we are today. Roger didn't invent punk either, but he takes that sensibility into his work. Similarly, the characters Larson invented aren't the first to have the attitudes or beliefs we see onstage, and they still translate today. What started as looking like removed nostalgia for today's audiences have clear parallels once you unravel them a bit.

We can flip some of this as an element of the show's positive representation. While the more challenging areas of racism are glossed over, it is perhaps an element of "leading by example" that can be useful in art—the idea that if you show what an alternative to how the world looks might be, then it helps the world move toward that. So perhaps a young academic like Collins would have struggled to get to where he is, or Benny would even struggle in a white-dominated industry like New York real estate. Joanne, as a Black female lawyer, would certainly encounter racism. However, these are positive role model aspects of the characters. While they may be "naively" written, they also offer a question of "but what if"? These people exist, after all: people of color in academic roles, Black lawyers.

If we speculate what the politics of *Rent* characters might be in 2021, envision Collins as part of the Black Lives Matter movement (whether we think of him as written as Black or not) or Extinction Rebellion. We should see Collins, too, as part of ACT UP. As we read *Rent* in its original form, Collins would have been one of the original members of the organization—it would be no surprise to see him in 2021 as one of the members still going strong—ACT UP still being actively supporting not only those with HIV/AIDS but also campaigning for various political causes. In 2020, ACT UP campaigned for action and research around COVID-19; the organization spoke up about government inaction's disproportionate impact on Black and other ethnic minority groups. The politics of Collins's alignment with ACT UP feel like a chapter from contemporary history as much as 1990s politics.

A parallel impossible to ignore are the AIDS/COVID-19 elements. In some ways, the pandemics can't be compared: there was a moral panic around AIDS illustrated by the decisive inaction that informed government responses and the still deeply engrained prejudices around the illness. That said, there are some similarities: government inaction in the early days of COVID-19, mismanaged public health policies, disproportionate effects on certain ethnic and socioeconomic groups, and fearmongering and prejudice. The biggest parallel, however, was that for the first time in a generation, young people feared and witnessed death on a grand scale.

Rent, along with other AIDS plays/musicals/films, has seemed slightly remote to anyone who didn't live through it. For people in their twenties and thirties, the idea of their peers being at risk of death was not prevalent for much of the late 1990s and 2000s. But in 2020, it once again became a possibility. Even if COVID-19 began in other countries and older demographics, it quickly and tragically affected all ages and populations. For the first time in a generation, young people faced the reality of losing people their own age. By 2021, very few people were unaffected by COVID-19 losses.

Unexpectedly and tragically, *Rent* has a contemporary, emotional resonance again. The sense of societal loss, the feeling of fear hanging over a community, grief and how you process it, facing loss with dignity, and continuing to love in the face of multiple losses and fear are all relevant themes again. During these times, community members cling to one another. Although many people were physically apart during 2020, there was—and still is—a strong need for community within the grief.

Rent has always connected with people individually when they experience loss at whatever point in life, but especially perhaps when it happens to young people. Individuals bond with the show—someone discovering it after a parent dies, for example, or finding comfort in it with the tragic early death of a friend. Post-2020 *Rent*, collectively, hits differently because of that collective sense and awareness of loss.

Alongside that, the collective anger fueled by COVID-19 (but certainly amplified by it), is reminiscent of many of the activist movements of the 1980s and 1990s that supported LGBTQ rights, AIDS awareness, and, the civil rights and women's rights movements before that. For a while there was a lull in large-scale grassroots activism but a combination of the political climate, the impact of the pandemic, and a growing awareness supported by online discussion and activism led to a resurgence. So while the politics of *Rent* might not be something at its forefront for audiences, that sense of standing up for a community, of protest, that thread running through the show, feels suddenly fresh again.

External factors aside, there is something to be said for simply discovering *Rent* fresh. So yes, while some elements might have rung true, hit deeper, and felt suddenly relevant again, there is the simple fact that *Rent* has had enduring appeal as a musical.

While *Rent* is a period piece for many, it is relatively new as a piece of musical theater. When we consider the "classic" revivals that still take up space on Broadway and in the West End, they are of the Rodgers and Hammerstein era, the early Sondheim era, and the occasional Andrew Lloyd Webber eras. Their sound is distinctive—as it should be to their era, not just of musical theater but to the broader era of music in which they sit. But *Rent's* fusing of pop-rock with classic musical scores has not gone out of style—instead, it continues to evolve and be part of Broadway's contemporary sound. Thus, shows from *Spring Awakening* to *Be More Chill* are part of *Rent's* legacy. The sound of Broadway changed in the years following *Rent*. This isn't to say everything became exclusively rock-music centered. Many new works stuck to more traditional styles and became hits in their own right, but the rock-musical endured. Despite the music *Rent* draws on going "out of fashion," the fusing of pop-rock with musical theater remains firmly in style for musicals trying to appeal to a younger demographic. A cursory look at some of the musicals aimed at younger audiences during the 2020 season which was cut short due to the pandemic suggests as much: *Moulin Rouge* (which uses existing pop songs rewritten and updated from the popular songs in the film to reflect contemporary tastes), *The Prom* (original music with a pop-feel), *Be More Chill* (similarly pop-rock), and *Six* (pop concert style retelling of the wives of Henry VIII which uses direct influences from specific pop divas). *Rent* is still very much *in*, and on hearing the songs, audiences are likely to be excited and inspired rather than finding it dated.

Conclusion

Why Rent *Matters*

The story of *Rent* is theatrical legend by now. Even those who don't know *Rent* likely know something or someone influenced by it; whether it's their favorite composer, actor, or musical, someone's life was altered by the musical.

If it sounds a bit romantic, it's probably because it is. *Rent* is romanticized because of the story we start with—Jonathan Larson's rise and the tragedy of his death. Larson became the touchstone of what being a young musical theater artist could entail. And as with many a tragedy, his death cemented the legend.

But as argued in this book, you don't get to be "the musical that defined a generation" with *just* a headline-grabbing story. A good story sells tickets, but it doesn't win a Pulitzer Prize. More importantly perhaps, a good story didn't sell over a decade's worth of tickets on Broadway. What sustained *Rent* was the power of the musical itself.

Larson managed what the brilliant musical theater writers of every generation do—he hit on the formula that appealed to new audiences.

Larson did what Miranda would do a generation later and found that alchemy of musical theater and contemporary sound. He then found the story that goes with that, as did Miranda, who was himself inspired by Larson.

Rent is a story about family and love. Like all great Broadway stories, this endures. *Rent* packaged it up and told it in the voice of the generation nobody was talking to. Nobody was telling the stories that mattered to the teens and the twentysomethings in musicals. Now, we're spoiled for choice with Broadway musicals for younger audiences from *Hamilton* to *Mean Girls* or *The Prom*. The list goes on and on, changing year after year like a revolving door of musicals that sound like music a teenager wants to listen to and has stories they can relate to.

Rent wove its way into the lives of fans beyond that moment in their teens or twenties when they fell in love with it. Whether that was on the street outside the Nederlander, or in their school auditorium, or in a theater on the other side of the world, hearing Larson's words in their own language captured hearts of audiences and performers.

Rent is a show that finds people when they need it. It's a show that maybe, if you don't *need* it when you first see it, you never fully understand it in the way people who need it do. For all the moments of "I didn't know people who looked like me could do that" onstage, there's also the stories of love, loss, and grief that this show walked through with fans. It is the catharsis of feeling a loss so fully that only a musical can facilitate. It is the relief and love of seeing queer people onstage and thinking, "That's me." It is watching the musical to escape painful moments in their lives. It is remembering the people lost. *Rent* has so many individual stories beyond the legend of Larson and how it got to Broadway. This is why *Rent* matters, twenty-five years on.

HOW DO YOU MEASURE A LIFETIME IN *RENT*?

Most musical theater kids have a *Rent* story. Everyone who loves it—who *really* loves it—has their reasons why. I'm no different. I came late to musical theater. Aside from Andrew Lloyd Webber chart toppers of the 1990s, musicals were not part of my world. But when I discovered *Rent* in college, it immediately became the center of my musical theater universe.

I bought the double-CD set of *Rent* at Indigo in Montreal. I first listened to it perched on a crowded bus traveling down Sherbrooke trying to unsuccessfully stop my portable CD player from skipping. I spent months listening to that CD, cracking the case, scratching it on my tiny CD player and listening through laptop speakers. I was living thousands of miles from home for college, and my father died that Thanksgiving. No wonder a tale of love and loss captured my young heart.

We all have that moment when we knew this was part of our hearts. December 26, 2005 (you don't know how much I wish it was December 24), I saw *Rent* for the second time. I sat in the balcony, having convinced my mum to buy a second set of tickets that morning. Midway through "Will I?" something cracked open. In the theater, I cried like I never had before. It was then that I knew I was connected to the show forever.

My sense of *Rent* imposter syndrome is rife. I live on the wrong side of the world to be hanging around the Nederlander stage door, though I did manage it once. I lived in a country with a notoriously checkered past with producing this musical I loved. But I devoured content about it, living vicariously through the internet message boards. They were my window to Broadway and the world of *Rent*.

Rent wasn't my first Broadway musical (that honor goes to Hugh Jackman and *The Boy from Oz*, incidentally another musical about AIDS), but it was the musical that made me a Broadway nerd. It's the musical that made me dive deeper, follow actors, and seek out their shows. I might never have ventured beyond the TKTS booth if it wasn't for *Rent*. Instead, I've found myself in basement rooms for concerts, traveling continents to see performers, and driving the length of the country to see the musical that started it all.

I didn't know I needed *Rent* until much later. I'd never seen two men dance together or two women kiss before *Rent*. I'd never seen queer women happy in a story. I'd never seen queer women being kick-ass and brilliant and belting out a song that would be the soundtrack to my twenties. I had never seen a community that accepted queer people like the one Larson created onstage. I still see it on occasion, and because of this, *Rent* feels like coming "home."

I went on to create a career around my love for this show. I spent four years writing a PhD on *Rent*, defending my work every step of the way against supervisors who thought a musical wasn't worthy and others at conferences who thought a musical couldn't be used to talk about AIDS. Even when it was done, the section of my thesis about *Rent* was always taken less seriously than the section about *Angels in America*. I stand by what I said for all those years: *Angels in America* is my head, but *Rent* is my heart.

My relationship with *Rent* is now very much like that of a sibling. I bicker with it (sometimes out loud). I know all its faults and can point them out at length, but I won't stand for anyone else coming for it. I know *Rent* is flawed and that it doesn't stand up to our twenty-first-century analysis. But that doesn't mean I don't love it with my whole heart still. It gave us the generation of Broadway performers that passed through its doors and the generation of people who love Broadway. *Rent* raised us as a generation of theater nerds, and so much more.

Most musical theater kids have a *Rent* story. Everyone who loves it, who loves it, has their reasons why. For me, it was being a twenty-year-old on the bus desperately trying to get my CD Walkman to play "What You Own" without it skipping. Then it was Boxing Day—you don't know how much I wish it was Christmas Eve—two months after my father died, sobbing like I never had before, and rarely have since, at a musical that felt like it reached out and fixed something in me. Look, it hardly takes a lot of work to figure out that, yes, a queer musical theater–loving teen loved *Rent*. But there was something about being part of a generation that "the musical that defined a generation" changed, that stayed with us all. And *Tick, Tick . . . Boom!* became part of that generation—and that the original cast album of *Tick* show is engrained not only in my mind, but deep in my soul. More so even than *Rent*, perhaps. I learned everything I know about being a writer from Jonathan Larson and these songs. They are a part of me in a way that so few pieces of art are. They taught me about love when it was an abstract concept, and they taught me about being a writer before I was one. And I know instinctively I'm not the only one who feels this way.

Tick, Tick . . . Boom! occupies a particular place for the now thirty-somethings of musical theater. In the early 2000s, it was part of a subset, not quite yet one of the "classics," not one of the big hitters, though we found our way there through *Rent,* of course. When we discovered *Rent*, we also discovered alternative musical theater. It was the era of Sh-K-Boom records, of Sherie Rene Scott, and Norbert Leo Butz in *The Last Five Years*. It was *Songs for a New World* and *I Love You Because*.

Later it was *See What I Wanna See* because Idina was in it. It was what-ever mix and match of those off-Broadway musicals you discussed on BroadwayWorld, or with your college friends. It was belting out "Come to Your Senses" or attempting to duet "Therapy" when you'd exhausted "Take Me or Leave Me." It was crying along with "Louder than Words" in your bedroom and dreaming of doing what Jonathan did.

Tick, Tick . . . Boom! has always been a life raft in a different way than *Rent*. For me, for most of us, *Rent* is a place for the big feelings, the love, the loss of our teens and twenties, and beyond. It's about finding yourself. *Tick, Tick . . . Boom!* is always been about something far more frightening: daring to dream.

It raised us. It was our beacon of "you can do this too."

I don't feel I would be the person I am without Jonathan Larson. I wouldn't be the writer I am; I know that. We all have our Holy Trinities of people who make us write but, more importantly, keep us writing. For me, Larson is the core of that. He showed me stories that moved me in ways I didn't understand then and gave me language for experi-ences I didn't have words for. He gave me a style to emulate. And in a world where I am often "too much" or "too sentimental" or "not edgy enough" for theater, I look to Larson with his openhearted sincerity and conviction to write the stories he knew he had to, and I say over and over again, "that's who I want to write like." What Miranda gave us in *Tick, Tick . . . Boom!* is the man behind that and a reminder to write your stories, to make your art, however difficult it might be.

Larson gave me my love of Broadway—of musicals, yes—but also a particular love affair with New York theater that endures even now. The years of traveling across the Atlantic to seek out obscure shows, often purely because they had some connection to someone who was once in *Rent*, raised me as a baby theater nerd. The shows my love of *Rent* led me to shape my love of theater and my life.

My love of Larson's work led me to write a PhD. My whole career and life as it looks now are literally because of Larson's work.

With *Tick, Tick . . . Boom!* Larson gave me the words to be a writer. I first saw it live the summer I moved to London to do my master's in theater. That moment of, "Yes, I'm going to jump in, I'm going to live this dream." But also now, as someone who has not only passed the *Tick, Tick . . . Boom!* moment of turning thirty, but also passed the age Larson was when he died, there's a question too of "Have I done enough?" but also the affirming nature of keeping going, of "cages or wings?"

I've watched everyone around my age do versions of Michael or Susan. Chasing the different dreams of security, family, and the "right time" to do things while I feel perpetually stranded between "Johnny Can't Decide," the "compromise or preserve" moments, and "Why," and thinking "I want to spend my life this way," always circling back to, "How do you know when it's time to let go?" The lyrics of "Johnny Can't Decide," are both burned into my consciousness and ripped from my diary. That desperate need to create, do what you feel you are here to do, and deal with the push-pull of "Real Life."

More than ever lately, I've found myself retreating into Larson's words, not *Rent*, but in *Tick, Tick . . . Boom!* And for those times, I get to think, "Hey, what a way to spend a day," having spent large portions of my time writing. In times of doubt, I remind myself, as Jonathan made that vow, "I'm gonna spend my life this way." Because one thing we all took from Larson's life was his tragic, untimely death and the reminder that maybe we should lean into our art, whatever gifts we might have there, just in case there's not that much time left.

In August 2021, I drove four hours to see *Rent* again at the Hope Mill Theatre with theater friends, the online friends we all made back in the days of *Rent* in the 1990s. I sat with one of my best friends (whom I wouldn't know without musical theater). We had been apart for a year and a half thanks to another pandemic. During "I'll Cover You (Reprise)," something cracked open again, and I sobbed on my friend's shoulder as I had only done once before.

Larson gave me my love of Broadway and New York theater that endures even now. The years of traveling there, seeking out obscure shows because they had a connection to someone who was once in *Rent*, raised me as a baby theater nerd. Jonathan Larson was the foundation of my love for theater, and he made me a writer.

Yes, *Rent* was the future of musical theater, but more importantly, Jonathan Larson was the foundation of our love for theater, and for so many of us, he made us writers.

How do you measure a lifetime in *Rent*? How about 525,600 little connections, moments of beauty, people, songs, shows—and love?

The little show that took over the world gave me, time and time again, something to cling to when I needed it most.

Rent gave me a creator and artist to look up to, who helped shape my life and work.

Thank you, Jonathan Larson.

Appendix

MUSICAL NUMBERS

Act 1

"Tune Up #1" — Mark and Roger

"Voice Mail #1" — Mark's Mother

"Tune Up #2" — Mark, Roger, Collins, and Benny

"Rent" — Mark, Roger, Benny, Collins, Joanne, and Company

"You Okay, Honey?" — Preachers, Angel, and Collins

"Tune Up #3" — Mark and Roger

"One Song Glory" — Roger

"Light My Candle" — Mimi and Roger

"Voice Mail #2" — Mr. and Mrs. Jefferson

"Today 4 U" — Collins, Roger, Mark, and Angel

"You'll See" — Benny, Mark, Roger, Collins, and Angel

"Tango: Maureen" — Joanne and Mark

"Life Support" — Gordon, Paul, Mark, and Company

"Out Tonight" — Mimi

"Another Day" — Mimi, Roger, and Company

"Will I?" — Steve and Company

"On the Street" — Preachers, Squeegee Man, Mark, Collins, Angel, and Homeless Woman

"Santa Fe" — Collins, Angel, Mark, and Company

"I'll Cover You" — Angel and Collins

"We're Okay" — Joanne

"Christmas Bells" — Company

"Over the Moon" — Maureen

"La Vie Bohème A" — Mark, Waiter, Roger, Benny, Mimi, Collins, Angel, Maureen, Joanne, Mr. Grey, and Company

"I Should Tell You" — Mimi and Roger

"La Vie Bohème B" — Maureen, Collins, Joanne, Mark, Angel, and Company

Act 2

"Seasons of Love A" — Company

"Happy New Year A" — Mark, Roger, Mimi, Collins, Angel, Maureen, and Joanne

"Voice Mail #3" — Mark's Mother and Alexi Darling

"Happy New Year B" — Mark, Roger, Mimi, Collins, Angel, Maureen, Joanne, and Benny

"Take Me or Leave Me" — Maureen and Joanne

"Seasons of Love B" — Company

"Without You" — Roger and Mimi

"Voice Mail #4" — Alexi Darling

APPENDIX

"Contact" — Angel and Company

"I'll Cover You" (Reprise) — Collins and Company

"Halloween" — Mark

"Goodbye Love" — Mark, Roger, Mimi, Collins, Maureen, Joanne, and Benny

"What You Own" — Roger and Mark

"Voice Mail #5" — Roger's Mother, Mimi's Mother, Mr. Jefferson, and Mark's Mother

"Finale A" — Preachers, Mark, Roger, Collins, Maureen, Joanne, and Mimi

"Your Eyes" — Roger

"Finale B" — Company

CHARACTERS

Mark Cohen: A struggling filmmaker and the narrator of the show. He is Roger's and Collins's roommate until Collins moves out; he is also Maureen's ex-boyfriend.

Roger Davis: A once successful but now struggling musician who is HIV positive and an ex-junkie. His girlfriend, April, killed herself after discovering out that she was HIV positive. He is roommates with Mark.

Mimi Márquez: A club dancer and drug addict. She lives downstairs from Mark and Roger. She is Roger's love interest, and like him, she has HIV. She is also Benny's ex-lover.

Tom Collins: Mark and Roger's former roommate and a professor. He has AIDS, is described as an "anarchist," and now dreams of opening his own restaurant. He meets Angel when he is beaten up on the street corner in front of Mark and Roger's apartment, and they form a relationship.

Angel Dumott Schunard: A young drag queen and street performer with AIDS. Collins's love interest.

Maureen Johnson: Mark's ex-girlfriend and Joanne's current girlfriend. A performance artist who stages a protest-performance.

Joanne Jefferson: Maureen's girlfriend, an Ivy League–educated public interest lawyer. Joanne has very politically powerful parents (one is undergoing confirmation to be a judge, the other is a government official).

Benjamin "Benny" Coffin III: Former friend and roommate of Mark and Roger; he is the owner of the building. He is also Mimi's ex-lover.

AWARDS

1995: Outer Critics Award, Best Musical (Off Broadway).

1995: Obie Award: Outstanding Book, Outstanding Lyrics, Outstanding Music.

1996: Tony Award, Best Musical, Best Book of a Musical, Best Original Score.

1996: Drama Desk Award, Outstanding Book of a Musical, Outstanding Music, Outstanding Lyrics.

1996: Drama Critics Circle Award, Best Musical.

1996: Pulitzer Prize, Drama.

TIME LINE

1996, New York Theatre Workshop, directed by Michael Greif.

1996, Nederlander Theatre, New York, directed by Michael Greif.

1996, National Tour "Angel Leg," USA, directed by Michael Greif.

1997, National Tour "Benny Leg," directed by Michael Greif.

1998, London, Shaftesbury Theatre, directed by Michael Greif.

1999, Australian Tour (beginning in Sydney)

2001, British tour.

December 4, 2001, to January 6, 2002, Prince of Wales Theatre, London (final leg of British tour)

2002, Swedish premiere, the Göteborg Opera in Gothenburg, Sweden.

2002, British tour.

December 6, 2002, to March 1, 2003, Prince of Wales Theatre, London (final leg of British tour)

2005 to 2008, American tours running concurrently across the country.

2005, *Rent* film release.

2005–2006 International tour started in Singapore and included Hong Kong, Beijing, Shanghai, Wuhan, Seoul, Taipei, Tokyo, Bangkok, Amsterdam, Rotterdam, Brussels, Antwerp, Barcelona, Madrid, Stockholm, Reykjavik, Oslo, Helsinki, Copenhagen, Cape Town, Johannesburg, St. Petersburg, and Moscow, Budapest.

2006, Manchester Palace Theatre.

2006, 10th Anniversary Concert, Nederlander Theatre.

2007, *Rent: Remixed*, Duke of York's Theatre, London.

2008, Closing performance Broadway.

2008, Manchester Palace Theatre, "Goodbye Performance."

2009–2010, American tour featuring original cast members Anthony Rapp and Adam Pascal. Tour stops included Los Angeles, Seattle, Costa Mesa, Toronto, Phoenix, Sacramento, Orlando, Miami, St. Louis, Milwaukee, Chicago, Des Moines, Cincinnati, Pittsburgh, Norfolk, and Houston.

2010, Hollywood Bowl Production, directed by *Rent* alumnus Neil Patrick Harris, two days of concert-format performance at the Hollywood Bowl.

2010, Hollywood High School, the first high school in America to perform *Rent*.

2011 Off-Broadway revival, New World Stages, New York, directed by Michael Greif.

2012, American Theater Company, Chicago.

2013, *Rent in Concert*, UK tour, a concert-staging version of the musical toured mid-sized concert halls across Britain.

2013, Greenwich Theatre, London.

2013, Tabard Theatre, London.

2013, Royal Welsh College of Music and Drama, the first use of *Rent* as a professional production staged in a university environment.

2014, New York City Center *Tick, Tick . . . Boom!* (starring Lin-Manuel Miranda, Leslie Odom Jr., and Karen Olivo)

2014, Melbourne, Australia.

2014, *Rent in Concert*, UK tour. The 2013 tour restaged with some casting changes.

2016, Off-Broadway revival of *Tick, Tick . . . Boom!*

2017, 20th Anniversary Tour (UK).

2019, *Rent: LIVE* (FOX network TV)

2021, NYTW Online 25th Anniversary Tribute.

2020/21, Hope Mill Theatre (Manchester).

2021, "Farewell" US tour.

2021, *Tick, Tick . . . Boom!* film released (Netflix); directed by Lin-Manuel Miranda.

These productions represent an overview of significant productions; current licensing is owned by Music Theatre International, who also holds the license for the school's edition.

Since the closure of the Broadway version and the end of the national tours, license in America is granted to professional and amateur productions wishing to stage *Rent*. In Britain, following the final tour in 2007, and the amended version in *Rent: Remixed*, the license to perform *Rent* has been bought by a variety of smaller theater companies, including the touring version and some key productions listed above.

JONATHAN LARSON PLAYS AND WRITINGS

Plays (as Writer/Composer)

A Darker Purpose, Naked Angels Theater, New York City, 1991 (Composer)

A Midsummer Night's Dream, New Jersey Shakespeare Festival, Drew University, Madison, 1991 (Composer)

Superbia, Playwrights Horizons Theater, New York City, n.d. (Writer/Composer)

Rent, New York Theatre Workshop, New York City, 1994, 1996 (Playwright, Composer, and Lyricist)

Rent, Nederlander Theatre, New York, 1996 (Writer/Composer)

J. P. Morgan Saves the Nation, New York City production, 1995 (Composer)

Tick, Tick . . . BOOM! New York Theater Workshop (Writer/Composer)

Other

Sesame Street, PBS, Various dates 1990s (Composer/Lyricist)

Away We Go! PBS, 1996.

An American Tail (Composer, book on tape), n.d.

Land Before Time (Composer, book on tape), n.d.

References

Adler, Steven. *Space in Performance: Making Meaning in the Theatre*. Ann Arbor: University of Michigan Press, 1999, p. 38.

———. *On Broadway: Art and Commerce on the Great White Way*. Carbondale: Southern Illinois University Press, 2004. Chapter 5, note.

Baker, W. *Then and Now*. Program for *Rent: Remixed*, 2006.

Barthes, Roland. *Image-Music-Text*, translated and edited by Stephen Heath. New York: Hill & Wang, 1978.

Bennett, Susan. *Performing Nostalgia: Shifting Shakespeare and the Contemporary Past*. New York: Routledge, 1996.

———. *Theatre Audiences: A Theory of Production and Reception*. Second edition. London: Routledge, 1997.

Carlson, Marvin. *Theatre Semiotics Signs of Life*. Bloomington and Indianapolis: Indiana University Press, 1990.

———. *The Haunted Stage: The Theatre as a Memory Machine*. Ann Arbor: University of Michigan Press, 2003.

Carter, Erica, and Simon Watney, eds. *Taking Liberties: AIDS and Cultural Politics*. London: Serpent's Tail, 1989.

Cline, Rob. "Jonathan Larson's Celebration of Life Keeps *Rent* Soaring."
Rent Performance Program. Iowa City: University of Iowa, n.d.

Clum, John M. *Still Acting Gay: Male Homosexuality in Modern Drama.*
New York: St. Martin's, 2000.

Crimp, Douglas, ed. *AIDS: Cultural Analysis/Cultural Activism.*
Cambridge: MIT Press, 1988.

De Jongh, N. *Not in Front of the Audience: Homosexuality on Stage.*
London: Routledge, 1992.

Derrida, Jacques. *Specters of Marx.* New York: Routledge, 1994.

Gould, Deborah. B. *Moving Politics, Emotion and ACT UP's Fight
against AIDs.* Chicago: University of Chicago Press, 2009.

Hills, Matt. *Fan Cultures.* London: Routledge, 2002.

Hodges, Ben, and Scott Denny. *On Broadway: From Rent to Revolution.*
New York: Rizzoli, 2016.

Hoffman, Victoria Leacock. "Rent Is Real." In *Rent: The Complete Book
and Lyrics of the Broadway Musical.* New York: Applause Theatre &
Cinema Books, 2008.

Hutcheon, Linda. *A Theory of Adaptation.* London: Routledge, 1988.

Jones, Therese, ed. *Sharing the Delirium: Second Generation AIDS Plays
and Performances.* Portsmouth, NH: Heinemann, 1994.

Kenrick, John. *Musical Theatre: A History.* London: Bloomsbury
Publishing, 2010.

Kirle, Bruce. *Unfinished Business: Broadway Musicals as Works in
Progress.* First edition. Carbondale: Southern Illinois University
Press, 2005.

Kramer, Larry. *Faggots.* New York: Random House, 1978.

———. *Reports from the Holocaust.* New York: St. Martin's Press, 1989.

Larson, Jonathan. *Rent by Jonathan Larson.* Interviews and text by Evelyn McDonnell with Katherine Silberger. New York: Rob Weisbach Books, 1997.

———. *Rent: The Complete Book and Lyrics for the Broadway Musical.* New York: Applause Theatre & Cinema Books, 2008.

———. *Tick, Tick . . . Boom!: The Complete Book and Lyrics.* New York: Applause Theatre & Cinema Books. 2009.

Lipsky, David. *The Creation of Rent.* Booklet distributed at the Nederlander Theatre, 1996.

McAuley, Gay. *Space in Performance: Making Meaning in the Theatre.* Ann Arbor: University of Michigan Press, 1999, p. 3.

Miller, J. Hillis. "Narrative." In Frank Letricchia and Thomas McLaughlin, eds., *Critical Terms for Literary Study.* Chicago: University of Chicago Press, 1995.

Murger, Henri. *Scènes de la vie de bohème.* FQ Classics (1851) 2007.

Panceo, Robert. "AIDS Activism and Sex in the Nineties." In *Tony Kushner in Conversation*, edited by Robert Vorlicky. Ann Arbor: University of Michigan Press, 1998.

Postlewait, Thomas, and Bruce A. McConachie, eds. *Interpreting the Theatrical Past: Essays in the Historiography of Performance.* Iowa City: University of Iowa Press, 1989.

Prince, Hal. *A Sense of Occasion.* Applause Books, 2017.

Rapp, Anthony. *Without You: A Memoir of Love, Loss, and the Musical Rent.* New York: Simon & Schuster, 2006.

Román, David. *Acts of Intervention.* Bloomington: Indiana University Press, 1998.

———. *Performance in America Contemporary U.S. Culture and the Performing Arts.* Durham, NC: Duke University Press, 2005.

Rowan, Tom. *Rent FAQ: All That's Left to Know about Broadway's Blaze of Glory.* Montclair, NJ: Applause, 2017.

Savran, David. "Rent's Due: Multiculturalism and the Spectacle of Difference." *Journal of American Drama and Theatre* 14 (Winter 2002).

Schulman, Sarah. *Stagestruck: Theater, AIDS, and the Marketing of Gay America.* Durham, NC: Duke University Press, 1998.

Sontag, Susan. *AIDS and Its Metaphors.* New York: Penguin, 1991.

———. *Illness as Metaphor.* New York: Farrar, Straus and Giroux. 1978.

Stempel, Larry. *Showtime: A History of the Broadway Musical Theater.* New York: W.W. Norton & Company, 2010.

Sutrken, Marita. *Tangled Memories: The Vietnam War, the AIDS Epidemic, and the Politics of Remembering.* Oakland: University of California Press, 1997.

Viertel, Jack. *The Secret Life of the American Musical: How Broadway Shows Are Built.* New York: Farrar, Straus and Giroux. 2016.

Vigas, Robert, and Louis Botto. *At This Theatre: 110 Years of Broadway Shows, Stories, and Stars.* New York: Applause Theatre & Cinema Books. 2010.

Wollman, Elizabeth L. *The Theater Will Rock: A History of the Rock Musical from* Hair *to* Hedwig. Ann Arbor: University of Michigan Press, 2006.

ARTICLES

Altman, Lawrence K. "Rare Cancer Seen in 41 Homosexuals." *New York Times,* July 3, 1981.

Barton, Matt. "*Rent* at the Hope Mill Theatre—Review." WhatsOnStage, August 9, 2021.

Benedict, David. "The American Musical Comes of Age." *Independent on Sunday*, April 19, 1998.

———. "Theatre: How the Wild West End Will Be Won. 'Rent' Has Reinvented the Musical on Broadway. Can an HIV Rock Opera Do the Same Here?" *Independent*, May 5, 1998.

———. "Rent Review" *Guardian*. October 16, 2007.

Berson, Misha. "'Rent' Holds Up Well in Tour at Paramount, with Refreshed Staging, Impressive Music." Entertainment. *The Seattle Times*, June 17, 2009.

Billington, Michael. "Rent Review" *Guardian*. May 14, 1998.

———. "Synthetic Makeover Robs Rent of Its Roots: *Rent*, Duke of York's Theatre." *Guardian*. (London), October 16, 2007.

Blumenthal, Ralph. "Calling All Unsung Superstars: 'Rent' Needs Singers." *New York Times*, July 13, 1996.

Brantley, B. "Rent Review." *New York Times*. February 19, 1996.

———. "Theatre Review: Rock Opera a la 'Bohème' and 'Hair.'" *New York Times*. February 14, 1996.

———. "Theatre Review: Enter Singing: Young Hopeful and Taking on the Big Time." *New York Times*, April 30, 1996.

———. "Soul Searching at the Milestone Age of 30" *New York Times*, June 14, 2001.

———. "Didn't We Just See This Revolution?" Theater Review: *Les Misérables*. *New York Times*, November 10, 2006. https://www.nytimes.com/2006/11/10/theater/reviews/10mise.html?searchResultPosition=1.

REFERENCES

———. "That Ragtag Bohemian Army Returns." *New York Times* August 11, 2011.

Butler, Robert. "Rent Review." *Observer*, May 17, 1998.

———. "Bohemian Travesty." *Independent on Sunday*. May 17, 1998.

Cavendish, Dominic. "Rent's Rousing Return." *Daily Telegraph*. December 11, 2001.

Chadderton, David. "Rent." British Theatre Guide, 2021.

Clapp, Susannah. "Rent Review." *Evening Standard*. March 13, 1998.

Coles, Joanna. "Author! Author? It Could Be a Storyline of fiction: Struggling Young Writer-Composter Dies on the Eve of Phenomenal Success." *Guardian* (London), March 15, 1998.

Cox, Chris. "Anthony Rapp: *Without You*." Theatre Review. *Huffington Post*, November 6, 2012.

Cushman, Robert. "*Without You*, Anthony Rapp's *Rent* Memorial Doesn't Hit Home." Theater. *National Post*, December 22, 2012.

De Jongh, Nicholas. "Rent Review" *Evening Standard*, London, March 15, 1998.

———. "Fear-Stained Laments in a Musical That Still Hooks." *Evening Standard*, December 6, 2001.

Dziemianowicz, Joe. "Rent Review: Classic Broadway Production Has All the Talent of the Original but Less Emotional Pull." *New York Daily News*, August 12, 2011.

Ebert, Roger. *Rent* (review). *Chicago Sun-Times*, November 22, 2005.

Edwardes, Jane. "Rent Review." *Time Out London*, May 20, 1998.

Fanshawe, Simon. "The American Musical Comes of Age." *Independent Sunday*. April 19, 1998.

Feingold, Michael, "Review: Rent." *The Village Voice*, May 18, 1993.

Fienberg, Daniel. "Fox's 'Rent': TV Review." *The Hollywood Reporter*, January 27, 2019.

Fricker, Karen. "Review: Rent Remixed." *Variety*, October 16, 2007.

Friedlander, Mira. "Review: Rent." *Variety*, January 4, 1998.

Framke, Caroline. "Why *Rent* Feels So Outdated 20 Years after Its Debut." Vox, April 29, 2016.

Gardner, Lyn. "Review: Theatre Rent*" The Guardian*, December 7, 2001.

Gates, Anita. "Evoking Triumph and Tragedy in the 90s." *New York Times*, September 18, 2009.

Gerard, Jeremy. "Review: Rent." *Variety*, February 19, 1996.

Golder, Andy. "Don't Watch 'Rent' as an Adult or You'll Realize How Annoying It Is." BuzzFeed, January 26, 2016.

Gritten, David. "Rent Review." *Daily Telegraph*, May 5, 1998.

———. "Rent Is Due but Will We Pay Up?" *Telegraph*. May 9, 1998.

Gussow, Mel. "Jonathan Larson, 35, Composer of Rock Opera and Musicals" *New York Times*. January 26, 1996.

Harris, Aisha. "*Rent Live* Review: How Do You Measure a Show You Were Never Meant to See?" *New York Times*, January 28, 2019.

Isherwood, Charles. "Review: Rent" *Variety*. July 15, 1997.

———. "Review: Rent" *Variety*. September 30, 1997.

———. "Review: Tick Tick . . . Boom!" *Variety*. July 13, 2001.

———. "525,600 Minutes to Preserve." *New York Times*. September 17, 2008.

———. "A Creator and His Doubts." *New York Times*. June 24, 2014.

Istel, John. "Jonathan Larson Talks about His Writing Process and Making 'Rent.'" *American Theatre*, July/August, 1996.

———. "Rent Check: Did Jonathan Larson's Vision Get Lost in the Media Uproar?" *American Theatre*, July/August, 1996.

Lahr, Jon. "Hello and Goodbye: Jonathan Larson's Rent Tries to Update the Musical." *New Yorker*, February 19. 1996.

Macaulay, Alistair. *Rent Review, The Financial Times* (London), May 4, 1998.

Marlowe, S. "Funky Makeover That Fails to Paper over the Flaws—Rent." *The Times* (London), October 17, 2007.

Maxwell, Dominic. "Theatre: Rent at the St. James Theatre, SW1." *London Times*, December 16, 2016.

Mayo, Douglas. "The Jonathan Larson Project." Music | Reviews. BritishTheatre.com, April 23, 2019.

Milzoff, Rebecca. "Rent: The Oral History." *New York*, May 2, 2016.

Miranda, Lin-Manuel. "Pushing the Muse against the Clock." *New York Times*, June 19, 2014.

Moynihan, Caitlin. "Jeremy Jordan on His *Rent* dream and Long *Little Shop* Intermission." Broadway.com, April 13, 2020.

Murray, Matthew. "Rent." Off Broadway Reviews. Talkin' Broadway, August 8, 2011.

Musical Theatre Review. "Rent—Hope Mill Theatre, Manchester." Admin, August 9, 2021.

Nightingale, Benedict. "Sympathy Missing for Long-Distance Runner—First Night Review." *The Times* (London), May 13, 1998.

———. "Mimi's Cult of Bit of Rough-Arts." *The Times*, May 14, 1998.

Nisbet, Ian. "Transposition in Jonathan Larson's Rent," *Studies in Musical Theater* 5, no. 3, 2011.

Otterman, Sharon. "As Rent Ends 12-Year Run, a Gathering of Fans Overflows with Emotion." *New York Times*, September 6, 2008.

Paceho, Patrick. "Life, Death, and Rent." *Los Angeles Times*, April 14, 1996.

———. "Many Are Called But Few Will Be Chosen for 'Rent'" *Los Angeles Times*, July 18, 1996.

Pasorke, Whiney. "Rent: The Cast Looks Back." *Entertainment Weekly*, April 10, 2008.

Pastorek, Whitney. "Rent Review." *Entertainment Weekly*, August 7, 2010.

Peter, John. "So Caring, Sharing and Wearing." *Sunday Times*, May 17, 1998.

Pierce, Jerald. "First Big Touring Musical Back in Chicago? 'Rent'—Including Cast Members on Return Visits." *Chicago Tribune*, September 30, 2021.

Portantier, Michel. "Rent Stablization." *Playbill*, May 1996.

Pulver, Andrew. "Rent Review." *The Guardian*, April 7, 2006.

Rich, Frank. "Journal: East Village Story." *New York Times*. March 2, 1996.

Rickwald, Bethany. "How David Auburn Rescued *Tick, Tick . . . Boom!* from Desk Drawer Obsurity." TheaterMania, October 5, 2016.

Riedel, Michael. "Every Day a 'Rent' Party: Hardcore Fans of the Hit musical Form a Squatters Camp at the Box Office." *New York Daily News*, March, 3 1997.

Robertson, Campbell. "Bohemia Takes Its Final Bows." *New York Times*, July 13, 2008.

Romano, Aja. "How do You Measure 20 Years of *Rent* Backlash?" Vox, April 29, 2016.

REFERENCES

Romano, Nick. "The Prom Celebrates 'First LGBTQ Kiss' in Macy's Thanksgiving Day Parade History." Yahoo!News. November 22, 2018.

Rooney, David. "Review: Rent." *Variety*, November 19, 2005.

Shuttleworth, Ian. "Theatre, Rent." *The Financial Times* (London), October 17, 2007.

Siede, Caroline. "A Not-Quite-Live *Rent* Is a Lovingly Imperfect Celebration of a Lovingly Imperfect Musical." AV Club, January 28, 2019.

Sierz, Alex. "Rent Review." *Tribune*, May 29. 1998.

Sokol, Tony. "The Rocky Horror Picture Show and Its Lasting Legacy." Den of Geek. August 14, 2019.

Sokolove, Michael. "The CEO of Hamilton Inc." *New York Times Magazine.* April 5, 2016.

Soloski, Alexis. "*Tick Tick . . . Boom!* Is Jonathan Larson's Run up to *Rent.*" *New York Times*, October 20, 2016.

Spencer, C. "Rent Review." *Daily Telegraph.* May 14, 1998.

Spencer, Charles. "'Rent Remixed' Unfair Punishment as Grunge Comes Clean." *Telegraph*, October 16, 2007.

———. "*Rent Remixed,*" *The Telegraph* (London), October 16, 2007.

Steiner, Rupert. "Musical Sets Stage for Profitable Plays—Musical Rent." *Sunday Times* (London), May 3, 1998.

Taylor, Paul. "A Low-Rent Entry to the West End Theatre—Extra Rent Duke of York's London, Rent: Remixed, Review." *The Independent* (London), October 17, 2007.

Thomas, David. "*Rent* a Hit." *The Times*, March 28, 1998.

Tommasini, Anthony. "A Composer's Death Eches in His Musical."
New York Times, February 11, 1996.

———. "The Seven-Year Odyssey That Led to *Rent*." *New York Times*,
March 17, 1996.

———. "Some Advice to *Rent* from a Friend." *New York Times*, July 28,
2002.

Trachtenberg, J. A. "How to Turn $4,000 into Many Millions: The
Story of *Rent*." *The Wall Street Journal*, May 23, 1996.

Van Gelder, Lawrence. "On the Eve of a New life, an Untimely Death."
New York Times, December 13, 1996.

Viagas, Robert. "*Rent* Wins Pulitzer." *Playbill*. April 10, 1996.

Weinert-Kendt, Rob. "Those Magic Changes." *American Theatre*, July/
August, 2014.

Wolf, Matt, "Rent Review." *Variety*, May 18–24, 1998.

Zoglin, Richard. "Lower East Side Story." *Time*, March 4, 1996.

Zuckerman, Esther. "Michael Greif, Director and Angela Wendt,
Costume Designer Revisit Rent." *The Village Voice*, July 29, 2011.

WEBSITES

ACT UP, www.actupny.com

Broadway.com, www.broadway.com

Broadway World, www.broadwayworld.com

Internet Movie Database, www.imdb.com

Playbill, www.playbill.com

Talkin' Broadway, www.talkinbroadway.com

Theatre Board, www.theatreboard.com

ARCHIVE DOCUMENTS

Larson, Jonathan. *Rent.* Directed by Michael Greif. Videotaped by
the New York Public Library's Theatre on Film and Tape Archive
at the New York Theatre Workshop, New York, NY, March 28,
1996; 2 videodiscs (DVD) (141 min.): sd., col.; 4¾ in. NCOV
1915.

Larson, Jonathan. *Rent.* Manuscript or Typescript, NCOF+ 99-3565.

Larson, Jonathan. *Rent.* Directed by Michael Greif. *Rent* 10th
anniversary concert performance [video recording] 1 videodisc
(145 min.): sd., col.; 4¾ in. (DVD) New York, c2006,
Nederlander Theatre, New York, NY, April 24, 2006.

Larson, Jonathan. *Rent.* Joey Fatone press reel, [video recording] 1
videocassette (3 min.): sd., col.; ½ in. (Beta SP). Videotaped at the
Nederlander Theatre, New York, NY, 2002 NCOX 1969.

Larson, Jonathan. Clippings *Rent*, Jonathan Larson Performing Arts
Foundation 1 folder of clippings, *T-CLP.

Larson, Jonathan. *Rent.* Interview with James C. Nicola [video
recording] 1 videodisc (DVD) (86 min.): sd., col.; 4¾ in.
April 28, 2010, NCOW 343.

Larson, Jonathan. *Rent.* Clippings, 1996, *MGZR.

Larson, Jonathan. *Rent.* Mixed material collection of newspaper
clippings of dramatic criticism, 2011/12, *T-NBL+ Collection
2011/12 (Rent).

Larson, Jonathan. *Rent.* Interview with Michael Greif (raw footage)
[video recording] directed by Michael Kantor, Videotaped in New
York, NY, on August 26, 2003, Thirteen/WNET. dnr Broadway
Film Project, Inc. dnr NCOX 2166

Larson, Jonathan, *Rent*. Interview with James C. Nicola (raw footage) [video recording], directed by Michael Kantor, 1 videocassette (VHS) (42 min.): sd., col. SP; ½ in. Videotaped at the New York Theatre Workshop at 79 East Fourth St., New York, NY, on September 9, 2003, NCOX 2168.

Larson, Jonathan. *Rent*. Interview with Idina Menzel (raw footage) [video recording], 1 videocassette (VHS) (17 min.): sd., col. SP; ½ in. Interviewer: Michael Kantor. Interviewee: Idina Menzel. Videotaped in New York, NY, on September 12, 2003, NCOX 2171.

ARCHIVE AND VIDEO RECORDINGS

Larson, Jonathan. *Rent*. directed by Michael Greif. Videotaped by the New York Public Library's Theatre on Film and Tape Archive at the New York Theatre Workshop, New York, NY, March 28, 1996, NCOV 1915.

Larson, Jonathan. *Rent*. Directed by Michael Greif, *Rent* 10th anniversary concert performance [video recording], New York, c2006, Nederlander Theatre, New York, NY, April 24, 2006.

Larson, Jonathan. *Rent*. Joey Fatone press reel [video recording]. Videotaped at the Nederlander Theatre, New York, NY, 2002 NCOX 1969.

Larson, Jonathan. *Rent*. Interview with James C. Nicola [video recording], April 28, 2010, NCOW 343.

Larson, Jonathan. *Rent*. Interview with Michael Greif (raw footage) [video recording], directed by Michael Kantor. Videotaped in New York, NY, on August 26, 2003, Thirteen/WNET. dnr Broadway Film Project, Inc. dnr NCOX 2166.

REFERENCES

Larson, Jonathan. *Rent*. Interview with James C. Nicola (raw footage) [video recording], directed by Michael Kantor. Videotaped at the New York Theatre Workshop at 79 East Fourth St., New York, NY, on September 9, 2003, NCOX 2168.

Larson, Jonathan. *Rent*. Interview with Idina Menzel (raw footage) [video recording], 1 videocassette (VHS) (17 min.): sd., col. SP; ½ in. Interviewer: Michael Kantor. Interviewee: Idina Menzel. Videotaped in New York, NY, on September 12, 2003, NCOX 2171.

Larson, Jonathan. *Rent*. Recorded at the Nederlander Theatre, March 28, 1996.

Larson, Jonathan, and Stephen Chobosky. *Rent*. Directed by Chris Columbus, Columbia Pictures, 2005, USA, DVD (2006).

Larson, Jonathan. *Rent: Live on Broadway*. Directed by Michael John Warren, Sony Pictures, February 3, 2009, DVD.

Index